CW00522209

The

SCENTED GARDEN

The
SCENTED
GARDEN

By

ELEANOUR SINCLAIR ROHDE

with illustrations by
Patricia Dale, R.M.S., F.S.B.A.

LONDON
THE MEDICI SOCIETY
7 GRAFTON STREET

First published in 1931 by The Medici Society.
Now reprinted from the 1931 edition
with the addition of 15 colour plates
and detailed captions
by Patricia Dale, R.M.S., F.S.B.A

Published by The Medici Society Ltd, London, 1989

British Library Cataloguing in Publication Data:

Rohde, Eleanour Sinclair
   The scented garden
   1. Gardens, Fragrant
   I. Title
   635.9'68   SB454.3.F7

ISBN 0-85503 099 2

Distributed by B. T. Batsford Ltd, PO Box 4, Braintree,
Essex CM7 7QY   *Telephone* 0376 21276

Set in Garamond type and printed on 'Cranham Lodge' Laid,
made specially to match the paper of the original edition.

Printed and bound in Great Britain at the University Printing
House, Oxford.

"I wish unto you by dayly Prayer and fruition of the Heavenly Paradise cravyng of the Omnipotent and provident God, the guider of that gorgeous Garden that hee would vouchsafe to graunte unto you the sweete savour of his chiefe fragrante floures, that is his comfort to cleave faste unto you, his mercy to keepe you and his grace to guyde you nowe and evermore."

(From the Epistle dedicatory addressed to William Cecil, Lord Burghley; Lord High Treasurer of England. *The Gardeners Labyrinth* 1577.)

PREFACE

I FIND it difficult to express my gratitude to the Hon. Vicary Gibbs and to Colonel Messel for all the help they have so kindly given me, particularly with the lists. To both of them I am further indebted for reading the book in proof. I am also indebted for much kind help to Mr. J. Comber.

Parts of this book have already appeared in article form in *The Spectator* and one part in *The Landmark*, and I am indebted to the editors for their kind permission to include these articles.

I have quoted some lines at the end of the book from a poem which I liked and copied a few months ago from one of the leading journals. Unfortunately, I made no note at the time of the source or the name of the writer, who, I hope, will forgive me for quoting without acknowledgment.

ELEANOUR SINCLAIR ROHDE

CRANHAM LODGE,
   REIGATE,
      SURREY.
February, 1931.

"One worlde is crowned with faire red rosys . . .
and the thyrd with lusty prymerosys and lylyes
entermellyed and graciously arrayed."

The Dreme of the pylgremage of the soule. . . . Emprynted
at Westminster by William Caxton.   And fynyshed the sixth
day of June the yere of our Lord MCCCCLXXXVI.   And the
first yere of the regne of Kynge Edward the fyfthe.

CONTENTS

LIST OF ILLUSTRATIONS

❦ *List of Illustrations* ❦

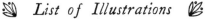

List of Illustrations

❧ *List of Illustrations* ❧

THE SCENTED GARDEN

INTRODUCTION

ON the old Roman Via Cassia, once one of the most important highways of Europe, and northward beyond the bridge (of which the central part is 2000 years old), a road, corresponding more or less to the ancient Via Flaminia, leads to Prima Porta and to all that remains of the Villa Livia. Here the Empress Livia, second wife of Octavianus Augustus,[1] had a summer retreat whence she could see, as one can see to-day, a wonderful view of the Tiber, Rome in the distance, and the Campagna stretching away to the blue Sabine Hills. Nothing remains of this villa save the spacious ' garden room,' with its barrel-vaulted roof and the walls, adorned all round with a singularly beautiful fresco representing a scented garden, possibly the Empress' favourite garden. Although painted 1900 years ago this wonderful fresco is in an exceptionally good state of preservation, for it is no ordinary fresco painting, with the colour laid on the wet plaster. The colour was worked in with wax, and it is probable that it was by no less an artist than Ludius, famous, according to Livy, in the days of Augustus. This no one can say for certain, but the fresco is the work of a master hand. Here we have depicted for us in arresting beauty an early morning scene in a scented garden of well-nigh two thousand years ago, and its fascination

[1] The ' Caesar Augustus ' of S. Luke II. 1.

I

is in no small part due to the skill wherewith the artist has given a sense of distance. Indeed, one feels one is actually in the garden. On every wall the garden is depicted in two parts—in the foreground a part planted with low-growing flowers fenced with wooden trellis-work in front, and on the further side with a small exquisitely patterned screen in stonework. Beyond this lies the garden proper. The early morning breeze stirs the trees, and the mist is rising from the ground. What a wonderful scene it is ! Orange trees laden with fruit and flowers, oleanders, palms, pomegranates, olive trees, roses and carnations, as they were two thousand years ago, and many other flowers. And the butterflies and birds ! The more one looks at this garden scene, and it is surely one of the loveliest, though one of the least known, ever depicted, the more entranced one becomes. So great is the artist's skill that not merely does one gaze through his magic casement into a scented garden of two thousand years ago, but one is transported into the heart of it.

As one wanders along this fresco one realizes something of the beauty of the gardens of far-off days, and one's thoughts fly to those still older gardens for which Egypt was famed over three thousand years ago. In the gardens of the ancient civilizations, shade, scent and water—water both seen and heard—were the essential features. Such were the gardens of ancient Egypt, and tomb-paintings reveal to us something of their stately magnificence. They excelled in the art of making gardens within gardens, and we can visualize the pleasure gardens with their painted pergolas covered with vines, their glorious water-gardens, the avenues of scented shrubs and their stately summer-houses. To the ancient Egyptian the flower of flowers was the sweet-scented blue lotus—*Nymphaea coerulea*. Few plants have indeed been held in such veneration, for to the Buddhists also the lotus was a sacred flower, symbolizing the purity of the spiritual life of man, for as the flowers have their roots in earth and water but float above in the sunlight, so the soul of man rises above the earth-life.

How great was the skill of the perfumers of ancient Egypt! In the tomb of the High Priest Ra Ouer (3000 B.C.), recently discovered near the Sphinx, were found, amongst other treasures of inestimable value (including a necklace of 4000 rubies and a large gold vase containing golden flowers), some unknown substance so sweetly scented after the lapse of 4700 years that, to quote the description in the report, ' one was surprised by the delicious scent of flowers, as if sweet-smelling bouquets had only recently been placed there. One would say that the alabaster itself had been impregnated with some unknown substance capable of preserving the perfume for centuries.' It is difficult for our modern and Western minds to grasp the importance of perfume in the religious rites of the most ancient civilizations. In a recent article[1] in *The Times*, the writer, after referring to the belief that in 7000 or 6000 B.C. the vast areas in Arabia and Africa now desert were productive and well populated, and that from their inhabitants came a culture which had elements in common with the prehistoric European culture known as Tardenoisian, pointed out that in the dawn of history in the Sudan (not later than 3000 B.C.) the most valued article of commerce, apart from gold, was incense or

[1] ' A Relic of the Ancient World. The Incense Trade.' *The Times*, 5th July, 1930.

frankincense—regarded as of divine nature. 'It came from Southern Arabia and the neighbouring parts of Africa, and from remotest antiquity was held to be a panacea for all ills. So highly was it esteemed that the trade in aromatic spices and herbs was guarded by the producers with the utmost secrecy, and the secrecy of the trade was augmented by the exclusiveness of the religious ideas and rites attached to it. Control of the Arabian incense trade was one of the leading features in the foreign policy of all the great empires of the ancient world, such as Babylon, Assyria and Egypt.' The writer points out further the interesting fact that it was probably due first to the jealousies surrounding the incense trade, to its sanctity and prestige, that Arabia remained, and has remained until now, almost *terra incognita* to the rest of the world.

Remembering the close connection between Egypt and the Holy Land, and that Solomon's chief wife was Pharaoh's daughter, it is more than probable that the gardens Solomon made for his pleasure closely resembled those for which Egypt had been famed for centuries, formal gardens with stately avenues, groves of pomegranates and scented shrubs, vine pergolas and water-gardens. From the Bible we know that Solomon's gardens were scented gardens, and the 'Song of Songs which is Solomon's,' the lyric of the scented garden, is full of the honeyed sweetness and aromatic fragrance of flowers and shrubs. It is noteworthy that Solomon, like Bacon, comments on the exquisite scent of newly opened vine blossoms, one of the most delicious of all scents.[1]

'Awake O north wind and come thou south; blow upon

[1] Cant. II. 13.

my garden that the spices thereof may flow out ' (Cant. IV. 16). The royal herb garden was a typical Eastern herb garden, that is a garden consisting chiefly of sweet-scented shrubs—' camphire with spikenard, spikenard and saffron; calamus and cinnamon, with all trees of frankincense; myrrh and aloes with all the chief spices.' The ' mountains of spices ' mentioned in Canticles VIII. 14, probably refer to the King's gardens of spices on the hill-sides round Jerusalem. In the days of his descendant Hezekiah ' spices ' were reckoned among the royal treasures, and as such stored in a special house. ' And Hezekiah had exceeding much riches and honour, and he made himself treasuries for silver and for gold . . . and for spices, and for shields and for all manner of pleasant jewels ' (2 Chron. XXII. 27, and see also 2 Kings xx. 13). Perfumes in Solomon's day appear to have been made from vegetable substances only, for no mention is made of ambergris, nor musk, nor indeed of any scent of animal extraction, with the sole exception of ' onycha ' (the operculum of a variety of mussel found in the Red Sea). The art of distilling was apparently unknown in Biblical times, but Job refers to the method of making perfumes by boiling vegetable substances in fat. Isaiah mentions the ' sweet balls ' (marginal reading) attached to long chains suspended either from the neck or at their girdles which the Hebrew women wore (Isa. III. 19). These probably resembled the pomanders of Elizabethan days.

Mediaeval gardens, like those of the East, were scented gardens, and it is pleasant to think of the great gardeners of those early days. Of Saint Radegonde, Queen of Clothair, who fled to Poitiers, and, with her nuns, tended the violets and roses in the garden they made on the sunny

slopes beneath the city walls ; of the Merovingian Chil-
debert's queen in whose garden ' the air was balmy with
the perfume of roses of Paradise ' ; and later, of the ninth
century monk, Walafred Strabo, who, above all, loved his
roses and lilies, and ' the glow of their sweet scent.' In
the gardens of our own mediaeval ancestors roses, lilies,
gilliflowers, wallflowers, violets and irises were the chief
flowers, besides the large number of aromatic herbs used
in medicine, in cosmetics and in cooking. Chaucer, in
The Franklin's Tale, immortalized the perfume and the
beauty of the garden that ' May hadde peynted with his
softé showers.'

> ' The odour of flowrés and the fresshé sighte
> Wold han makéd any herté lighte
> That ever was born, but if too greet siknesse,
> Or too greet sorwé, helde it in distresse ;
> So full it was of beautee with plesance.'

We know that as early as the twelfth century the French
perfume makers were of sufficient importance to be
granted a charter. There was no such trade in England for
centuries later, and even in Chaucer's day it was only
possible to buy perfumes from the mercers. From
Crusading days the far-famed perfumes of the East were
valued gifts, but in England they never found so much
favour as on the Continent, and when perfumes became
the fashion in Elizabeth's reign, it was to their gardens
the women-folk of England turned rather than to the
products of Eastern lands. The use of perfumes in every
way became so popular that even the smallest country
houses had their still-rooms and the old gardening and
still-room books are full of fragrant recipes for rose-
water, honey of violets, lily of the valley spirit, conserve

6

of the flowers of lavender, and lavender water, syrup of clove carnations, jasmine water, and sugar of damask roses, musk rose water, rosemary water and spirit of rosemary, Madonna lily water, balm water, cowslip syrup, elderflower water, and so forth. The luxurious scented their baths according to the season, with rose leaves, lemon peel, orange flowers, jasmine, rosemary, lavender, mint or sage. In her still-room the lady of the house made perfumed powders, wash-balls and pomanders, scented ointments and sweet bags. The most delightful recipe I know for a sweet bag is to be found in *Ram's Little Dodoen* (1606), and it runs thus : ' A Bag to smell unto for Melancholy or to cause one to sleep. Take drie Rose leaves, keep them close in a glasse which will keep them sweet, then take powder of Mints, powder of Cloves in a grosse powder, and put the same to the Rose leaves, then put all these together in a bag, and take that to bed with you, and it will cause you to sleep, and it is good to smell unto at other times.' Our great-grandmothers filled their sweet bags (which they hung on ' wing ' arm-chairs) with lavender, sweet scented geranium leaves and verbena, and a more delicious mixture it would be difficult to find.

The most famous of the old gardening books are full of the writers' delight in the scent of flowers. ' If odours may worke satisfaction,' wrote Gerard, ' they are so soveraigne in plants and so comfortable that no confection of the apothecaries can equall their excellent Vertue.' In his *Sylva Sylvarum*, as in his famous essay, ' Of Gardens,' Bacon almost suggests the close connection between scent and music. ' Scents and other odours are sweeter in the Air at some distance. For we see that in Sounds likewise they are sweetest when we cannot hear

every part by itself. . . . For all sweet smells have joined
with them some earthy or crude odours and at some
distance the sweet which is the more spiritual is perceived
and the earthy reaches not so far.' Is the passage about
scent in the garden, in the stately essay, too well known to
quote ? ' And because the breath of flowers is far sweeter
in the air, where it comes and goes, like the warbling of
music, than in the hand, therefore nothing is more fit
for that delight, than to know what be the flowers and
plants that do best perfume the air. Roses, damask and
red, are fast flowers of their smells, so that you may walk
by a whole row of them, and find nothing of their sweetness ; yea though it be in a morning's dew. Bays likewise
yield no smell as they grow ; rosemary little, nor sweet
marjoram. That which, above all, yields the sweetest
smell in the air is the violet, especially the white double
violet, which comes twice a year ; about the middle of
April and about Bartholomew-tide. Next to that is the
musk rose ; then the strawberry leaves dying, with a most
excellent cordial smell ; then the flower of the vines ;
it is a little dust, like the dust of a bent, which grows upon
the cluster in the first coming forth ; then sweet-brier ;
then wallflowers, which are very delightful, to be set under
a parlour or lower chamber window ; then pinks and gilliflowers, especially the matted pink, and clove gilliflowers ;
then the flowers of the lime tree ; then the honeysuckles,
so they be somewhat far off. . . . Those which perfume
the air most delightfully not passed by as the rest, but
being trodden upon and crushed, are three ; that is
burnet, wild thyme and water mints. Therefore, you are
to set whole alleys of them to have the pleasure when
you walk or tread.'

8

'There be some flowers make a delicious Tussie-Mussie or Nosegay both for sight and smell.' *(See page 9)*

facing p. 8

'... cottage-folk delight to load their friends who have the misfortune to live in towns.' *(See page 9)*

And I love the passage in the *Paradisus*, where the lives
of 'vertuous men' are compared to the fragrance of
flowers : 'That as many herbes and flowers with their
fragrant sweet smels doe comfort and as it were revive
the Spirits and perfume a whole house ; even so such men
as live vertuously, labouring to doe good, and to profit the
Church of God and the commonwealth doe as it were
send forth a pleasing savour of sweet instructions, not
only to that time wherein they live and are fresh, but
being drye, withered and dead, cease not in all after
ages to doe as much or more.'

> 'Farewell, dear flowers ; sweetly your time ye spent,
> Fit, while ye lived, for smell or ornament,
>   And after death for cures.
> I follow straight, without complaints or grief ;
> Since, if my scent be good, I care not if
>   It be as short as yours.'

'There be some flowers make a delicious Tussie-Mussie
or Nosegay both for sight and smell.' Thus John Parkinson in his *Paradisus*. Is there, I wonder, any part where
this pleasant and expressive old word for nosegay is still
used ? The word is suggestive of the generous bunches of
sweet-smelling flowers wherewith cottage-folk delight to
load their friends who have the misfortune to live in
towns. We all know those delicious bunches—in the
spring wallflowers and bunch primroses, honesty, columbines, Solomon's seal and lilac ; in the summer a peony or
two, roses and pinks, gardener's garter, valerian, honeysuckle, lad's love, ferns, sweet rocket and London pride,
and later roses again with pansies, thyme, marigolds, bergamot, lavender, Aaron's rod and phlox. Who would
exchange one of these posies for the most faultlessly and

9

painfully well-arranged effort from a florist's shop? I wonder what happens to flowers in florists' shops, for somehow they invariably look entirely different from their own kind growing in the garden. Personally they always give me the uncomfortable feeling that I am with complete strangers. I sometimes think it would be fun just for a week or so to have a barrow loaded with real country bunches of all the sweet-smelling old-fashioned flowers so difficult to buy in any city, and to sell them in one of the London streets or preferably in one of the few remaining old-time squares—Edwardes Square in Kensington, for instance. But the nosegays would have to be real country bunches, not the imitations of these one sometimes sees, and no two bunches would be alike. I don't think much would be left on the barrow by the end of each day! For it is the flowers Chaucer, Spenser and Shakespeare loved which still hold first place in our affections. They are the flowers, too, which figure so largely in the books which everyone cherishes, not only for their intrinsic beauty, but because they are so redolent of the country and country gardens—books such as Mrs. Ewing's *Mary's Meadow* and *Daddy Darwin's Dovecot* and Miss Mitford's *Our Village*.

Anyone writing in the last century on scented plants would certainly have written of musk. Now for many years past it has been impossible for anyone to find a plant with anything more than the faintest suspicion of scent. So far no explanation of this unsatisfactory phenomenon, indeed, no guess even at what may be the explanation has been offered, so far as I know, by any botanist. An old Etonian told me that in his day musk was a favourite carpeting plant for the window-boxes of Eton boys, and used to fill their rooms with fragrance. How vividly, too, one remembers the musk plants lovingly tended on cottage window-sills. Their owners trained them up tiny thin ladders, narrow at the bottom, to fit the pot, and wide at the top, and when the ladder was completely covered no one could desire a prettier or more fragrant pot-plant. Small wonder that they were such a source of pride and pleasure to their owners. And how ' at home ' those little pots looked on sunny window-sills. Musk is not the only flower which has lost its scent. Clusius,[1] writing in the sixteenth century, describes the largest of the snowdrops (*Galanthus plicatus*) as being scented, but it is apparently scentless now. This snowdrop is a native of the Crimea, and was the flower which gave our soldiers in the Crimean War so much pleasure when they first saw it in bloom, for it reminded them of our own native snowdrops.

It is curious how the same flower scent affects people differently according to circumstances. The scent of gorse flowers, especially of the double flowered gorse, would not, I think, give us much pleasure in summer, yet in spring it seems to hold captive as by a miracle the glory of a whole day of sun and warmth. The rather crude scent of cow-parsley in mass is not a favourite scent with country-folk. But to town-folk it is delightful, simply because it is one of the most familiar scents of an English lane in May. To anyone returning from a tropical country it is probably far more welcome than any rich Eastern scent, and for no other reason than that it is one of the homely country smells with which he has

[1] *Rariorum aliquot Stirpium per Pannionam et Austriam. Ex officina Christophori Plantini.* 1583.

been familiar from childhood. Few people appreciate the scent of broad bean flowers, simply because the broad bean is a ' vegetable,' yet it is one of the most beautiful of flower scents. Broad beans are usually regarded as the only ' vegetable ' with scented flowers, but sea-kale flowers have almost as attractive a scent, for although less sweet it is nut-like and mellower. The only other ' vegetables ' with scented attractions are, I think, the delicate morel mushrooms, which appear very early in the year, and have a most pleasant scent. The scent of elder, when one encounters it on the highway, is ' heady ' and overpowering, but in a hayfield, when it blends with the newly-mown hay curing in the sun, it is a pleasant smell. Meadowsweet in the mass is a dull and rather heavy smell, but if one is in a boat and the scent is wafted by a passing breeze across water this perfume is sweet, and suggestive of the fulness and richness of summer. The smell of the peppermint plants by the stream-side, crushed by the boat against the river bank, is also pleasantest when water-borne. To town-dwellers the scent of hay in haymaking time must be almost unbearable, for surely no other smell makes them realize with the same poignancy that their lot is that of prisoners, no matter how gilded their cages may be. For the scent of hay in all its stages is one of those all-pervading primitive scents of which it is more true to say that one is enfolded in it rather than that one smells it. Even a whiff of hay scent from a passing cart in a city has a magical effect, for the street disappears and one sees instead the shimmering heat in the hayfield at noonday, the hedgerow starred with wild roses and the first bramble flowers, the butterflies flitting to and fro, the lowly many-hued undergrowth of daisies, lady's bedstraw and trefoil and tufted vetch in the depths of the sea of grass. Sweetest of all is meadow hay. The scent of a newly-made stack is fresh, but the scent of an old stack has perhaps the finer aroma.

Certain flower scents appeal to some people but not to others. To some folk the scents of marigold and phloxes are disagreeable, but to those of us who like these ' cottage smelling ' flowers they are delightful. There is no trace of sweetness but these vigorous wholesome scents have a charm of their own. There are people who actually describe privet flowers as ' honey-scented,' but to most of us these near relations of the ' lilac ' family have a singularly unpleasant smell. (*L. Quihoui* is the exception, for this privet has sweetly-scented flowers.) Again, there are certain scents which are apparent to some people but not to others. Snapdragons, for instance, are not usually regarded as ' scented ' flowers, yet to many they have a particularly delightful, though only faint, scent. Some scents are perceptible only at a little distance. For instance, the bracts of *Davidia involucruta* are not scented, but often at a distance of about 10 feet from the tree there is a decided although fugitive fragrance. The flowers of *Rhododendron Roylei* are scentless, but a few feet away there is an aroma (only an occasional whiff) which is very like that of Russian leather. Scents vary also according to locality. Moss roses grown in the plains of India quickly lose their mossiness, and with it the peculiarly exquisite scent of the mossy calyces ; but transferred to the hills, the same plants regain their moss and with it the scent. Forget-me-nots in the British Isles are not scented, but only this morning I had a letter from a friend who

13

lives in Yukon Territory, and writing from Carcross, within the Arctic circle, she says, ' Last week a party of us climbed a mountain. What struck us most were the glorious flowers we found above timber line. The forget-me-nots were the bluest I have ever seen, and they smelt so sweet.'

We talk of ' looking ' for spring, but I think we country-folk smell the oncoming spring long before any signs are visible. These first scents are manifold and usually fleeting —the smell of the earth on those rare sunny days which rejoice our hearts early in February, the scent of the wind when it blows from the south after a long spell from the north-east, the scent of young grass when it first pushes up in the pastures, the scent of the first spring rain on wind-dried earth, the indefinable but sweet scent of birch and larch when they first come into leaf. To lovers of sweet scents these familiar smells are as much part of the music of spring as the songs of birds, the busy hum of bees and the bleating of young lambs.

Fragrance in flowers may, indeed, be described as their music, and it is none the less beautiful because it is silent. In every scented flower and leaf the perfume is exhaled by substances so perfectly blended that they give the impression of a single scent, just as several different notes make a chord. We are all familiar with the dual sensation produced by smelling any sweet-scented flower—both an appreciation of the perfume and the still deeper pleasure afforded by something so delicately balanced and, as it were, faultlessly rounded that it seems almost beyond our mere human senses to enjoy it fully. Think of the scent of a rose—preferably a cabbage or a damask rose. Can the chemist with all his skill produce anything which

14

even faintly resembles this? In the essential oil of the rose there are at least eight substances, the ' dominant note ' being geraniol. These eight substances are so exquisitely balanced and ' in tune ' with each other that the preliminary sensation is of a single scent, whereas it is, in fact, a perfect chord of scent. There are many differences between flower and leaf scents. All flower scents give themselves, but leaves must be bruised before they yield their scents. The containers of flower scents lie almost on the surface of the petals, but the containers of leaf scents are deeper and hence the leaf must be bruised before we can appreciate its scent. Most leaf scents, too, are simpler in their composition than flower scents, and they contain substances which rarely occur in flowers, and which give leaf scents the pungent qualities we so much enjoy, in, for instance, the aromatic herbs.

The melodies of the flowers—the music of fairyland—cannot be heard by mortal ears. Yet throughout the year this lovely music is being played. When the snowdrops appear, do we not feel we are listening to fairy bells, the ' horns of elfland faintly blowing,' telling us of the coming spring, when the golden trumpets of the daffodils will take up the refrain? I think to most of us the scents of the different seasons are as characteristic as their colours. The purest scents are those of spring, for no summer scents have the fresh ethereal purity of primroses, cowslips or white violets. These scents are suggestive of worlds fairer even than our own. Unlike many of the richer perfumes we can never have enough of these scents, and their elusive charm haunts us throughout the year. The scent of apple blossom has, I think, this quality more than any other of the early flowers. Were

15

I condemned to live in the tropics, I should be heart-sick every May for the scent of apple blossom. The same quality of purity and wholesomeness is characteristic of the less ethereal scents of bean-flowers, of clover and new-mown hay, and beyond all of heather under a hot sun. The scents of the summer flowers are rich and joyous and sweetest of all are the scents of the ' old ' roses. The scent of the cabbage rose is more than a scent. It is the beauty of life itself, of its sorrows as well as its joys. And what of the melodies of wondrous beauty wafted from the snowy trumpets of the Madonna lilies—songs of praise unknown to mortal ears ? The summer flowers laugh and sing and the earth is filled with gladness. No two scents are alike, and yet how perfectly they blend in the garden. ' There is neither speech nor language but their voices are heard among them.'

" **The roses and lilies speak Thee.**"[1]

[1] George Herbert.

CHAPTER ONE

EVEN in the early days of January deliciously scented flowers are already in bloom. On my table is a wide shallow bowl filled with damp moss, stuck with sprigs of *Chimonanthus fragrans*, and my little writing-room is filled with their fragrance. There is always something fascinating in the appearance of delicate leafless branches arrayed with flowers, and the flowers of *C. fragrans* are peculiarly beautiful. Both the outer parchment-coloured petals and the small inner petals, which are maroon-coloured, are very thin in texture, but even at a distance of two feet the outer petals have a thick wax-like look, owing to the curious way in which they are curled inwards and longitudinally. This wax-like appearance is enhanced by the rich honeysuckle perfume. The tiny maroon-coloured circle of inner petals, the yellow stamens, the rough knobby surface of the pale fawn calyces and the exquisite pale green of the branches combine to make this Chinese treasure extraordinarily attractive. The grandiflora variety has larger flowers, but they do not seem to me so fragrant. The fresh honey-scent of the flower has long since secured it its charming English name of 'Winter sweet,' the leaves are also pleasantly scented, and perhaps in time it will be as popular as it deserves. It can be grown in the open border, but, naturally, it is usually given the protection of a wall, as then the flowers are produced

17

earlier. Theoretically it likes a rich light soil, but on a heavy soil it grows rampantly. All the attention it needs is to prune back the flowering branches to within one inch of the base in February (when the flowers are over), leaving, of course, those needed to make more branches. On poor soils an application of weak liquid manure when the leaves are out, or mulching in October, is useful.

Two of the winter-flowering shrubby honeysuckles (*Lonicera fragrantissima* and *L. Standishii*) are sweetly scented, but in a small garden one would certainly choose *L. fragrantissima*. It takes very little space (it grows to about six to eight feet) and spread out against a wall is very attractive. Fresh green leaves abundantly produced in mid-winter are always a joy, and the small golden-stamened cream-coloured flowers give us rich honeysuckle scent in January. The flowers are borne in pairs, but so closely are they set together that they look like a single flower. *L. fragrantissima* cannot be described as free-flowering, but in the cold of January one is grateful for the sweetly-scented flowers, almost concealed by the leaves. *L. Standishii* takes up too much room where space is limited, for it is a fair-sized bush (about six feet high and quite four feet through). The flowers of *L. fragrantissima* are well protected by the leaves, but those of *L. Standishii* are unprotected, and, consequently, they soon assume a brown shrivelled appearance unless planted where there is shelter. In a mild January several of the daphnes are in bloom. The best-known one —*Daphne mezereum*—produces its deliciously fragrant blossoms in colours ranging from pure white to deep purplish pink. It remains in bloom for about two months. But the best of the early-flowering daphnes is *D. Japonica* (syn *odora*). The flowers are larger than those of *D. mezereum ;* it is even more fragrant, and it is also in leaf in January. But this variety, which one often sees in Devon and Cornwall, can only be grown out of doors against a very warm, sheltered wall. *D. laureola* and *D. pontica* produce their yellow-green flowers in February and March. For the few there are *D. fioniana* and *D. retusa,* but even in skilful hands the former usually looks a rather unhappy little object !

D. mezereum and *D. laureola* are supposed to be indigenous in England. A paragraph in Philip Miller's *Gardener's and Botanist's Dictionary* (1807), on the subject of *D. mezereum,* is so interesting—especially the reference to ' Mr. White in Selborne-hanger, Hants '—that I quote it :

' Native of Lapland, Sweden, Denmark, Germany, Switzerland, France, Carniola, Savoy, Piedmont, Great Britain. Mr. Miller is the first who mentions that it is a native of our island, namely, near Andover, in Hampshire. Since that it has been found by Mr. Woodward at Laxfield, in Suffolk ; by Mr. White in Selborne-hanger, Hants ; and it has been frequently observed in the beech woods of Buckinghamshire. As it has escaped all our old herbarists and even the indefatigable Ray and his immediate successors, and birds are remarkably fond of the berries ; I should suspect that they may have disseminated this beautiful shrub ; unless we may suppose that it remained unnoticed on account of the early flowering, before herbarists sallied forth on their vernal excursions. Gerard says that he had plenty thereof for his garden from Elbing, in Poland. He calls it Germaine Olive Spurge, or Spurge Olive, Spurge Flax and Dwarf Bay, and says that

19

the Dutch call it Mezereon. Parkinson calls it Dwarf Bay or flowering Spurge.'

Of the early flowering berberises, *Berberis japonica* var. *Bealii,* is worth growing, however limited the space may be. Its large handsome leaves, standing out almost like rays, and the lily-of-the-valley-like scent of its racemes of yellowish white, make this a most attractive bush. The flowers are followed by grape-like fruits, which remain on till late summer. *B. japonica* has shorter racemes of flowers, and is not nearly so attractive. *Clematis cirrhosa* is a winter-flowering climber for every garden, doing well either on pillars or walls, and producing its lovely swinging cups of pale green flowers in the coldest and shortest days of the year. Though impervious to severe cold this clematis abhors cutting winds, and should be planted where it is protected from them. *C. cirrhosa* is a native of Spain, where it was observed by Clusius in 1565. Gerard, who had it in his Holborn garden in 1596, called it 'Traveller's joy of Candia'; Johnson, in his enlarged edition of Gerard's *Herball,* called it 'Spanish Traveller's Joy,' and Parkinson, 'Spanish wild Climber.' *Viburnum fragrans* opens its richly scented, wax-like, pinkish cymes sometimes as early as November, and this shrub should find a place in every scented garden for its interesting associations. The late Mr. R. Farrer, who discovered it, says it was grown 'all over Northern China; old specimens are seen in almost every palace or temple yard, and its loveliness and fragrance carried it to Pekin, where it was among the most prized specimens in the Imperial Gardens until the death of the Dowager Empress, and after the fall of the Dynasty only was it allowed out at last into the eager hands of the common cultivator.' Mr.

20

R. Farrer describes it as growing wild ' only in the small hill range between Shi-ho and Shi-Ja-Jaung.' *V. fragrans* strikes freely from cuttings. The Japanese witch hazel (*Hamamelis arborea*) and the Chinese witch hazel (*H. mollis*) are not exactly scented, but for those who appreciate it there is something very pleasing in the ' dusty ' Eastern perfume of the spider-like yellow blossoms with which they wreathe their branches so fantastically in January and February. Both *H. arborea* and *H. mollis* are perfectly hardy.

For the gardens of the few who can give them warm walls in the most sheltered parts of Great Britain, two scented January-flowering treasures are *Edgeworthia chrysantha* and *Freylinia cestroides*. With its globe-shaped head of flowers, ranging from deep butter to cream-colour on the same head (the flowers turn cream-colour as they fade), its sweet scent and the length of time it remains in bloom, *E. chrysantha* is a most attractive plant, and the buff-coloured flowers of *F. cestroides* fill the air with fragrance in mid-winter. There are gardens where *Acacia dealbata* (the ' mimosa ' of Covent Garden) flowers in the open, but as a rule it is only possible to grow this lovely evergreen against a wall in sheltered parts. *A. armata* one rarely sees growing out of doors, although it is hardier than *A. dealbata*. Grown indoors, *A. armata* is, I think, certainly the more attractive of the two.

Amongst the humble flowers one of the most sweetly scented is the one least frequently seen—*Tussilago fragrans*. I wonder why this sweet-scented tussilage has gone out of fashion. A hundred years ago, when it was first introduced into England (it is a native of Italy), it was grown not only out of doors, where it becomes a rampant weed, but also in pots, for the scent of the whitish lilac flowers is almost indistinguishable from that of ' cherry-pie.' It was apparently very fashionable as a pot plant, for an early nineteenth century writer observes loftily, ' The modest flowers of this plant were too insignificant to have attracted the notice of the ignorant, who have not souls to admire humble merit, whether in men or flowers, until it has received the sanction of fashion or the patronage of the great.'[1] The scent of the flowers is indeed sweet, a bowl of them in midwinter looks pleasantly old-fashioned, and perhaps some day this relation of the humble coltsfoot will again ' be patronized by the great.' In spite of its scent, *T. fragrans* should only be planted in a wild part of the garden, for once it has taken hold it is difficult to eradicate.

Considering the number of flowers one can pick from a square foot of *Iris stylosa*, this iris should find a place even in the smallest garden. The lovely lavender-blue flowers seem to bring summer into midwinter, for the blue of their scented petals is almost the blue of a summer sky. These plants, which are natives of Algeria, like being starved in a sunny spot by a wall in light soil with plenty of lime rubble. Put into ordinary garden soil they produce leaves and no flowers, but given the conditions they like they produce abundantly, and their masses of long leaves give the flowers a considerable amount of protection. *I. stylosa* will not flower the first season, for it requires a little time to settle down comfortably. The flowers for indoor decoration should be picked in bud, for though the masses of long leaves give

[1] H. Phillips. *Flora Historica.*

a certain amount of protection, they are apt to be ruined by heavy rain. There is a white variety (*I. stylosa alba*) which is not so attractive ; also, as a rule, it flowers later. *I. stylosa speciosa* has even larger lavender flowers than the ordinary *I. stylosa*. The lovely *I. histrioides cilicia*, which is a native of Palestine, and grows on Mount Lebanon, also flowers in January both in the north and south of England. It does well facing west in full sun, and makes a splash of colour with its flash of orange gold down the centre of each fall. The violet-scented *I. reticulata* is one of the easiest of the early-flowering irises to grow, and even where space is limited it is well worth giving room to a tiny group of them. The deep violet-coloured form (the original type) is not a very attractive colour out of doors in midwinter, but the flowers look beautiful in a shallow bowl with variegated holly, as the yellow leaves show up the violet blooms, and the scent in a warm room is delicious. The origin of the deep violet-coloured *I. reticulata* is uncertain, for it is unknown in a wild state. In the opinion of the late Mr. Dykes, it may have been a hybrid from *I. reticulata* × *I. histrioides :* the deep reddish-purple form *I. reticulata* var. *Krelagei* comes from the Caucasus. Of the two pale blue forms, *I. cyana* is the wild pale blue, and *Cantab*, a garden seedling. There were some wonderful seedling irises shown this month (February) at one of the R.H.S. shows. One exhibit of new seedlings (*I. reticulata* × *I. Krelagei*) varied in colour from pure white to gentian blue, wine, purple and maroon, all with a gold flash on the fall. Another exhibit all of sapphire blue looked, as someone said, 'like a pool of blue water ruffled by the wind.'

In February the constellations of the crocuses shine

23

forth in their firmament of green. Most crocuses have a faint warm scent, but only on really sunny days or in a warm room. Many people do not regard them as scented flowers, but Virgil knew their exquisite scent in Italian sunshine. Sometimes one wonders whether our modern eyes are dimmed to the amazing beauty of these flowers, especially the orange-coloured ones. Homer's carpet of the gods was of hyacinths, crocuses, and lotus flowers, and all the classical writers used ' crocus-coloured ' to describe a glowing orange golden colour, for which indeed there is no other word. The golden crocus turns the earth to sheets of living flame. To quote Homer, ' the flaming crocus made the mountain glow.'

Saffron yellow, the colour of light, was apparently the royal and sacred colour of the most ancient days. The Persian kings wore saffron yellow shoes in imitation of the still older Babylonio-Median costume. In Aeschylus' *Persians* Darius is summoned from the nether-world by the chorus, ' Rise, ancient ruler, rise ; come with the saffron-dyed sumaris on thy feet . . . a royal tiara on thy head.' When Jason prepared to plough the field in Colchis with the fire-breathing bulls, he threw off his saffron-coloured garments. Bacchus wore *Krokotos*, the saffron dress. The new-born Herakles Pindar describes as swathed in crocus-yellow. The crocus dress of Pallas Athene the Attic maidens embroidered with many colours. Antigone let fall her crocus-coloured stole in her despair at the death of her mother and brothers. Helena took with her from Mycenae her gold-embroidered *palla*, a crocus-bordered veil. In the Epics, Eos, the dawn, is ever saffron-veiled. The companions of Europa, when Jupiter approached her in the form of a bull, were

24

gathering the fragrant hair of the golden crocus. When Pan and the nymphs passed singing through the meadows, the fragrant crocus and hyacinth bloomed in the tangled growth of grass.[1] It was ever the crocus of the East, *Crocus vernus*, which was so highly esteemed, not the humbler native kind. When Roman luxury was at its height, crocus scent and crocus flowers were used as lavishly as rose leaves. Heliogabalus bathed in saffron-water, and his guests reclined on cushions stuffed with crocus petals.

Crocuses are natives of the south and central Europe, the Levant and western Asia. We do not know when they were introduced, but it is quite likely that the Romans brought bulbs of such favourite flowers to adorn the gardens of their villas in England during the first centuries of our era. In the Middle Ages, when they were again introduced, the autumn-flowering *C. sativus* was certainly known and grown in this country long before the spring-flowering varieties. *Croh* was the Middle English word for saffron. According to tradition the saffron bulb was introduced into England in the reign of Edward III by a pilgrim, who brought it concealed in the hollow of his staff. Even in the sixteenth century herbalists described the spring-flowering crocus as saffron of the spring—'Saffron of the Spring with yellow flowers.'

Three hundred years ago Gerard wrote of the crocus, ' It hath floures of a most perfect shining yellow colour, seeming afar off to be a hot glowing coal of fire. That pleasant plant was sent unto me from Robinius of Paris, that painful and most curious searcher of simples.' Is there any other flower which so wonderfully gives us at

---

[1] See Victor Hehn, *Wanderings of Plants and Animals.*

least a faint idea of the meaning of the words, ' And the
streets of the city were pure gold like as it were transparent glass ' ? Crocuses are indeed amongst the loveliest
and most gladsome of spring flowers. Each crocus cup is
not only of exceeding beauty, but within its petals it
seems to hold the quintessence of sunlight in luminous
gold, and their scent is the scent of sunlight. Many years
ago that great flower-lover, Mr. Forbes Watson, wrote of
them, ' Whilst the Snowdrop enters with so quiet a
footstep that it might almost pass unobserved amidst
the remnants of the melting snow, the Crocus bursts
upon us in a blaze of colour like the sun-rise of the
flowers. . . . Though at first sight apparently alike in
colour, close attention will show that the inner segments
are of deeper hue and more distinctly orange than the
outer. But we must carefully observe the colour itself.
Like most things that are very beautiful it varies greatly
in different aspects ; the petals to a careless eye, and
especially in a dull light, may seem but a surface of glossy
orange. Yet look carefully and they are lighted with rosy
reflections, pencilled with delicate streaks and nerves of
shade and, above all, bestrewed with little gleaming points,
a host of microscopic stars, which cast a fiery sheen like
that of the forked feathers of the Bar-tailed Humming-
bird, as if the surface were engrained with dust of amber
or gold.'

Crocuses never look happy if they are continually being
attended to. Thick close clumps of them, fifteen and
twenty together, growing naturally with masses of their
lovely golden chalices full of sunlight, look gloriously
happy, but planted out singly there is always something
depressing about them. They look forlorn and tidy.

Crocuses are companionable flowers, and they seem to enjoy huddling together. Grown separately, the flowers are, or should be, larger (I have never observed this to be actually the case, but there is such a thing as taking all the rules and theories one finds in gardening manuals too seriously !) Picking crocuses planted out singly makes one feel guilty of a crime, but picking them from fat neglected clumps is a joy.

I am writing for the first time this year out of doors, on one of those glorious sunny days which always come in February and for which one is so much more grateful than for a whole week of summer sun. And I have just been counting the number of flowers on the largest clump of golden crocuses (*C. vernus*) by the apple trees in our garden. There are at least seventy-eight flowers fully out, though how they have managed to crowd themselves into a space measuring only about 9 inches by 12 is little short of a miracle. The flowers are as large as any grown singly and very long-stalked (some of them certainly 5 or 6 inches long), and, pushing aside the fully expanded flowers, one could see there were masses more coming on. When I came there were eight or nine bees working at the flowers, and watching the bees for some time it was delightful to see how often the same bees, after a hurried visit to smaller clumps near by, returned to feast on the riches spread before them on the largest clumps. The words of an Elizabethan madrigal come into my mind :

> ' I like the bee with Toil and Pain
> Fly humbly o'er the flow'ry Plain
> And with the Busy Throng
> The little sweets my Labours gain
> I work into a song.'

The scent of the crocuses would be almost imperceptible from the single flowers, but from the masses it is warm and exquisite, and in the sunlight the clumps look like masses of translucent gold caught not out of the sunlight but out of the sun itself. It is curious how colour seems to alter the character of a crocus flower. Yellow and golden crocuses look almost riotously happy, but all the mauve varieties have a placid dreamy appearance. Of the very early-flowering varieties *C. imperati* is always described as scented, but it does not seem to be more scented than some of the other varieties, especially the commonest of the yellow and gold-coloured kinds. From the point of view of decorative effect nothing touches the Dutch yellow crocus (*C. vernus*). No one knows its origin. It is probably of garden origin, for it is sterile, and it has never been found growing wild. It increases by throwing off little corms. If planted in grass the grass should never be mown till the crocus leaves have quite withered, otherwise the corms will suffer badly. Though the bees love crocuses grown in clumps the birds do not seem to attack them as much as crocuses planted singly, or if they do, their depredations are not so apparent. What the birds love in them is the tiny drop of nectar to be found in each flower. What with one thing and another crocuses have many enemies. Field mice, the mischievous grey squirrel and rats all enjoy eating the corms, and if planted near the surface nothing will stop pheasants pecking them out.

The scents and sounds of spring remind one of St. Bride, the patron saint of the first flowers, young children and lambs. For February is the month of St. Bride of the kindly flame, the gentle mother of all young and tender things Her ways are ways of gentleness. Through

28

the mists of centuries we see her gracious figure, her lamb in her arms, a lamp in her hand. When the bitter winds are still blowing, the kindly flame of her flower, the dandelion, shines out and tells us that spring is near. She watches over mothers and their new-born babes, and on the hill-sides she brings the shepherds to the new-born lambs. She is loved in all Celtic lands, from the western highlands and islands of Scotland to Kildare, where, for centuries, her lamp was kept always burning.

St. Bride's father was Dubtach, twelfth in descent from Fedlimidh Rechtmar, King of Ireland in the second century. Her mother was a beautiful slave. When St. Bride took the veil seven virgins followed her example, and each of them chose a Beatitude representing the grace she specially desired. St. Bride chose ' Blessed are the merciful for they shall obtain mercy.' The various lives of her recount many tales of her gentle pity for all young creatures, and for weak and suffering folk. She was noted for her love of animals and birds, and she particularly delighted in calling the wild duck and geese to her and caressing them.

When her fame was at its height Iollan, King of Leinster, offered her land to build a monastery. She chose the clay ridge above the plain of Magh Breagh, and there, by an ancient and venerated oak, she established her *cill*, afterwards famous as Kildare, the ' cell of the oak.' Innumerable folk of both sexes came to her *cill* and, according to Cogitosus, Kildare became ' the head of nearly all the Irish churches and the pinnacle towering above all monasteries of the Scots, whose jurisdiction spread throughout the whole Hibernian land, reaching from sea to sea.' St. Bride was joined by her kinsman,

Conlaeth, a hermit who was famed for the bells he made. He became bishop ' to govern the church with her in episcopal dignity.' Even when he was a bishop Conlaeth continued to work at his anvil, and made many croziers and bells. Whether St. Bride loved bells we do not know, but it is on record that St. Gildas sent her a bell from Brittany. Numerous churches are named after this beloved saint, amongst others, St. Bride in Fleet Street.

Beyond St. Bride we see another form, still more remote and almost lost in the darkness of antiquity—Bride the Beautiful, the Gaelic goddess of poetry. A goddess of flame also, for she was born at sunrise, and has never ceased to light the hearts of poets with divine fire. She, too, lights the kindly flame of the dandelion, the first fire of spring. In the clouds which shroud the hill-sides the shepherds hear the crying of the young lambs she is bringing earthward, and they rejoice at her coming. She watches over young children in their cradles, and when they smile it is because they have seen gentle St. Bride's face.

Long before the royal gold of the buttercups, the joyous gold of the dandelion gladdens our eyes. She scatters her humble lovable flower even by trodden paths to enliven the heart of the wayfarer, and all lovers of simple, lowly flowers are cheered when they see her kindly flame.

CHAPTER II

VIOLETS, PRIMROSES AND WALLFLOWERS

'A YOUNG MAN in green, with a Garland of Mirtle, and Hawthorn Buds, Winged, in one hand Primroses and Violets, in the other the sign Taurus.' So run the instructions in a seventeenth-century book for embroidering a figure representing Spring.

'Violets are the spring's chiefe flowers for beauty, smell and use.' The sweet-scented violet (*Viola odorata*) is a native not only of Europe, but also of Persia, Palestine, Barbary, Arabia, Japan and China. In the East as in the West it has been beloved from time immemorial. Violets preserve in their scent the memory of Orpheus, for one day, being weary, he sank to sleep on a mossy bank, and where his enchanted lute fell, there blossomed the first violet. The magic music of his lute still haunts the scent of violets. Deep-toned melodies from faerie linger in

'the sweet sound
That breathes upon a bank of violets,
Stealing and giving odour.'

The violet is regal in its humility, and what a splendour of purple radiates from the petals of this shy flower. It glows with the fragrance and warmth of its beauty. 'And the more vertuous the flower thereof is the more it bendeth the head thereof downward. The lyttlenesse thereof in substance is nobly rewarded in greatnesse of

31

savour and vertue.' And to violets the old herbalists ascribed the gift of sleep. 'For them that may not sleep for sickness, seethe the violets in water and at even let him soke well hys feete in the water to the ancles ; when he goeth to bed bind of this herb to his temples and he shall slepe well by the grace of God.' We are all familiar with the curious effect produced by smelling violets. The keen delicious perfume in a few seconds becomes fainter and similar to that of a mossy bank and in another moment the scent has apparently vanished. But the violets are of course still full of fragrance and it is our sense of smell which is exhausted, not the perfume of the violets. The dominant note in their scent is ionone, which has a tiring, almost soporific effect on the sense of smell. Shakespeare refers to the fleeting nature of the pleasure given by this exquisite scent :

> ' Sweet, not lasting
> The perfume and suppliance of a minute.'

Garden varieties of the sweet-scented violet have a richer scent, but they have not the exquisitely keen, pure, almost rarefied scent of wild violets. As a child one thought that the white violet was even more sweetly scented than the purple, and the first time one read the immortal essay ' Of Gardens ' it came as a pleasant surprise to find one's childish belief confirmed by no less a personage than the great Francis Bacon. ' That which above all yields the sweetest smell in the air is the Violet, especially the white double violet which comes twice a year, about the middle of April and about Bartholomew-tide.'

'Pansies and violas, ... a cluster of either gives out a sweet though faint perfume.' *(See page 35)*

I love Henry Vaughan's lines about violets:

> ' As harmless violets, which give
> 　　　　　　　Their virtues here
> For salves and syrups while they live,
> Do after calmly disappear,
> And neither grieve, repine, nor fear :
>
> So dye his servants ; and as sure
> 　　　　　　　Shall they revive.
> Then let not dust your eyes obscure,
> But lift them up, where still alive,
> Though fled from you, their spirits hive.'

The violet is the symbol of humility. Over thirteen centuries ago the bishop-poet Fortunatus sent to Queen Radegonde of saintly fame violets and other scented flowers, and with his gift he wrote, ' He who offers violets must in love be held to offer roses. Of all the fragrant herbs I send none can compare in nobleness with the purple violet. They shine in royal purple : perfume and beauty unite in their petals. May you show forth in your life what they represent.' In Giovanni di Paolo's paradise the redeemed wander in meadows blossoming with the violets of humility and the lilies of purity. In the Adorations by the great masters, notably Botticelli, the violet symbolizes above all the humility of the Son of God, Who came to this earth as a little Child. In like manner the jasmine flowers tell us of the starry Heavens He left, and roses of the Divine love which sent Him to this earth. In an altar-piece by Lochner the Holy Child seated on His Mother's lap stretches up to take a violet held by her. In Signorelli's Madonna, in the Cathedral of Perugia, transparent vases

33

of jasmine, roses and violets are depicted, the roses
denoting Divine love, the violets His humility, and the
jasmine the starry heavens He had left to come to this
earth. In the beautiful Adoration of the Shepherds, by
Hugo van der Goes, in the Uffizi Gallery, purple and white
violets are in the centre of the foreground with lilies,
columbines, carnations, and blue and white irises. The
Infant Christ, bathed in light emanating from Himself,
lies on the ground, beside Him kneels His Mother,
around them are angels with jewelled circlets on their
brows, to the right adoring shepherds and on the left St.
Joseph. Between the Infant Child and the flowers lies a
sheaf of corn, symbolising the Bread of Heaven. The irises
denote His royal birth, the carnations His divine love in
coming to this earth, the columbines the seven gifts of the
Holy Spirit, and the violets His humility.

No one has written more beautifully of the effect produced on the mind by violets than old Gerard : 'March
Violets of the Garden have a great prerogative above
others, not only because the mind conceiveth a certaine
pleasure and recreation by smelling and handling of those
most odoriferous Flowers, but also for that very many by
these Violets receive ornament and comely grace : for
there bee made of them Garlands for the head, Nosegaies
and posies which are delightfull to looke on and pleasant
to smell to, speaking nothing of their appropriate vertues ; yea Gardens themselves receive by these the
greatest ornament of all, chiefest beautie and most
gallant grace ; and the recreation of the minde which is
taken hereby, cannot be but very good and honest : for
they admonish and stir up a man to that which is comely
and honest ; for floures through their beautie, varietie

of colour, and exquisite forme, doe bring to a liberall and gentlemanly minde the remembrance of honestie, comeliness, and all kinds of vertues. For it would be an unseemly thing for him that doth looke upon and handle faire and beautifull things, and who frequenteth and is conversant in faire and beautifull places, to have his minde not faire.'

Our great-grandmothers not only candied violets as we do, but they made various confections scented with violets, chiefly violet syrup and violet tablet. Violet syrup was made by macerating two pounds of fresh violets in five pints of distilled water for 24 hours. Then the liquor was strained off, sugar added (allowing a pound of sugar to each pint of liquor) and then boiled to a syrup. Violet tablets were made by steeping violets in lemon juice, adding sugar in the same proportion as above, and then boiling till when cold it set firm. They also used to eat young violet leaves fried and served with slices of lemons and oranges. No less an authority than John Evelyn describes this as ' one of the most agreeable of all the herbaceous dishes.'

Pansies and violas, which are so nearly related to violets, have, with few exceptions, little scent when smelt singly, but a cluster of either gives out a sweet though faint perfume. The soft mauve-blue Maggie Mott is fragrant, and Mrs. E. A. Cade, which is quite the earliest of the rayless yellow violas, is very fragrant. It flowers at least a fortnight earlier than the other rayless yellows, and does well again in early autumn. There are probably few plants with so many curious old country names as pansies,—Heart's-ease, Love-in-idleness, Herb Trinity, Three-Faces-under-a-Hood, Jump-up-and-Kiss-me,

Pink - of - my - John, and Call - me - to - you. Pansies are amongst our oldest favourites in the garden, and our Anglo-Saxon ancestors called the flower ' bone-wort.' We do not know for how many centuries the flower has been associated in fairy lore with the magical qualities which Oberon ascribed to

> ' the little western flower
> Before milk-white, now purple with love's wound,
> And maidens call it love-in-idleness.'

As early as January the first primroses shine forth in their ethereal loveliness, but they never attain their full beauty till April sun and showers have developed their soft beautiful leaves. Woodland primroses are such shy flowers that they never look quite at their ease in gardens except in a wild part or on a bank. What is the colour of the primrose? There is an exceeding softness and delicacy about the flowers, enhanced by the down of their stalks and the faint green of the under surfaces of their leaves. About them is the mystery and purity of the far expanses of the gardens of space. In the pure light of their petals they seem to reflect the luminous majesty of the flowers in the starry meadows of the Pleiades. How curiously arresting is the pale yet vivid green eye of the primrose with its circle of orange. Violets' eyes are full of dreams, aconites' of demure laughter, wood anemones' of fairy secrets, but in the delicate sensitive eye of the primrose there is something of almost human appeal. It is sweet and grave and child-like, thoughtful without a trace of sadness. Beyond all this is the elusive other-world expression which always baffles us. We may look at them, but their eyes never meet ours. The first ambassadors of spring in the woodlands bring with them

a nameless quality from worlds infinitely remote and
beyond our ken. Their secret is held in their faint
ethereal perfume, so delicate that one never tires of it,
so fresh that no other scent can be compared to its un-
earthly purity. They are redolent of the paths of the
angels. Primroses shine with a sudden gladness lacking
in flowers far more brilliant in hue. But their light does
not seem to be of this earth, and memories of them haunt
us even when the merry bluebells carpet the greenwood.

In the legend of St. Oswain primroses are mentioned
with roses, and lilies amongst the fairest flowers in the
gardens of the Earthly Paradise :

> ' Fair were her erbers with flowres,
> Rose and lily divers colours,
> Primrose and parvink :
> Mint, feverfoy, and eglantere,
> Columbin, and mother wer
> Than ani man mai bethenke,
> It berth erbes of other maner
> Than ani in erth groweth here,
> Tho that is lest of priis ;
> Evermore that grene springeth,
> For winter no somer it no clingeth,
> And sweeter than licorice.'

Primroses have such thick fleshy rootstocks that they can
lay up store in the previous summer for early flowering
the following year. The root has a strong smell of anise,
and it is a curious fact that nearly every animal rejects the
plant as food. Yet primrose leaves were used as late
as the nineteenth century in salads and primrose and
comfrey ointment is still made in out of the way parts
of the country.

What a wealth of real spring colour the masses of the different coloured primroses give. The range now is wonderful—blues of every shade, pinks, the 'Wisley red' which is so attractive, and the whole range of Juliae hybrids. *P. Juliae* itself is a native of the Caucasus, and all the hybrids are free-flowering and easily grown—'Jewel' (rosy purple and of even stronger growth), 'Pam' (ruby crimson, the brightest of all), 'Peg' (deep beautiful wine colour), 'Lingwood Beauty' (clear ruby), 'Mr. Neave' (velvety crimson), 'Juliana' (reddish purple), 'Bunty' (a dark purple-blue, one of the best), 'Crispie' (a bright crimson), and 'Wanda' (deep wine colour). 'Wanda,' I think, is one of the best, and is in bloom so early. This last mild winter 'Wanda' was in full bloom in mid-January, though of course very short-stalked—2 inches long only, instead of the 4 inches of her later flowering sisters. All the wine-coloured primroses look charming in shallow bowls of pale green moss. A real treasure which is comparatively new but which I should imagine will soon be seen in every garden is Barrowby Gem—a true 'primrose' but of a deep butter colour, the petals slightly thicker with just a suggestion of being frilled and very fragrant. At Wisley this primrose was continuously in bloom from mid-December to June, and then again for a brief spell in October. It is free-flowering, very striking outdoors and delightful for indoor decoration. The raiser, Mrs. McColl, told me that several years ago she noticed a seedling primrose in her garden of a very charming shade of soft yellow. She waited till by division she got about a dozen plants and then collected seed from them. Out of 200 seedlings from these plants only one produced flowers of the same soft yellow, but it was of an even deeper and better shade. This is the primrose now known in the catalogues as Barrowby Gem. There are already 'improved' (dreadful word!) varieties being shown, but though they have all the modern qualities of immense size, and striking colour, they are not, I think, nearly as pleasing as the original 'Barrowby Gem' which in spite of its deep lemon colour still preserves something of the ethereal delicacy and charm of the wild primrose.

The beautiful old double primroses are by no means easy to grow, for the English climate is too dry for them, but they flourish in Ireland. The bunch primroses (a cross between primroses and the old polyanthus) are deliciously scented, and given the cool rich soil they like, they are amongst the most beautiful of spring flowers. The range of colours now available is wonderful, ranging from white to deep velvety crimson, and nearly all of them with a beautiful orange eye. The true polyanthus has for centuries been a favourite in our gardens, and best of all are the old yellow-throated scarlet 'hose in hose,' which figure in Parkinson's *Paradisus*, and which, fortunately, have not been improved out of existence. Of the 'new' polyanthuses one of the very best for scent of the named varieties is 'Tangerine.' The name exactly describes the colour and the scent is as strong and as sweet as the scent of freesias. It is very free flowering and desirable in every way. So many of the spring flowers, such as tulips, need a thick edging round the beds, otherwise they are apt to look 'thin,' and there is nothing more delightful than a good border of polyanthus. It makes the bed look like a nice old-fashioned basketful of flowers.

39

A path bordered with masses of polyanthus of every colour is not only a joy to behold but looks so characteristic of Britain.

Indeed of all garden flowers there are few which are more truly of pure British stock than polyanthus and bunch primroses. In an authoritative article on the origin of these flowers Mr. Miller Christy pointed out that though they have been favourite garden flowers for nearly three centuries it is impossible to identify the plant we know as Polyanthus with any plant described in the works of the earlier herbalists (Fuchs, Turner, Dodoens, Matthiolus, de l'Obel, etc.), or even in Gerard and Parkinson. This, however, he acknowledges, is far from being conclusive evidence that the polyanthus as we know it was unknown then, owing to the vague nomenclature then employed. Early in the eighteenth century there was a polyanthus mania, and Philip Miller, writing in 1760, stated that ' in some parts of England they are so much esteemed as to sell for a guinea a root ; so that there may be still a much greater variety raised, as there are so many persons engaged in the culture of this flower.' At the end of the eighteenth century auricula and polyanthus shows were as common as rose shows to-day.

The interesting point which Mr. Miller Christy emphazises in conclusion of his theories as to the possible origin of the polyanthus is that whether this plant is an improved cultivated form of the hybrid between a red primrose and a red cowslip, or whether there may possibly be a slight foreign strain owing to being crossed with the Eastern red-flowered primrose (which is more brightly coloured than our native red primrose), the polyanthus is

40

a plant of British origin, having been evolved solely by the skill of British growers. And on the Continent the polyanthus is always known as the 'English primula.' It is interesting to remember that when the polyanthus was a prime favourite, Lancashire and Cheshire growers were celebrated. In his *Flora Historica* (1824) Phillips says : ' In no part of the world is this flower so successfully cultivated as in England, particularly by the zealous florists of Lancashire and Cheshire, who have, in the instance of this flower, left the Dutch bloemist considerably in the background. The neighbourhood of Manchester and Macclesfield is justly celebrated for producing the finest specimens of this flower, and in these manufacturing districts the criterion of a fine polyanthus is ascertained with as narrow a scrutiny as the sportsman regards his pointer or setter dog ! '

We have five species of primula native in Great Britain —the common primrose (*P. vulgaris*), the Bird's-eye primrose (*P. formosa*), the Scottish primrose (*P. scotica*), the oxlip (*P. elatior*), and the cowslip (*P. officinalis*). Of these the common primrose is the only one which can be described as accommodating. Three hundred years ago Parkinson wrote of the Bird's-eye primrose : ' It will hardly endure in our gardens, for all the care and industrie we can use to keepe it,' and this is as true to-day. For this lovely little primrose, which with its rosette of leaves covered on the under-side with a meal-like excretion, its umbel of lilac-purple flowers with a yellow eye (some varieties are pink or deep crimson) upborne on slender stems 3 to 12 inches high, is such a joy in the rock garden. Native of the mountainous pastures of Yorkshire and Westmorland, it requires a moist atmosphere and a

moist, deep, well-drained soil. The Scottish primrose
grows wild only in Orkney, Caithness and Sutherland,
and it requires the same conditions as the Bird's-eye
primrose. Oxlips are rarely seen growing wild nowadays,
except just occasionally in out-of-the-way parts of the
Eastern countries. The Caucasian oxlip, *P. leucophylla*,
is a much stronger grower than our English oxlip,
very hardy and splendid for naturalizing. There are
giant cowslips now, but nothing can equal the wild cowslip grown for its beauty and fragrance in our gardens for
centuries, but it is essentially a creature of the wild and
out of place in gardens. Cowslips and nightingales have
always been connected and there is an old saying, ' No
cowslips, no nightingales.' Most children have made
cowslip-balls or tisty tosties, as they-call them in the
West Country.

> ' I call, I call ; whom do ye call ?
> The maids to catch this cowslip ball :
> But since these cowslips fading be,
> Troth, leave the flowers and maids, take me.
> Yet if that neither ye will do,
> Speak but the word and I'll take you.'

Our ancestors used cowslips in countless ways, the young
leaves and flowers in salads, in puddings and tarts. They
candied and pickled the flowers, they made cowslip wine,
tea, syrup and complexion washes from them. In Turner's
Herbal (1551) there are singularly few beauty recipes—
only four altogether. One of them concerns cowslips,
and Turner observes sternly, ' Some weomen sprinkle ye
floures of cowslip w^t whyte wine and after still it and
wash their faces w^t that water to drive wrinkles away
and to make them fayre in the eyes of God, whom they

are not afrayd to offend.' Cooper, who was cook to
Charles I, gives a recipe for cowslip cream, which must
have been a dish fit for a king, though it horrifies one to
think of anyone eating cowslips. According to his recipe
he bruised the young cowslips and beat them up with a
quart of cream, the yolks of two or three eggs, fine sugar
and orange flower water, and served the dish strewn with
the flowers.

The American cowslip, or 'Shooting Star' (*Dodecatheon Meadia*), which is a native of many parts of
North America, was introduced into England over
200 years ago, for it was sent from Virginia to Bishop
Compton (then Bishop of London) in 1704. Philip Miller
mentions having seen it in bloom in the Bishop's garden
at Fulham Palace in 1709. After that it was apparently
lost. In 1744 it was again introduced by a Mr. Catesby,
who named it after Dr. Richard Mead, a celebrated doctor
of the day. Linnaeus gave it the name *Dodecatheon*,
though why he should call this flower 'twelve gods' it is
difficult to understand. 'Shooting Star' is descriptive
of the graceful pendent flowers which certainly remind
one of the fireworks known as 'shooting stars.' There
are several species, *D. giganteum* being one of the best.
The American cowslip is not particular as to soil, though
it likes plenty of leaf-mould, but part shade is essential.
It can easily be raised from seed or increased by division
of the roots in September. In at least two books *D.
Meadia* is described as having a clove-like scent (though
in no book by an American authority have I ever found
such a statement). The scent strikes me as fainter than
those of almost any of the primula family, and certainly
not clove-like!

Auriculas, which are so nearly related to primroses, were only introduced into gardens in the sixteenth century, largely owing to the French botanist, de l'Escluse, to whom also tulip-lovers owe so much. The Emperor Maximilian II was himself a great garden-lover, and when de l'Escluse accepted the Emperor's invitation to become botanist at the Court of Vienna, he was able to spend much time climbing in the Tyrol and Styria in search of fresh treasures. He had a special affection for the genus primula and naturalized *P. auricula*, *P. glutinosa*, and others in his garden. He gave the name *Auricula ursi* to these species owing to the resemblance of the leaves to bears' ears. De l'Escluse sent roots to his friend, van de Delft, in Belgium, whence they were spread, and early in the seventeenth century they were already established in English gardens. It is interesting to remember that we owe their popularity in England largely to the Huguenot refugees, who brought so many of their favourite flowers with them. Their old names still survive in different parts of the country. In Gloucestershire they used to call them ' Vanners' Aprons.' During the latter half of the seventeenth century auriculas became quite a cult, and Samuel Gilbert, in his *Florist's Vade Mecum* (1683), states that enthusiasts paid as much as twenty pounds for a root. Samuel Gilbert himself was an auricula enthusiast, and he gives great praise to those raised by ' Mr. Jacob Roberts who keeps the Physick garden in Oxford,' also to those ' in the Pallace Garden at Worcester.' He writes at length on their cultivation, and of the many quaint little poems in his book, that in praise of his favourite flower ' with their parti-coloured coats and pleasing scents,' is perhaps the most attractive :

' See how the Bears' Ears in their several dresses,
  That yet no Poet's pen so high expresses,
  Each head adorned with such rich attire,
  Which Fools and Clowns may slight, whilst skill'd admire,
  Their gold, their purples, scarlets, crimson dies,
  Their dark and lighter hair'd diversities,
  With all their pretty shades and Ornaments,
  Their parti-coloured coats and pleasing scents,
  Gold laid on scarlet, silver on the blue,
  With sparkling eyes to take the eyes of you,
  Mixt colours, many more to please that sense,
  Others with rich and great magnificence ;
  In double Ruffs, with gold and silver laced,
  On purple crimson, and so neatly placed.
  Ransack Flora's Wardrobes, none sure can bring
  More taking Ornaments t'adorn the spring.'

In later years auriculas became especially popular with the Lancashire weavers, who called the flowers ' Baziers.' There is an old Lancashire song :

' Come listen awhile to what we shall say
Concerning the season, the month we call May,
For the flowers they are springing, the little birds they are singing,
And the Baziers are sweet in the mornings of May.'

Another pleasant old name for the auricula was Dusty Miller, and it is fortunately still possible to get the old red Dusty Miller and the old yellow Dusty Miller.

Altogether there must be quite a hundred members of the primula family in cultivation in Great Britain, and one can only envy those with sufficient space to make a primrose garden and able to give the Asiatic varieties the moist situations so many of them require. A primrose garden is full of beauty for quite six months in the year, for the early primroses, both the single and double

45

varieties, are followed by the bunch primroses, the polyanthuses, the auriculas, and then the exotic varieties,
mostly of the candelabra type. I shall never forget a
small garden I once saw, which must at some time have
belonged to a primula enthusiast. From the house, a
square unpretentious building (so often far more attractive and full of character than the obviously ' picturesque '), a small garden sloped down to a stream, which
ran partly along the bottom and partly along the side of
the garden. And the banks were thickly planted with
primulas of every sort. It was in June, and the candelabra
varieties were in their full beauty, their colours ranging
from the palest cream to deep ruby crimson. It was an
unforgettable sight. The house was uninhabited, the
place had obviously been neglected for some months, and
one could only hope that the new owners would preserve
the beauty of that stream-side garden.

What treasures are continually being added to the
already numerous species of Asiatic primulas in our
gardens, yet some of them look already as though they
had been at home with us for centuries. Best of all for the
scented garden is *P. Florindae*, the giant of the Sikkimensis
primulas (it sometimes attains 4 feet) found in S.E.
Tibet by Mr. Kingdon Ward at an altitude of 12,000 feet.
Although only found in 1924, this glorious cowslip-
scented primula, producing its bright yellow trusses of
flowers in August, is already well known. It can scarcely
have too much moisture so long as the water is not stag-
nant. *P. Cockburniana*, with its gorgeous orange scarlet
flowers (the only member of the primrose family with
this colour), has unfortunately proved to be practically
biennial. Some of the hybrids, however (crossed with

46

P. pulverulenta) are perennial, *P. Bulleyana* being perhaps the best. *P. pulverulenta*, sometimes with as many as ten whole whorls of its gorgeous velvety crimson flowers, is still one of the most beautiful. Then there are *P. Beesiana* (purple with orange eye, 1½ feet), which crosses so readily, *P. anisodora* (deep maroon with yellow eye), found by Mr. Forrest in Yunnan, at an altitude of over 10,000 feet (it smells strongly of aniseed), *P. Chrysopa* (scented lilac blue flowers), and *P. Littoniana* (red and violet flowers grouped like a torch), *P. sikkimensis* (pale yellow flowers) from the Himalayas, *P. pudibunda* (the dwarf type of *P. sikkimensis*, which Mr. Kingdon Ward found at an altitude of 15,000 feet in Tibet), *P. nivalis sino-purpurea*, also from Tibet, *P. microdonta* var. *alpicola* and Mr. Kingdon Ward's No. 5746, with fragrant yellow flowers powdered white ; *P. chionantha* (related to *P. nivalis*), with drooping sweetly scented white blooms with a dark centre and yellow tube flowering in May. The last is of moderate growth (1½ feet), and likes a cool, rich, moist situation. *P. involucrata* (6 inches) one of the early introductions from the Himalayas, a true perennial, very free-flowering and vigorous, and with very fragrant white flowers, is still one of the best of the scented primulas.

There is, I suppose, no flower which gives greater pleasure to town-dwellers than wallflowers. To thousands of country-bred folk, who have the misfortune to live in cities, a bunch of wallflowers is a pleasure so great that it is almost pain. For their scent transports one instantly into the gorgeous sunlight of an old-fashioned garden, and one sees not only the wallflowers but the lilacs in full bloom, the peonies and lad's love, the flowering currants and apple blossoms, and instead of the noise of

47

the city one hears only the pleasant sound of the bees. Scientists tell us that wallflowers comprise the elements of many scents in their petals, even rose and violet scents, and possibly this accounts to some extent for the sensation they give that one is enjoying a garden full of flowers. But there is something in the scent of wallflowers beyond anything for which science can account.

Nowadays one seldom sees wallflowers treated as perennials, left to grow in peace and to live their full span of life, but how sturdy and attractive and full of character they are. A bed of wallflowers raised from seed the previous year give a feast of colour, but they cannot compare with a fine old plant full of years. Such a plant, covered with blossoms and with the bees hovering over it, is a delight. Wallflowers are beloved by bees and hence the old name of ' bee-flower.' As Gervase Markham wrote over three hundred years ago, ' The Husbandman preserves it most in his Bee-garden, for it is wondrous sweet and affordeth much honey.'

We do not know when wallflowers, ' which are very delightful to be set under a parlour or lower chamber window,' were introduced into our gardens, but it must have been in very early days. They are natives of the south of Europe. When found growing wild on old buildings the flowers are invariably yellow, and yellow therefore is evidently the original colour. ' Yellow violet ' was formerly a common name for them among country-folk. Gerard, in his *Herball* (1597), mentions only yellow wallflowers—' most pleasant sweete yellow flowers very double '—Parkinson, in his *Paradisus*, being the first to record those with striped or variegated petals. It is interesting to remember that both Turner and

'A primrose garden is full of beauty for quite six months in the year.' (*See pages 43, 45*)

Lyte call wallflowers 'Hertes Ease.' In his *Names of Herbes* (1548), Turner says, 'Called in English Cheiry, Hertes ease or wal Gelefloure, it hath yealowe floure.' In his *Herbal* (1551), he says: 'Viola that hath the yelow floure is called in English Wal gelefloure or hartes ease.' Lyte, in his translation of Dodoen's *Herbal*, says, 'The yellow Gillofer is called in English wall floures and Hartes ease.' Lyte also speaks of them as gillofer-wallflowers, and wall-gillyflowers was a common name for them in the sixteenth century. Parkinson gives the alternative English names, Bee-flowers, Wall-gilloflowers, Winter Gilloflowers and yellow Stocke-Gilloflowers. In Bulleins' *Bulwarke of Defence* (1562), wallflowers are called 'yellow violets,' 'hartes ease' and 'Swete Williams.' In the delightful dialogue between Hillarius (the gardener) and Marcellus, the former wishes the latter 'hearts ease,' to which Marcellus replies: 'I do hartely thanke you, for wishing to me so precious a jewell: so rich a treasure and so heavenly a comforte. For what is more to be desired then hartes ease, and who doe so sodainly slide or slippe awaie as hartes ease: Nothyng. For when adversitie come in at the one doore, eft soones, hartes ease doe run out at the other.'

In Lincolnshire they used to call the dark double wallflower 'Bloody Warrior,' and in Wiltshire 'Bleeding Heart.' It is said that the name 'Cheiranthus' was given by Linnaeus because the flowers had for so long been a favourite for nosegays. As Parkinson said of them, 'The sweetnesse of the flowers causeth them to be generally used in nosegays and to deck up houses.' Wallflowers were valued formerly not only for their beauty and scent, but also for their medicinal properties. In the sixteenth

49

and seventeenth centuries an oil was made from them
which the apothecaries sold under the name ' Cheirinum.'
Mixed with honey the petals were used to cure ulcers,
the juice was dropped into the eyes to remove dimness of
sight, the leaves bound to the wrist with bay salt were
accounted good for ague, and a conserve made of them
was a remedy for palsy.

Wallflowers which grow out of the crevices of walls are
naturally hardier than those of the garden. The stems
of the former become firm and woody, whereas the stems
of the latter are too succulent to resist severe frost. Owing
to the florist's skill we can now have wallflowers almost
the year round, for the early flowering varieties sown
under glass in February and March flower early in October
and in a mild season will continue flowering throughout
the winter. The Siberian Wallflower (*Cheiranthus
Allionii*) is valuable not so much for its fragrance as for its
gorgeous orange colour. One does not so often see *Erysi-
mum Perofskianum*, which is more fragrant, has flowers of
as brilliant an orange, and grows $1\frac{1}{2}$ feet. The old ' fairy-
wallflower ' (*E. rupestre*) is a charming little perennial for
sunny parts on a rockery. Also *E. linifolium*, the little
Portuguese wallflower, with slightly fragrant mauve-
coloured flowers, a hardy perennial about 6 inches high,
and flowers the first year from seed. The most sweetly
scented of all is the little old-fashioned Harpur Crewe.
It is curious how seldom one sees this, yet one little spike
of its double yellow flowers smells like the quintessence
of a whole bunch of wallflowers with just a trace of
mignonette scent also. There is also the little *C.
alpinus compactus*, which is smothered in spring with little
yellow flowers. A few days ago I was looking at some

' wallflowers ' in a friend's garden. They had been raised from a packet of wallflower seed, but a large number of them looked almost like stocks. The plants were stock-like, and so were the double and very large golden, strongly scented flowers, rather like the flowers of Harpur Crewe, only quite four times the size. They were curious and interesting, but how sad we should all be if our old wallflowers suffered any change !

One cannot help wishing that we had kept the prettiest of the old names for wallflowers—' Chevisaunce.' For this is the name Spenser used :

> ' Strowe me the ground with Daffadowndillies
> And Cowslips and Kingcups and loved Lillies,
> The pretty Paunce
> And the Chevisaunce
> Shall match with the fayre flowre Delice.'

We have long since lost the art of giving flowers names. Old flower-names are not only full of meaning, but they describe the essential character of the flower so simply and yet so perfectly that sometimes one cannot help wondering whether these names grew like the flowers themselves, or were they given in more leisured ages when people had time to ' consider ' flowers in the Biblical sense of the word ? In spite of the learned authorities (who tell us there is no such word as ' cherisaunce ') possibly ' chevisaunce ' is a misprint for ' cherisaunce,' which means ' comfort.' ' Comfort ' describes the true character of this beloved flower, for surely of all flowers wallflowers are the most comforting. The various mean-ings of ' chevisaunce ' all centre round the idea, ' achieve-ment,' and applied to a flower they are meaningless. Is it likely that so great a flower-lover as Spenser would have used a meaningless word when he had the whole range of sixteenth century names from which to choose? Remembering that two of the greatest botanists of his day called wallflowers ' Hertes ease ' one cannot help cherishing the belief that Spenser used a name which describes the wallflower as no other name could describe it— ' comfort.'

We have lost many of our pretty old English names of flowers. Some were applied to different plants, and in many cases it is difficult to identify them at all. The old names were naturally in common use as much in the New as in the Old World. But there, as with us, many are forgotten. For instance, in describing the gardens of ' New Amsterdam,' Adrian van der Donck mentions ' Jenoffelins, ' Baredames,' ' Maritoffles,' ' Summer sots,' etc. What flowers do these pleasant names represent? I like particularly ' Jenoffelins ' and ' Maritoffles.' Van der Donck describes yellow maritoffles as ' a very sweet flower.'

How satisfying the old flower names are, and how true. Forget-me-not preserves the memory of a beautiful old legend. There came a day when the Heavenly Father bestowed on all the flowers their names. But a pale blue flower, a little dreamer, forgot her name. She looked in the clear water at her feet and up to the blue Heaven above her, but try as she would she could not remember.

When night came on, and the stars shone out, it filled her with wonder to think that her Heavenly Father knew the number of those dazzling myriads in the infinite gardens of Heaven, and called them all by their names. ' I cannot remember my name. Do you know it? ' she whispered to one of the fairest stars. ' Not yet,' said the star, gazing down on the exquisite beauty of his new little sister on earth. ' But our Heavenly Father knows your name. Ask Him and He will tell you.' In the morning when she woke she saw a group of daisies near her throwing back their lovely crimson-tipped petals to be kissed by their big brother the Sun. ' Do you remember your name ? for I have forgotten mine,' she said to one of them, a gay little fellow with more crimson tips on his petals than any of the others. ' I did not hear your name,' he replied, ' but ask our Heavenly Father and He will tell you. We are daisies. What other name could be ours, for see how like we are to our big brother.' And he turned his laughing little face up to the Sun.

In the cool of the evening God walked in the garden. In time He came to the little blue flower and with adoring love and wonder she beheld His face. Presently she said very humbly, ' Alas ! that I should have forgotten the name Thou gavest me.' The Heavenly Father smiled on her, but He did not tell her the name she had forgotten. He answered her, ' Forget-*Me*-not.'

The little blue flower was silent with happiness. So beautiful a name would have crowned the furthest star in the Heavens, yet her Heavenly Father had chosen to bestow it on a little flower of this earth. The forget-me-not is still a dreamer. Through the centuries she dreams and forgets continually, but she does not forget her name. So earnestly does she obey her Heavenly Father's command that not only is the blue of Heaven in her petals, but something of its peace and joy as well. And to all who look on her she gives a peculiar joy.

CHAPTER III

SPRING-FLOWERING BULBS
AND SHRUBS

A GRAND old cherry tree (it is well over a hundred years old) loaded with its snowy cloud of exquisite blooms and in the grass beyond and all around a glory of daffodils —millions of them—covering the ground so thickly that the grass is almost invisible. This is what I am looking at now. There are only a few fleecy clouds in the blue sky, and the sunshine is so warm that were it not for the daffodils it would seem like a day in June rather than April. This daffodil garden has been forty-two years in making, and during all these years all flower-lovers have been welcomed by the kindly, generous owners of ' Wiggie.' The place still bears the quaint name that it bore in the sixteenth century. In John Norden's map of Surrey, made by order of Queen Elizabeth, Wiggie is one of the few places marked in the ' Reygate Hundred.' Something of the peace and quiet of those days still haunts Wiggie. Shortly before the war one of those employed here was a man, Daniel Gumbrell by name, who had entered the service of Mr. Trower's grandfather, in the reign of William IV, as a child of nine, and had worked for the family for 75 years. Four other men had been in their service for over 50 years. Old Daniel (who had served them for 75 years) by the time he had reached 90 years of age had 120 descendants, and I shall not easily forget Mr. Trower telling me of the Sunday afternoon when

54

Daniel was photographed with his 'family.' After this impressive ceremony the old patriarch headed the procession and they all went to Wiggie to offer their respects to Mr. Trower and his brother. Men such as Daniel Gumbrell do not die, for they live still in the hearts of their old masters.

At Wiggie the old 'Wilmer's Double daffodil' (*Narcissus Telamonius plenus*) is grown in abundance. This daffodil is thus described in the *Paradisus* (1629). 'The stalke riseth to be two foote high, bearing at the toppe one great faire double flower, each leafe whereof is twice as large and broad as the former, diversly intermixt with a rowe of paler and a rowe of deeper yellow leaves, wholly dispersed throughout the flower, the pale colour as well as the deeper yellow.' Of the origin of this daffodil, which has now been grown in our gardens for over 300 years, Parkinson gives the following interesting account. 'We first it had from Vincent Sion, borne in Flanders, dwelling on the Bank side, in his lives time, but now dead, an industrious and worthy lover of faire flowers, who cherished it in his Garden for many yeares, without bearing of any flowers untill the yeare 1620, that having flowred with him (and hee not knowing of whom he received it, nor having ever seene the like flower before) he sheweth it to Mr. John de Franqueville, of whom he supposed he had received it (for from beyond Sea he never received any) who findeth it to bee a kinde never seene or knowne to us before, caused him to respect it the more, as it is well worthy. And Mr. George Wilmer of Stratford Bowe Esquire in his lives time having likewise received it of him (as my selfe did also) would needes appropriate it to himselfe, as if he were the first founder thereof, and call it by his owne name Wilmer's double Daffodill, which since hath so continued.'

The richly-scented poet's narcissus is still known in some parts of the country by its pretty old names of Sweet Nancies and None-so-pretty, but one never hears the old name, ' primrose peerless,' recorded by Lyte. ' These pleasant flowers are called in Englishe Narcissus, White Daffodils, and Primrose pierelesse.' In the British Museum Library there is Lyte's own annotated copy of the French version of Dodoen's *Herbal* (translated by Lyte in 1578), and over the figure of *N. poeticus* one may read in Lyte's own writing, ' White primrose pyerles, Laus tibi, and of some Daffodille.' This same book has on the title-page the quaint inscription, ' Henry Lyte taught me to speake Englishe.' It is pleasant to remember that the true poet's narcissus, if not indigenous in England, has probably been grown here without a break since the days of the ancient Romans. Phillips in his *Flora Historica* (1824), says, ' This Narcissus seldom produces seed in England, even by the assistance of cultivation, and we are therefore of opinion that the few plants which have been found at Shorne, between Gravesend and Rochester, as well as those discovered in Norfolk, are the offsets from imported plants, probably of as early a date as the time of the Romans, who, we may naturally conclude, would not fail to plant the flower of their favourite poet, when we discover that they paved the floors of their dwellings in this country with tessellae that represented his tales.'

None of the modern varieties of the poet's narcissus seem to have the wonderful scent of the old ' Pheasant's Eye ' (*N. poeticus recurvus*). And the orange-coloured ring is being increased in breadth with the result that the striking effect of the aptly named ' Pheasant's Eye ' is wellnigh spoilt. Shall we ever recover the long-lost art of giving flowers names ? Modern daffodil catalogues are full of sophisticated names which sometimes manage to be impressive, but they never succeed in giving one a word-picture of the flower in question. But who could improve on ' Pheasant's Eye,' ' Butter and Eggs,' or ' Codlins and Cream ? ' They describe the flowers to the life and they are names no one can forget.

Jonquils and their hybrids flower somewhat later and of the former the old single sweet jonquil with its clusters of deliciously scented yellow flowers is still one of the best. A treasure either for the rockery or for growing in tiny pots for indoor decoration is the fairy-like and very sweetly scented *Juncifolius*. This native of the Pyrenees with its rush-like leaves and small yellow flowers in clusters only grows about 6 inches high, and grown for indoor decoration it is charmingly effective.

The most delightful lines about daffodils are, I think, those by Michael Drayton, but he does not say which of our native varieties the shepherd used to make his ' wreath of daffodillies.'

BATTE.

' Gorbo, as thou camest this way
By yonder little hill,
Or as thou through the fields didst stray,
Saw'st thou my Daffodil ?

She's in a frock of Lincoln green
Which colour likes her sight ;
And never hath her beauty seen
But through a veil of white.

Than roses richer to behold
That trim up lovers' bowers,
The pansy and the marigold
Tho' Phoebus' paramours.'

GORBO.

' Thou well describ'st the Daffodil :.
It is not full an hour
Since by the spring, near yonder hill,
I saw the lovely flower.'

BATTE.

' Yet my fair flower thou didst not meet
Nor news of her didst bring,
And yet my Daffodil's more sweet
Than that by yonder spring.'

GORBO.

' I saw a shepherd that doth keep
In yonder field of lilies
Was making as he fed his sheep
A wreath of daffodillies.'

BATTE.

' Yet, Gorbo, thou deludst me still
My flower thou didst not see ;
For I know my pretty Daffodil
Is worn of none but me.

To show itself but near her feet
No lily is so bold,
Except to shade her from the heat
Or keep her from the cold.'

GORBO.

' Through yonder as I did pass
Descending from the hill,

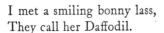

I met a smiling bonny lass,
They call her Daffodil.

And all the shepherds, that were nigh,
From top of every hill
Unto the valleys loud did cry,
" There goes sweet Daffodil." '

BATTE.

' Ay, gentle shepherd, now with joy
Thou all my flocks dost fill,
That's she alone, kind shepherd boy ;
Let us to Daffodil.'

None of the narcissi family take kindly to formal beds.
A thick row of nodding ' daffadowndillies ' bordering a
path leading to a cottage door look lovely, but those same
daffodils solemnly planted out in a stiff bed fail to be
even interesting. The real fact is that our ' formal ' beds
are not nearly formal enough ! A series of ' beds ' is
an unfinished affair and consequently falls between two
stools, for it is neither pleasant homely cottage gardening,
nor is it more than an elementary beginning of formal
gardening. Our ancestors, who excelled at this art, did not
stop half-way, and there was a great variety in the means
they used. Daffodils, or for that matter any of the
spring bulbs, look delightful in a bed laid out as a ' knot
garden.' Plenty of designs for these are to be found in
the old gardening books. The broad lines depicted in
these designs are planted with thyme or any other low-
growing shrub and the open spaces filled with the bulbs.
A bed planted in this fashion bears no resemblance to the
carpet bedding of Victorian days, but is a real pleasure to
the eye. The beauty of the flowers is distinctly enhanced

59

by the 'knot' of low-growing green stuff. Modern gardeners plant bulbs—hyacinths and tulips for instance—all of one colour in one bed, but our ancestors preferred (and I think they were right) a posy-like arrangement of mixed colours 'so that the place will seem like a piece of tapestry of many glorious colours to increase every one's delight.' One of the most attractive knot gardens I know is at Muntham Court. It is called 'the crown garden' and it is truly a royal garden, for the design is taken from the 'crown' of a baby's cap of 200 years ago.

Judging from the contemporary illustrations of them, Oriental hyacinths three hundred years ago bore little resemblance to the coarse type which the florists have managed to evolve. The 'hyacinth' of the classics is uncertain, but it is probably the same flower, for Pliny describes it as having grass-like leaves and the scent of the grape flower, and Homer mentions it with other fragrant flowers of the same season. Other poets write of its sapphire-coloured, crimson, purple and white bells. It is at least possible that the hyacinth was grown in England in Roman days, for Gerard speaks of wild hyacinths (they called them by the prettier name of Jacinth in those days) of 'a faire Carnation colour,' and these may have been survivals, for our native *Scilla nutans* is never flesh-coloured. We do not know for certain when the garden hyacinths were introduced, but it must have been about the middle of the sixteenth century, for Gerard does not speak of them as newly introduced. He says of them : ' These kinds of Jacints have been brought from beyond the seas, some out of one country, and some out of others, especially from the East countries, whereof they tooke their names *Orientalis*.'

They are natives of the Levant, Aleppo, Bagdad, etc., and in their native haunts they flower in February. Phillips in his *Flora Historica* suggests that they were introduced early in Queen Elizabeth's reign, for in 1561 she enabled Anthonie Jenkinson and others to visit Persia. The Dutch took up the culture of hyacinths with almost as great enthusiasm as that of tulips. Phillips mentions a certain Peter Voerhelm as the first to introduce the double hyacinths, one of which he named *The King of Great Britain.* This was early in the eighteenth century, and a bulb of this novelty cost £100. There was in fact a hyacinth mania as well as a tulip mania, and even in the early years of the nineteenth century £10 was an ordinary price for a fine bulb.

Some of the muscari are in bloom as early as February—*Hyacinthus azureus* for instance—but most of them during April and May. One always remembers Ruskin's description of the scent of the grape hyacinths—' the grape hyacinth, which is in south France, as if a cluster of grapes and a hive of honey had been distilled and compressed together into one small boss of celled and beaded blue.' Parkinson, who so frequently tells us the names given by women to flowers, tells us that ' English Gentlewomen call the white Grape-Flower Pearles of Spain.' The most sweetly scented of the muscari are the musk hyacinths, in bloom in April. They prefer a rich soil. The little spikes of inconspicuous bells both of the ordinary musk hyacinth and the large-flowered variety are veritably a quintessence of honey scent. A rare variety is *Moschatum flavum*, which has spikes of yellow bells. None of the muscari, alas! take really kindly to sandy soil.

61

Crown imperials, some would say, are not for the scented garden, but their strong 'foxy' smell is rather pleasing, and I think, as a contrast to the sweetness of most of the spring scents, it has an attraction of its own. This 'gallant flower,' as George Herbert described it, is certainly one of the handsomest of spring flowers and it has been a favourite since Elizabethan days, when it was introduced from Constantinople (it is a native of Afghanistan, Persia and the Crimea). Few flowers are so aptly named, for when the weighty seed-pods are formed they rise and form a perfect crown. John Lawrence gives another old name for the flower. ' The Crown Imperial,' he says, ' is by the Vulgar called Crown and Pearl by way of Corruption of the Word.' Gervase Markham in *The English Husbandman* (1613) says, ' The Crowne-Emperiall is of all flowers both Forraigne and home-bred the delicatest and strangest ; it hath the true shape of an Emperiall Crowne, and will be of divers colours, according to the Art of the Gardner. In the middest of the flower you shall see a round Pearle stand, in proportion colour and orientnesie like a true naturall Pearle, onely it is of a soft liquid substance : This Pearle if you shake the flower never so violently will not fall off, neither if you let it continue never so long will it either encrease or diminish in the bignesse, but remayneth all one ; yet if with your finger you take and wipe it away, in lesse then an houre after you shall have another arise in the same place, and of the same bignesse. This Pearle if you taste it upon your tongue is pleasant and sweet like honey.' The legend that the crown imperial now for ever bows its head because in the Garden of Gethsemane it failed to do so on the night of Our Lord's Agony in the Garden,

62

and that its pearl-like tears can never be permanently removed by human hands is well known. There is also a Persian legend according to which the crown imperial was once a queen. Her husband unjustly doubted her fidelity to him and she left him to wander the earth alone. An angel in pity changed her into this flower, but until she is restored to her husband her tears will remain.

Tulips hold pride of place in the spring garden and amongst them there are treasures for the scented garden. Of the early single tulips the sweetly scented Yellow Prince and Fred Moore (syn Thomas Moore) are, I suppose, the best. The latter is notable not only for its scent, but it is also one of the best of the orange terra-cotta shades and equally good either outdoors or for indoor bowl culture. It also forces well. Of the Darwin tulips, ' Cordelia ' (a gorgeous reddish violet with blue markings), ' Nauticus ' (deep rose with a violet centre), ' Philippe de Commines ' (a glossy dark plum), and the stately ' Sophrosyne ' (soft rose with white margin and blue centre) are all fragrant. Amongst the cottage tulips ' La Merveille ' is one of the finest. With her lovely cherry-rose petals, scarlet orange within, her exquisite shape when closed and her fine scent there are few tulips to compare with her. *Macrospila*, the sweet-scented scarlet tulip, never looks better than when planted in rough grass. ' Marvel ' (canary yellow within and soft rose outside), ' Mrs. Moon ' (butter yellow with a faint sweet scent), and the late-flowering ' Rosalind,' ' Primrose Beauty ' (a soft creamy, primrose and sweetly-scented), are all well worth a place in the scented garden. The so-called wild tulip, *T. sylvestris*, and its near relation *T. australis*, are both sweetly scented, and the lovely little *T. persica*, which likes a very warm spot on the rockery. Sir Daniel Hall says of *T. persica* : ' *T. persica* is presumably only a cultivated form of *T. australis*. It has certainly been known for two or three centuries in gardens, and Dr. Stapf thinks it may be identified as a form which Clusius described as sent to him from the south of France. There is no authority for the specific name *persica* ; the early writers like Parkinson called *T. Clusiana* by this name. Nor is any wild habitat known. Actually it is a very distinct form, marked by the fact that it is one of the latest tulips to flower, opening only as the late flowering garden tulips are going over.'

Nothing is yet known of the origin of the tulip beyond the fact that it is undoubtedly Eastern and a garden flower when first seen by Europeans. Certainly no flower has caused a greater sensation amongst plant lovers than the tulip when it was first introduced into the gardens of western Europe. Of its history before 1550 we know nothing, except that it was one of the most esteemed flowers in Turkish gardens, but for how long the Turks have cultivated it we do not know. Busbequius, the ambassador of the Emperor Ferdinand I to the Sultan, mentions in a letter written in 1554 that he saw tulips flowering in a garden between Constantinople and Adrianople. ' As we passed we saw everywhere abundance of flowers such as the Narcissus, Hyacinths, and those called by the Turks Tulipan, not without great astonishment on account of the time of the year, as it was then in the middle of winter, a season unfriendly to flowers. Greece abounds with narcissus and hyacinths, which have a remarkably fragrant smell ; it is indeed so strong as to hurt those that are not accustomed to it. The Tulipan, however, have little or no smell but are admired for their beauty and variety of colour. The Turks pay great attention to the cultivation of flowers, nor do they hesitate, though by no means extravagant, to expend several aspers for one that is beautiful. I received several presents of these flowers, which cost me not a little.' Conrad Gesner, the great German botanist, states in his *De Hortis Germaniae* that he saw tulips growing in a garden in Augsburg in 1559. This is the earliest record of their flowering in western Europe. ' In this year of our Lord 1559,' he says, ' at the beginning of April in the garden of the ingenious and learned Councillor John Henry Herwart, I saw there a plant which had sprung from seed which had been procured from Byzantia, or as some say from Cappadocia. It was growing with one large reddish flower, like a red lily, having eight petals of which four are outside, and just as many within, with a pleasant smell, soothing and delicate, which soon leaves it.' We do not know the exact date when tulips were introduced into England, but it must have been before 1582, for Richard Hakluyt in his *Remembrances of Things to be Endeavoured at Constantinople* (1582) says, ' And now within these foure years there have been brought into England from Vienna in Austria divers kinds of flowers called Tulipas, and these and others procured thither a little before from Constantinople by an excellent man called M. Carolus Clusius.' Clusius (de l'Escluse) came to Leyden as Professor of Botany in 1593, and from his garden the bulbs were either sold or stolen till tulips were soon commonly grown throughout the United Provinces.

Gerard mentions Mr. Garret, the London apothecary, as an enthusiastic tulip breeder.

In Paris tulips were the flowers most favoured by ladies to wear in their low-cut dresses, and gifts of the rarest were prized as though they were jewels. Parkinson in his *Paradisus* (1629) describes flower lovers as being ' more delighted in the search, curiosity, and rarities of these pleasant delights, than any age I thinke before. But indeede this flower, above many other, deserveth his true commendations and acceptance with all lovers of these beauties, both for the stately aspect, and for the admirable varieties of colours, that daily doe arise in them. But above and beyond all others the Tulipas may be so matched, one colour answering and setting of another, that the place where they stand may resemble a piece of curious needlework or a piece of painting : and I have knowne in a Garden, the Master as much commended for this artificial form in placing the colours of Tulips, as for the goodness of his flowers or any other thing. . . . But to tell you of all the sorts of Tulips (which are the pride of delight) they are so many, and as I may say, almost infinite, doth both passe my ability and, as I believe, the skill of any other. . . . Besides this glory of variety in colours that these flowers have, they carry so stately and delightfull a forme, and do abide so long in their bravery (enduring above three whole moneths from the first unto the last) that there is no Lady or Gentlewoman of any worth that is not caught with this delight or not delighted with these flowers.'

The ' tulip mania,' which was at its height between 1630 and 1640, is of little real interest to flower lovers. Collegiums or clubs were formed and held at the inns, which became tulip exchanges. A rare print of this period entitled ' The Fool's Wagon ' satirized the mania by showing a chaise-like car with Flora holding in one hand a horn of plenty containing tulip blooms and in the other three separate blooms. Three florists, named ' Good for Nothing,' ' Eager Rich,' and ' Tippler,' all decked with tulips, are with her, and a crowd runs after the car, trampling on their weaving looms etc., and calling out, ' We will all sail with you.' The only interesting feature of this gambling in tulips is the fact that the tulip ' fraternities ' took as their patron saint St. Dorothea. This information is, I think, given in only one book, *The Dutch Gardener*, translated into English in 1703. The author, Henry van Oosten, was an enthusiastic tulip grower and he describes his favourite flower as ' the Queen of Flowers and the chief Jewel of Flora,' and throughout the tulip grower is called ' the Lover.' But, alas! he does not tell us why St. Dorothea was chosen to be the patron saint of the tulip fraternities.

Forsythias are, I suppose, more commonly grown than any of the other spring flowering shrubs, and if only their golden bells were scented they would be even greater favourites. Flowering at the same time as the Forsythias are those established old favourites the American flowering currants, still amongst the best of the scented spring flowering shrubs. These natives of western North America were introduced in 1826, and very soon became so popular that they were grown in every cottage garden. Their instant popularity is not surprising, for apart from their intrinsic beauty and warm aromatic scent, they give a mass of rosy-red colour in the garden at a time when that colour is very scarce. They all root easily from cuttings. Of the different varieties of *R. sanguineum* the best are those which are true to type with brilliant blood-red flowers. Where there is space one would like to grow them all. The evergreen *R. viburnifolium* (a native of S. California) is interesting, for the scent of its leaves is peculiar. There is no suggestion of the strong, aromatic fragrance of *R. sanguineum*, but they have a very attractive scent, even though it be decidedly suggestive of turpentine.

Then there is that invaluable Chinese shrub—*Osmanthus Delavayi*—a beautiful shrub to look at and with very sweetly scented small white flowers. Even more pleasingly scented are the skimmias (*S. japonica* and the male form *S. fragrans*). The scent of their tiny flowers is indistinguishable from that of lilies of the valley. *Nuttallia cerasiformis* produces its racemes of creamy-white almond-scented flowers about the same time. This is a good shrub even for small gardens and very hardy. The red, cherry-like fruits in autumn are attractive, but to ensure these both the sexes must be planted just as with the skimmias. One of the most attractive of the March-flowering scented shrubs is *Corylopsis spicata*, a native of Japan and introduced into this country in 1863. It is one of the earliest shrubs in bloom and very delightful with its woolly leafless stalks and clusters of cowslip-scented flowers. It is curious that one does not see this shrub more often in small gardens, for though wide-spreading it is not more than about 6 feet tall. *C. pauciflora* is not so hardy, but for protected districts it is a charming shrub. *Azara microphylla*, with its tiny vanilla-scented flowers, blooms in February in a very mild season, but as a rule not till March and April.

Although the flowers are so small, they scent the air for yards round. It is one of the most attractive of small trees and was introduced from Chile for Messrs. Veitch in 1861. In April, *Viburnum Carlesii*, the most sweetly scented of all the viburnums, flowers. This is a valuable shrub for small gardens, for it grows only about 3 or 4 feet, is very hardy, and its white wax-like flowers with their rich scent are so freely produced. The scent of *V. Carlesii* is not, I think, quite so attractive as that of *V. fragrans*, for the scent of the former is curiously artificial. The handsome spring-flowering andromedas are not sweetly fragrant, but for those who like it there is something strangely fascinating in the strong, aromatic, nut-like scent of their thick white sprays of flowers. Flowering somewhat later is the handsome *Choisya ternata* (the Mexican orange blossom). Then there are the scented heaths, the honey-scented *Erica arborea*, also *E. australis* and *E. Veitchii*. *Fothergilla Gardeni* takes little space and its flowers are sweetly fragrant. The delicately scented Japanese apricot (*Prunus Mume*) and the violet scented American crab (*Pyrus coronaria*) give surely the most fairy-like of the spring scents. Amongst the showiest of the early flowering shrubs is the commonly grown *Berberis Darwinii*, an invaluable shrub both in large and small gardens. Its long arched sprays, massed with small orange-golden blossoms, faintly scented, are a joy both in the garden and for indoor decoration. It succeeds well in any soil. Many of the countless Berberis hybrids are very sweetly scented, usually a lily of the valley-like fragrance. Where space is limited, I think most people would include of the early flowering scented shrubs at least *Chimonanthus fragrans, Lonicera*

69

fragrantissima, *Berberis japonica* var. *Bealii*, *Ribes sanguineum*, *Osmanthus Delavayi*, *Viburnum Carlesii*, *Choisya ternata*, *Prunus Mume*, *Pyrus coronaria*, and lastly, and amongst the best of all, rosemary.

Even in December and January the rosemary bushes are full of buds, and in March, April and May, the long branches are so thickly clustered with their lovely mauve-blue aromatic flowers that at a distance the bushes look as though they were wreathed in lavender-blue mist. How the bees love these flowers! On sunny days the bee-music never ceases amongst them, and seems to add even greater richness to their warm, pungent fragrance. It is difficult to understand people who clip rosemary into trim, tidy bushes. Pruning it to prevent the plant from growing too straggly is one thing, but to keep it so trim that one loses the beauty of its long branches laden with flowers, especially when one considers how long they last in bloom, seems sheer foolishness. There is an erect-growing variety of rosemary, but I think the old-fashioned kind, formerly prized for its medicinal qualities, is the more attractive. *R. prostrata*, being dwarf, and spreading, is charming on a rockery. It does not flower till April or May and is not very hardy. *Rosmarinus angustifolius*, the thin-leaved rosemary, makes a more 'feathery' bush and a large specimen of it is very attractive. I once saw bushes of it growing all along the edge of a sunk garden, and in flower they were a lovely sight.

Mr. Trower, of 'Wiggie' fame, pointed out to me one day a bush of rosemary growing in his garden and told me its 'pedigree.' When George Eliot went to Stratford-on-Avon she was given a sprig of rosemary, from a bush said to have been there in Shakespeare's day. She took it back to Wimbledon and planted it herself in her garden. Mr. Trower was given a slip from this bush, which he, like George Eliot, planted himself, and he was kind enough to give me a slip from the bush. I in turn carefully planted it, and when large enough I will joyfully give slips to anyone who cares for them.

I am always hoping some day to light on the 'gilded rosemary' (presumably a variegated rosemary) which Parkinson mentions in his *Paradisus*. It was evidently grown in England in Elizabethan and Stuart days, for Parkinson describes it thus : 'This Rosemary differeth not from the former, in forme or manner of growing, nor in the forme or colour of the flower, but only in the leaves, which are edged or striped, or pointed with a faire gold yellow colour, which so continueth all the yeare throughout, yet fresher and fairer in Summer than in Winter ; for then it will looke of a deader colour, yet so, that it may be discerned to be of two colours, green and yellow.' Parkinson is always careful to state when he knows a plant only by repute, for of the double-flowered rosemary he says : 'This I have only by relation, which I pray you accept, untill I may by sight better inform you.'

Rosemary was probably first introduced into England by the Romans, but there has always been the tradition that it was re-introduced by Queen Philippa of Hainault. In the library of Trinity College, Cambridge, there is a most interesting MS., translated from the original (written by 'a clerk of the school of Salerno'), which was sent to Queen Philippa by her mother 'the Countess of Henaud,' and the translator ('danyel bain') states that rosemary was unknown in England until the

Countess of Hainault sent some to her daughter, the Queen of England. The MS. is entirely devoted to the virtues of rosemary, and contains interesting lore about the herb. Rosemary, we are told, never grows higher than the height of Christ when He was a man on earth, and after thirty-three years the plant increases in breadth but not in height. ' Lavender and rosemary,' says the writer, ' is as woman to man and White Rose to Red. It is an holy tree and with folk that be just and rightfull gladlye it groweth and thryveth.' Of its virtues, the compiler of Bancke's *Herbal*, the earliest herbal printed in the English language, tells us that it gladdens all who use it, that the leaves laid under one's pillow deliver one from evil dreams, that powder of the flowers bound in a linen cloth to the right arm makes one light and merry, that washing one's face in a decoction of the leaves boiled in white wine makes one fair to look upon, that the flowers laid amongst clothes and books keep away moths, that burnt rosemary wood used as powder keeps the teeth free from all evils and that even to smell it keeps one ' youngly.'

Rosmarinus—' dew of the sea '—has any plant a lovelier name ? However, far inland rosemary bears the memory of the sea, near which it grows naturally, in the bracing fragrance of its leaves and flowers. Rosemary has always been regarded as a herb endued with mysterious powers. In the old French language of flowers rosemary represents the power of rekindling lost energy. Did they not try to waken even the Sleeping Beauty by its magic power ? In Portugal rosemary is called *alecrim*, a word which carries us back to the days of the Vandals, for *alecrim* is derived from the

Scandinavian *ellegren*—literally 'elfin plant.' In very early days, therefore, rosemary was connected with elves, and in Sicily they tell one that the baby fairies sleep in the rosemary flowers. The lowest petals of the flowers are certainly perfect cradles for the baby fairies, and one loves to think of them swinging in them. According to a Spanish legend rosemary flowers were originally white, but during the Flight into Egypt the Holy Family rested beside a rosemary bush, and the Virgin Mary, having thrown her robe over it, the flowers preserved the memory of her having thus honoured them by turning the colour of her robe.

In Tudor days no herb was more widely grown and used. Hentzner mentions in his *Travels* (1598) that in English gardens the walls were frequently covered with rosemary, and at Hampton Court he says ' it was so planted and nailed to the walls as to cover them entirely.' Both in cookery and medicine the uses of this herb were manifold. The flowers were candied, a conserve was made of them and rosemary cordial was used in every household. Rosemary was one of the chief ingredients in the famous ' Hungary Water,' the recipe for which, tradition says, was given to Queen Elizabeth of Hungary by a hermit. The original recipe is treasured in what was formerly the Imperial Library of Vienna. Hungary Water was the favourite toilet water in most European countries for at least two centuries.

It is curious how few people trouble to dry and keep rosemary seeds, but their pungent, aromatic fragrance is most pleasant when kept in bags in the same way as lavender. Bushes which have been allowed to grow without severe clipping are as massed with these fragrant

73

seeds in August and September as they were with flowers throughout spring and early autumn. They should be collected on a dry day in September and thoroughly dried by spreading out on tissue paper placed on sieves. When dry they can be tied up in ' sweet bags ' for the house. Rosemary does not often propagate itself by seed in Britain, but a self-sown rosemary has appeared by the side of a path in our garden, and as it has chosen such poor soil I am watching it hopefully, and wonder whether it will grow into a ' gilded rosemary.'

Gilded branches of rosemary tied with different coloured ribbons were given as ' favours ' to the guests at a wedding, and the bridesmaids wore sprigs of gilded rosemary tied to their left arms. Why do not we revive this pretty old custom ? Churches were decorated with boughs of rosemary at Christmas, and it was also the custom to strew the floor with it for its pleasant savour. Rosemary and bays were commonly used with holly, ivy and mistletoe for indoor decoration at Christmas time, and in accordance with tradition carefully removed on Christmas Eve.

> ' Down with the rosemary, and so
>   Down with the bays and mistletoe,
>   Down with the holly, ivy, all
>   Wherewith ye dressed the Christmas hall,
>   That so the superstitious find
>   No one least branch there left behind ;
>   For look, how many leaves there be
>   Neglected there, maids, trust to me,
>   So many goblins you shall see.'

Above all rosemary was the herb of friendship. ' As for rosemary,' wrote Sir Thomas More, ' I lette it runne all over my garden walls, not onlie because my bees love

it, but because it is the herb sacred to remembrance
and to friendship, whence a sprig of it hath a dumb
language.'

In a little-known seventeenth century poem, the writer,
Judge Hale, prays His Lord that He will enter his humble
heart :

> ' And with Thy leave, I'll fetch some flowers that grow
> In Thine Own Garden—Faith and Love to Thee.
> With these I'll dress it up, and there shall be
> My Rosemary and Bays. Yet when my best
> Is done, the room's not fit for such a Guest.
> But here's the cure—Thy presence, Lord, alone
> Can make the stall a Court, the cratch a Throne.'

CHAPTER IV

THE SCENTS OF EARLY SUMMER

THE lily of the valley is, I think, the very first of the flowers whose scent is a true summer scent, for the ' May lily,' as our ancestors called it, never flowers till the bitter winds we so often get in late spring are over When the lily of the valley flowers we know in truth that summer has come :

> ' The hills tell each other, and the listening
> Valleys hear ; all our longing eyes are turned
> Up to thy bright pavilions ; issue forth,
> And let thy holy feet visit our clime ! '

Only in shade is it possible to see lilies of the valley in their beauty, with the softened light shining through their leaves on to the bells, hung like ' fairy lamps of snow.' In the shade of the woodlands so exquisite is this light that it seems as though the leaves were fashioned of the softest and richest velvet. Small wonder that to Keats, with his deep love of mysterious colours, the ' sweet lily of the lowly vale' was 'the queen of flowers.' Is any other flower set in such an exquisite aura of radiant yet hushed light ?

Lilies of the valley figure exquisitely in the magnificent ' Adoration of the Mystic Lamb ' by the van Eycks. The Mother of Our Lord is depicted with a crown of rubies, sapphires and pearls set in gold. The rubies alternate with the sapphires, the former being square-cut and surrounded with pearls. Above each ruby are set two columbines surmounted by a Madonna lily, and above each sapphire are roses surmounted by three stalks of

76

lilies of the valley. Around her head, seen as through a cloud, are twelve stars. The Madonna lilies denote her purity, the roses the divine love which sent Our Lord to this earth, the columbines the seven gifts of the Holy Spirit, and the lilies of the valley the humility of 'the handmaid of the Lord.'

The lily of the valley grows wild almost throughout Europe from Italy to Lapland. According to a Sussex legend, they grew first in St. Leonard's forest, where the Saint encountered and vanquished the dragons or 'fire drakes,' which devastated that part of the country. When this lowly flower was first made a garden flower we do not know, but Thomas Hyll, the author of the earliest book on gardening in our language, tells us (in 1568) that they had recently been 'bought and planted in gardens.' 'The wood Lillie or Lillie of the valley,' he says, 'is a flower mervallous sweete, florishing especially in the spring time, and growing properly in woods, but chiefly in valleies and on the sides of hilles. But now for the great commoditie and use known (of the floure) the same of late yeares is bought and planted in gardens.' The pink-flowered variety, which was known in Parkinson's day, was apparently and fortunately as rarely seen then as it is now. In the *Paradisus* he says of it that 'it groweth only in the Gardens of those that are curious lovers of rarities.' The flowers were formerly used in many ways. Distilled in wine they were accounted in Gerard's time 'more precious than gold.' Parkinson says, 'The flowers of the white kind are used with those things that help to strengthen the memory and to procure ease to Apoplectic persons. Camerarius setteth down the manner of making an oyle of the flowers hereof, which he saith is very

77

effectuall to ease the paines of the Goute, and such-like diseases, to be used outwardly, which is thus : Having filled a glasse with the flowers, and being well stopped, set it for a moneth's space in an Ants hill, and after, being drayned cleare, set it by to use.'

It is interesting to remember that a little over a hundred years ago the lily of the valley was a comparatively common wild plant near London. Philip Miller, writing in 1807, gives the following as the places where it was to be found :

' In Britain, near London on Hampstead Heath, but now sparingly, since the trees have been destroyed ; in Lord Mansfield's wood near the Spaniard ; between Shooter's-hill and Woolwich ; Norwood abundantly, where I have frequently seen large patches with very few flowers and no berries ; Bushy-heath, Cashioberry in Hertfordshire ; near Chiselhurst in Kent ; near Lee in Essex ; Woburn in Bedfordshire, whence the markets in London are generally supplied with the flowers. Whichwood forest in Oxfordshire, and in Beechwood, near Stokenchurch ; White-wood, near Gamlingay in Cambridgeshire ; Norfolk ; Buddon and Okeley woods in Leicestershire ; King's Cliff in Northamptonshire ; Kendal in Westmoreland ; County of Durham ; Ingleborough in Yorkshire ; Scotland.'

We have a piece of waste shady ground in our little garden, which we have planted with lilies of the valley, Solomon's seal, and bluebells (which are all in flower at the same time), ferns and foxgloves. The most sweetly scented of the wild geraniums, ' herb robert ' (our only wild flower called after Robin Hood), sows itself plentifully and is more or less (principally less !) diligently weeded out. Solomon's Seal (*Polygonatum officinale*) is one of the pleasant old-fashioned scented flowers one does not often see nowadays. I love their graceful arching stems, their flowers like wax tassels, and the curious rich ' thick ' smell, quite unlike that of any other English flower. Solomon's Seal is one of our indigenous plants, and it has many pretty old names—David's Harp, Ladder-to-Heaven, Lady's Seal, White Root or Whitewort (so called from the thick white roots). In French, Italian and Spanish it is called Solomon's Seal, the old belief being that the curious marks to be seen if one cuts the roots tranversely bear the impress of Solomon's own seal. The roots were formerly commonly used as a poultice for knitting broken bones, also for bruises. Gerard in his *Herball* says, ' the root stamped while it is fresh and green and applied taketh away in one night or two at the most any bruise, black or blue spots, gotten by falls or woman's wilfulness in stumbling upon their hasty husbands fists ! ' The distilled water of the plant was also in great demand for removing freckles, ' leaving the face fresh, fair and lovely after it has been a few times washed therein.' Parkinson in his *Theatrum Botanicum* tells us it was a favourite complexion wash among ' the ladies of Italy.' I have never seen the narrow-leaved Solomon's Seal (*P. verticillatum*), but it is said to grow wild, although very rarely, in Scotland.

The ' softest ' of the early summer scents is surely that of apple blossom. The individual blossoms have little perfume, but in the mass it is exceeding sweet, although delicate. But I think its most attractive quality, beyond even its sweetness, is its softness. To walk in an orchard of apple trees in full bloom is to be enfolded in an invisible soft cloud of most delicate yet all-pervading perfume. A great deal has been written about night-scented flowers, but lovely as they are, the early morning scents are, I think, the lovelier. The scent of apple blossom is sweetest and most pervading in the early morning. Indeed, it is so strong that it overpowers all other scents, for the whole air is filled with it. And how delightful it is to watch the pollen-bearing bees loaded with the pale yellow pollen of the blossoms. This year the apple blossom, according to the country-folk, is more wonderful than within living memory. Indeed, it is difficult to find on the young trees one wood-making shoot, and the flowers are so closely set that seven to ten flowers in a cluster are quite common. The apple orchards, especially of the West Country, have been surely one of the most glorious floral spectacles in Europe. Their beauty is unsung, and mercifully un-advertised, but to those who love them there are few sights of more endearing beauty than an English orchard in full bloom. How much has been written of the plum and cherry blossom of Japan, but what can compare with the opalescent loveliness and the ethereal scent of apple blossom ? When the trees are almost hidden by the wealth of white foam and given by the rosy-fingered dawn her first caress, a magic casement into fairyland is opened. An apple orchard in bloom is indeed one of the loveliest sights on earth. The beauty of cherry and plum blossoms appeals to the imagination, but the child-like loveliness of apple blossom appeals to the heart. Moreover, in spite of the ethereal beauty and fragrance of the flowers, there is a quality of homeliness about apple trees which endears them to us all.

The apple tree may indeed be described as the tree

Sweetly scented lilacs beloved by Mrs McKelvey. *(See page 83)*

symbol of an English home, for there is no other tree which embodies in its quiet happy beauty and its simplicity all that the word home means to our race. How largely this tree figures in the domestic history of our race, and how interesting it would be to trace the story of it in these islands from the days of our British ancestors through Saxon, mediaeval, Tudor, Stuart and Georgian days. What pictures flit before one of our indigenous apple trees in the beauty of their bloom before the days of the Romans, when the sacred island of Avalon was so called because of the apples which grew there in such abundance ; of the orchards of our Anglo-Saxon ancestors and the picturesque scenes when they made cider (which they called sieder) of the well-cared for orchards belonging to the monasteries ; of the fame of the cider orchards of Herefordshire even in Elizabeth's reign. Gerard enthusiastically advocated the planting of yet more orchards. ' Gentlemen, that have lands and living put forward in the name of God ; graffe, set, plant, and nourish up trees in every corner of your grounds ; the labour is small, the cost is nothing, the commoditie is great, yourselves shall have plentie, the poor shall have somewhat in time of want to relieve their necessitie and God shall rewarde your good mindes and diligence.' Apples and apple trees figure largely in our folk-lore and the custom of wassailing trees was kept up to within living memory.

' Here's to thee, old apple-tree ;
Hence thou mayst bud, and whence thou mayst blow,
And whence thou mayst apples bear enow !
. Hats full ! caps full !
Bushel, bushel sacks full !
And my pockets full, too ! Huzza ! '

81

Apples, too, were widely used, not only in the medicines prescribed by the physicians, but also in homely remedies, and the smell of apples was accounted very wholesome. John Key, who was physician to Queen Mary, and later to Elizabeth, had great faith in even the smell of apples. In his book, which was published in 1552, he counselled his patients, when feeling weak after a dangerous illness, to ' smell to an old swete apple for there is nothing more comfortable to the spirits than good and swete odours.' Apple juice and pulp were widely used in cosmetics and ' comfort apples,' as they were called (apples stuck with cloves), were the poor man's substitute for the orange stuck with cloves of the rick folk. One recalls a passage by Ralph Austen, that great lover of orchards and of the scent of their blossoms : ' Sweet perfumes work immediately upon the spirits for their refreshing ; sweet and health-full ayres are special preservatives to health, and therefore much to be prised. The most pleasant and wholesome odours are from the blossomes of Fruit-Trees, which having in them a condensing and cooling property are therefore not simply Healthfull, but are accompted Cordiall, chearing and refreshing the Heart and vital spirits.'[1] I wonder why we do not revert to the mediaeval custom of growing fruit trees in small pleasure gardens. There are thousands of small gardens where there is only space for a few shrubs and very frequently one sees shrubs which are in beauty for only one season. But fruit trees have two seasons of great beauty. A Captain John Taverner, writing as early as 1600, advised that all the highways in England should be planted with fruit trees, and he added the sensible suggestion that anyone should

[1] Ralph Austen. *A Treatise of Fruit Trees*, 1653.

be allowed to pick and eat the fruit, but that if he carried it away he should be punished.

Amongst the sweetest scents of early summer are those of the wistarias, lilacs, azaleas, *Phillyrea angustifolia*, *Buddleia globosa*, and that grand old shrub, the much ill-treated 'Portugal laurel' (*Prunus lusitanica*). Few climbers can compare with the beauty and the scent of the wistarias, but although *W. chinensis* was introduced well over a hundred years ago, the wistarias still look like strangers and aliens in our gardens. But who can imagine a cottage garden in May without a lilac tree laden with its fragrant blossoms? For over 300 years this shrub, which is a native of south-eastern Europe, has been grown in our gardens. The greatest wanderer of the species, however, is the Persian lilac. As Mrs. McKelvey says in her monograph, *The Lilac*, 'the fact that its name is a geographical misnomer indicates the long period of time in which it was assumed to be a native of Persia, and it was not till 1915 that the true home of this lilac was made known, namely, the mountain slopes of southern and south-eastern Kansu.' But in what far-off days was the cut-leaved Persian lilac brought from China by that ancient trade route through the heart of Asia to Persia and thence to the gardens of Europe? As Parkinson noted in his *Theatrum Botanicum* (1640), the scent of this lilac, which he calls 'The Persian Jasmine or Persian Lilac whether you will,' has an even sweeter scent than the common lilac. Gerard thus quaintly describes the scent of the common white lilac: 'a pleasante and sweete smell, but in my judgement too sweete, troubling and molesting the head in a very strange manner. I once gathered the flowers and laid them in my chamber

83

windowe, which smelled more strongly after they had been together a few howers, with such a ponticke and unacquainted savour, that they awaked me from sleepe, so that I could not take any rest till I had cast them out of my chamber.' The scent of the purple lilac he described as ' an exceeding sweet savour and scent but not so strong as the former : the flowers are of an exceeding faire blewe colour, compacted of many small flowers, in the forme of a bunche of grapes.'

Phillyrea angustifolia (a native of N. Africa and S. Europe) has been grown in our gardens for well over 300 years. Of it Gerard says, ' These plants doe grow in Syria neere the city Ascalon, and were found by our industrious Pena in the mountains neere Narbone and Montpelier in France ; the which I planted in the garden at Barne Elmes neere London, belonging to the right Honourable the Earle of Essex : I have them growing in my garden likewise.' A new treasure for lovers of sweet scents is *Osmarea Burkwoodii*, a bigeneric hybrid, the result of crossing *Osmanthus Delavayii* with the pollen of *Phillyrea decora*. The flowers are exquisitely scented, and this lovely new evergreen is very hardy.

The old Portugal laurel (*Prunus lusitanica*) is one of our finest evergreen hardy shrubs, but one usually sees it so mutilated and clipped that it is a depressing spectacle. When its fine, smooth, noble limbs are allowed to grow freely, it is one of the grandest shrubs. A specimen about 20 to 30 feet high, with its lustrous foliage and its profusion of slender racemes of scented flowers in June, is one of the most striking spec- tacles in the garden. It is finer even than *Laurus nobilis*, another shrub which is also usually maltreated, but not to the same extent as the Portugal laurel.

The peonies will soon be in their full splendour, and there is a succession of scented varieties flowering from the first week in June. Amongst the earliest are ' Sunrise ' (peach-coloured without and rose and yellow within), ' Lady of the West ' (rose without and cream-white centre petals), and a little later the glorious ' Lady Alexandra Duff.' By the end of June there is a wealth of splendour amongst the scented peonies—' Bunch of Perfume ' (rich rose-colour, and the most sweetly scented of all), ' Limosel,' ' Empress of India ' (creamy white and pink without), ' James Kelway,' ' Lady Curzon,' ' Joy of Life,' the tall-growing ' Dorothy Daniel,' ' Mountebank,' and the spice-scented varieties, ' British Beauty ' and ' President Poincaré.'

The peony is not only one of the most beautiful, but one of the oldest cultivated flowers in the world. Over a thousand years ago the Chinese gave the flower the name which it still retains in that language, and which means ' most beautiful.' To them the peony stood for all that the rose does to us—the very queen of flowers—and the fourth month of the year was called ' the moon of the peony,' just as we speak of June as ' the month of roses.' They grew the peony partly for medicinal purposes, but the flower has for centuries been the hobby of wealthy Chinese garden-lovers. They prided themselves on the age of choice specimens in their gardens. Some years ago there were peonies in the temple gardens of Peking, which were said to be over 200 years old. Even in the eighth century the Japanese were growing both tree and herbaceous peonies, having imported them from China. We still speak of a 'paean of praise,' and in this word we retain the origin of the peony's Western name—from Paeon, the pupil of Aesculapius, to whom Leto gave the flower and taught its marvellous virtues on Mount Olympus. Pliny, who gives the earliest known description of the peony, speaks of it as the most ancient of all plants, and he details at least twenty diseases for which it was a cure.

The lovely old-fashioned crimson peony (*P. officinalis*), which still flaunts its splendour so bravely in garden of to-day, was one of the most familiar flowers in the days of our Anglo-Saxon ancestors. *P. officinalis* has a quiet, rich charm which gives it a unique place in our affections. Its only drawback is its curiously unpleasant scent. The varieties of *P. officinalis* somehow lack the fascination of the original red flower. In the Middle Ages it was valued not only for its loveliness, but used, as we know from Langland's *Piers Plowman*, for flavouring purposes. They also used it in medicine. The seeds were carried as a charm against evil, a custom which survived until at least as late as the last century. In the gardens of our Elizabethan and Stuart ancestors peonies were largely grown ; Gerard gives eight illustrations of the varieties, and he tells us that they were all commonly grown in London gardens. Parkinson in the *Paradisus* says of them, ' They are endezined in our gardens, where we cherish them for their beauty and delight of their goodly flowers as well as for their physical vertues.'

Yet until recently how sadly the peony had fallen from its high estate ! Cottagers remained true to this glorious old favourite, but for many years it was not so commonly seen in larger gardens. But peonies now have come into their own again, and we realize that this flower is truly

' the rose of spring-time.' Unlike so many other perennials the peony has, alas ! no second period of blooming during the same season, but the dazzling beauty of its flowers more than compensates for the comparatively brief time during which it is in its splendour. How seldom one sees the very early flowering *P. tenuifolia*, which our grand-mothers called the Adonis peony. It came originally from the Caucasus. Its fern-like leaves are very finely cut, and the glorious flower is a blood-red colour, not found in any other peony. The plant is only 18 inches high, but the flower is very striking at a time when red is a scarce colour in the garden. After its blooming period is over *P. tenui-folia* dies right down and gives no sign of life till the following spring. In this it differs from all the other species, for peony foliage as a rule is a decorative feature in the garden throughout the summer and early autumn.

Why irises are not more grown on the dry sun-baked waste parts to be found in so many gardens, especially in the south of England, it is difficult to understand. Given a very dry position and ample sunshine they will flower magnificently in the poorest soil. They are the only flowers I know which will bloom profusely planted along the foot of a privet hedge. We have a whole row planted almost on top of the privet roots, and they give a wealth of bloom, so that at least while they are in flower that ugly hedge is bearable ! In fact, the drier the soil and the more sun-baking their rhizomatous roots get the better they flower. Theoretically they need lime, but on the sandiest soils devoid of lime the majority of them flourish exceedingly. There are few of the lovelier flowers which require so little attention and which have so many other attractive qualities. They are nearly all perfectly hardy, they will thrive in almost any soil (except peaty soil), manure is not only unnecessary but fatal to them, they can be planted at almost any time, except when actually in flower (though it is better to avoid transplanting in midwinter and August), and under normal conditions they are almost disease-proof. Lastly, if one has an iris garden, it can be a thing of beauty for nine months in the year. That delightful seventeenth century writer, Samuel Gilbert, who was both an auricula and an iris enthusiast, tells us that there are more colours to be found in irises than in the peacock's tail. What would he say to the modern range of hybrids? Of the April flowering irises *statellae*, *formosa* and *lutea* (the best of the early yellows) are all faintly but sweetly scented. *I. arenaria* (bright yellow flower), which also flowers in April, is very sweetly scented. This iris, which comes from the sandy plains of Hungary, needs a very well-drained spot in the rock garden. It needs protection in winter. In May we have the lovely scented Florentine iris *florentina*, whose root has for centuries supplied the ' orris root ' of the perfumery trade (the scent is not developed till the rhizomes have been dried for several months), ' istria,' the even more beautiful white iris (raised by the late Mr. Dykes) with sometimes as many as six blooms on a stem and beautifully scented, and the sweetly scented yellow Soledad. Amongst the June flowering irises there is a range of colour for the scented garden. The gem of the early flowering varieties is the late Mr. Dykes' ' pink ' Aphrodite, one of the very best of all the modern irises. How very lovely it is! Pinkish violet flowers of a very clear colour on stems quite 4 feet high and scented. At present 'Aphrodite' is rather a costly treasure, but she is a strong grower, and will

presumably soon be grown in every garden. ' Leonato,'
very large-flowered, and fragrant and a strong grower, and
Mr. Dykes' ' Moonlight,' with standards of the palest amber and with smoky yellow falls and a striking yellow beard,
are also amongst the earliest flowering scented irises.
Flowering rather later are *germanica alba*, the white and
sweetly-scented variety of the common blue flag iris,
' Shelford Chieftain' (*I. pallida* × *I. troyana*), 'Magnifica'
(raised by Messrs. Vilmorin), a strong grower with exceptionally large and beautiful flowers, the standards being
light blue and the falls reddish purple with yellow beards,
'Perdita,' a sweetly-scented cream self, ' Ringdove,' a soft
lilac blue, *pallida*, growing 4 feet; and ' White Knight,'
generally acknowledged to be the best of the white irises,
sweetly scented and a strong grower. Latest of all comes
the rather shy flowering but popular ' Lord of June '—one
of the few irises which resents excessive sun-baking, for on
a hot dry soil and in full sun he droops his petals; ' Myth,'
a clear lavender violet self, ' Medrano ' (raised by Messrs.
Vilmorin), a rich violet blue and more pleasingly scented,
I think, than any other iris, not exactly sweet, but more
like a muscatel grape. Of the Spanish irises (*Iris xiphium*)
the only scented one seems to be the dark blue. Of the
late-flowering scented beardless irises the most pleasingly
scented is *I. graminea*, which spreads its clumps in generous weed-like fashion. I think this humble little honey
and fruit-scented iris is most attractive when it is fading,
for then the style branches turn a lovely pink and look
exquisite nestling amongst the masses of green foliage.
I. graminea is a sun lover, and likes a damp soil, but will
flourish and spread even on a hot sandy soil if given part
shade.

Columbines in the mass have a faint, attractive, rather peculiar perfume, but the only columbine which can be described as scented is *Aquilegia fragrans*, a native of Kashmir. It grows about 16 inches high, and has cream-coloured flowers deliciously scented. *A. fragrans* has attracted so much attention lately that it is interesting to find this treasure was introduced for the first time into England nearly a hundred years ago. It is exquisitely figured in *The Botanist* (1840) with the following note : ' This is a most valuable addition to a well-known ornamental European genus, furnished by the mountainous chains of the north of India, a country analogous in many of its vegetable productions to the alpine districts of the south of Europe. With all the singularity of form and elegant growth of our own columbines, this species presents a colour of flower very unusual in the genus, and exhales a fragrance so much a desideratum in those hitherto cultivated. In its botanical affinities the plant comes nearest to *A. pubiflora* of Wallich, but the flower is twice as large, and spurs of the petals very much more hooked, besides which, *pubiflora* appears to have the flowers of a rusty purple. The *A. fragrans* is one of a number of North Indian plants raised by the Horticultural Society of London, from seeds presented by the Honourable East India Company. It has only flowered this spring (1840) for the first time, and has been hitherto kept in a conservatory or under a frame, but there is every reason to hope that it will prove as hardy as its congeners already in cultivation.'

Grown in quantities, columbines make a wonderful display of varied colour and it is curious that they are not more commonly potted up for indoor decoration, as

they can be had without any forcing at all in full flower
by the end of April. A 'bank' of them in mixed colours
is a glorious sight. Mr. Wall, who had such a wonderful
show of them in full flower at the R.H.S. Show, told me
that the plants were lifted in January and some of them
brought into a temperature of 45° (this is the highest
they will stand), and then put into quite cold greenhouses. His show was a joy to behold. Of columbines it is,
alas! as true to-day as it was three hundred years ago, when
Parkinson wrote : ' Columbines are flowers of that respect as that no Garden would willingly be without
them, that could tell how to have them, yet the rarer the
flowers are, the more trouble to keepe ; the ordinary
sorts on the contrary part will not be lost, doe what one
will.'

Few people grow the old-fashioned scented sweet peas
although at least one of the leading firms lists them.
Sweet peas and mignonette were a favourite mixture for
indoor decoration in Victorian days. Mignonette (a
native of Egypt) is only a comparatively old-fashioned
flower in our gardens, for it was not introduced till the
middle of the eighteenth century. According to the
Flora Historica—' By a manuscript note in the library
of the late Sir Joseph Banks, it appears that the seed of
the mignonette was sent in 1742 by Lord Bateman from
the Royal Garden at Paris to Mr. Richard Bateman at
Old Windsor ; but we should presume that this seed was
not dispersed, and perhaps not cultivated beyond Mr.
Bateman's garden, as we find that Mr. Miller received
the seed from Dr. Adrian van Rozen of Leyden, and
cultivated it in the Botanic Garden at Chelsea in the
year 1752. From Chelsea it soon got into the gardens

of the London florists so as to enable them to supply the
metropolis with plants to furnish out the balconies, which
is noticed by Cowper, who attained the age of twenty-
one in the year that this flower first perfumed the British
atmosphere by its fragrance. The author of *The Task*
soon afterwards celebrated it as a favourite flower in
London :
      ' the sashes fronted with a range
    Of orange, myrtle, or the fragrant weed.'

One frequently sees directions for growing mignonette
as a pot plant, but I have only once seen directions for
growing it as a perennial for indoor decoration. These
directions were given in one of the gardening journals,
and I copied them, but regret to find that I made no
note of the source. They are as follows : ' Sow two or
three seeds in rich light loamy compost in pots size 60.
From May to September is the best time. When the
seedlings are up leave only one in each pot. When they
begin to show flower pinch out the top and one week
after shift to a 48 size pot. Pinch as before, and pot once
again into 32 size pot. Water with care. Keep in a warm
place near the glass during winter and allow the flowers
to open. Directly one seed pod appears, cut off all the
flowers and prune tenderly to keep the plant shapely.
Keep near the glass. When another show of bloom is
promised water with liquid manure. But as soon as a
seed pod is produced it must be pinched and pruned as
before.' I have never tried this, but I remember the
writer said it was possible by this method to have large
pots of mignonette indoors almost throughout the year
and to keep the same plants for several years. Mignonette
is a lime lover, and where lime is lacking in the soil it is

essential to supply it in some form. Old mortar rubble is excellent.

One of the most attractive leaf scents at this time of year is that of the scented poplar (*Populus trichocorpa*). A young tree fills the air around it with a strong fragrance commonly described as ' balsamic.' I asked an artist friend (the painter of the delightful ' Piper of Dreams,' of which one sees reproductions everywhere) how she would describe the scent of this leaf, and after sniffing it for a few moments she replied : ' Walnut, faint musk and the skin of a sweet pear,' which seems to me a far more accurate description than the vague ' balsamic.' In winter the slender buds are coated with a gum, which has the same scent. It is the quickest grower of the balsam poplars and the finest of them, but except in the early stages of its growth it is only suitable in a very large garden. In its native habitats in the north-west of America it is said to attain a height of 200 feet. The greatest fascination of the leaves to my thinking is not their delicious scent, but the exquisite veining on the underside. There may be leaves with lovelier veining, but I cannot think of one which is such a miracle of loveliness as this. As in all the countless instances in plant life of the infinitely beautiful and faultless workmanship of the Divine Hand one realizes how impossible it is for our finite human intelligence to apprehend the mystery of even one leaf.

The leaves of *Drimys Winteri* are also pleasantly aromatic. *D. Winteri* is one of the most interesting shrubs, for it is, I believe, the only plant we grow in our gardens associated with the name of Sir Francis Drake. Captain Winter (after whom it is named), and who was in command of one of Drake's ships, brought back the bark from the Magellan Straits in 1578. Its smooth shoots (reddish when young), its strongly aromatic leaves and clusters of sweetly-scented, ivory-white flowers, are all attractive, but it is, alas! an evergreen which does well only in fairly sheltered parts. In this part of Surrey it does very well. *D. aromatica* is only suitable for sheltered parts in Cornwall, etc.

Sweetest of all leaf scents is that of sweet-briar. How delightfully shrubs of it planted by the windows fill a whole room with their clean, sweet fragrance, especially after rain. The sweet-briar or eglantine (*R. rubiginosa*), whose leaves are ' very greene and sweete in smell above any other kinde of rose,' grows wild throughout Europe and has been naturalized in the Eastern parts of the United States of America. This is the ' eglantine ' immortalized by Chaucer, Spenser and Shakespeare. Both the former mention its sweet scent. Chaucer calls it eglantere :

> ' Where she sate in a fresh greene laurey-tree,
> On that further side right by me,
> That gave so passing a delicious smell,
> According to the Eglantere full well.'

Turner calls it Cynorhos, Sweet Brere, and Eglantyne in his *Libellus* (1538). Lobel calls it Rosa sylvestris odorata in his *Icones* (1581), and in Gerard's catalogue (1596) it figures as the common sweet-briar. For centuries therefore this wild rose has been grown in our gardens. In olden times the young shoots were candied and eaten as a sweetmeat. We are grateful for the Penzance Briars, but, alas, for the sweet-briars we have lost ! In the early years of the nineteenth century there were numerous

94

varieties. We still have *R. rubiginosa magnifica*, which Andrews calls *R. eglanteria major*, ' the large eglantine rose or Tree Sweetbriar ' ; he says of its origin that it was ' a spontaneous effusion of nature in the nursery grounds of Mr. Williams of Turnham Green, who informs me he found it on his premises in 1768, growing luxuriantly in the midst of a hedge of sweetbriar. Its growth is so rapid that it will form shoots of 7 and 8 feet in one season, which joined to the largeness of its flowers and foliage induced us to adopt the specific appellation of *R. eglanteria major*.'

We seem to have lost the following varieties which are figured by Andrews.[1] I give them because it is so interesting to try and identify any one may find in an old garden.

R. eglanteria concava. The flowers as well as the leaves are all concave and resemble little spoons. It flowers during the latter part of summer and until the middle of autumn.

R. eglanteria pubescens. The downy-leaved Eglantine rose, the only sweetbriar with this characteristic. ' The drawing was made at the Nursery of Mr. Lee in 1819, where it was then called the Maiden's Blush Sweet-briar. It blooms towards the end of July, during the months of August and September.'

R. eglanteria multiplex. The double Eglantine rose or Williams' Sweet-briar. ' Of all the fragrant leaved Roses this is certainly the finest and for which we are indebted to Mr. Williams, who discovered it in his nursery about 23 years ago, growing promiscuously with the *eglanteria major* ; and although found vegetating at the same time,

[1] H. C. Andrews. *Roses,* 1817.

and under the same auspices, yet is its character altogether very different, this being as slow in growth as the other is quick. It is the only Eglantine rose at present known with perfectly double flowers, and is with difficulty increased by layers, which are a long time in forming a root ; and the seeds which it very rarely ripens, remain in the ground a long time dormant.

This variety was also known to Gerard, for he says of it : ' We have in our London gardens another sweet Brier, having greater leaves and much sweeter, the floures likewise are greater, and somewhat doubled, exceeding sweet of smell.'

R. eglanteria muscosa. Mossy Eglantine roses. ' These Eglantine roses are rather delicate plants and difficult to preserve. The palest coloured is known by the appellation of Manning's Sweet-briar, being first raised by a gardener of that name. It is also by some called the Mossy Sweet-briar. The other is called the Double Mossy Sweet-briar and we have never seen it in any other collection but that of Messrs. Whitley and Brames, whence our figure was taken in 1810. By whom, or in what manner it was originally raised we have not been able to learn, but have been told it first made its appearance about fifty miles from London.'

R. eglanteria robusta. Strong growing Eglantine rose. ' This fine dwarf Eglantine rose is the strongest growing and most luxuriant sweetbriar as yet in cultivation. The flowers are very fragrant, large, double, and follow each other in abundant succession from the month of June till September. Our drawing was taken in the summer of 1817 from plants in the Hammersmith Nursery.'

96

'Sweet Nancies' and 'None-so-pretty', with the common wallflower and
the eighteenth century azalea. *(See pages 47, 56, 281)*

R. eglanteria marmorea. The marble flowered Eglantine rose.

R. eglanteria rubra. Red flowered Eglantine rose. 'This Eglantine rose resembles some of the smaller species of centifolia, Rose de Meaux, etc. It is not so fragrant in the foliage as the generality of sweet-briars but the flowers are of a richer colour. It is in fine bloom from July till October. Our figure was taken from a plant at the Hammersmith Nursery, where it is known by the appellation of Lee's Duchess.'

R. villosa, one of our true natives, though now found wild only in a few places in the north, is well worthy of a place in the garden, not only for the beauty of its flowers, but also for its splendid, picturesque growth. There is an interesting account of this rose in Andrews, who describes it growing in a garden near Farnham, with sixteen other roses grafted on it all in bloom at the same time. 'The semi-double flowered Villosa is mostly known by the appellation of the Tree Rose, an appropriate title, as it may be frequently seen from ten to fifteen feet high, and in the gardens at Sheen House near Richmond, there is a Tree Rose near thirty feet high and fifteen feet wide, with a profusion of flowers, but much smaller leaves than are generally seen on the younger plants. It is a species of Rose well adapted for grafting or budding, as we found a plant of it in the gardens of the Hon. Wm. Irby, near Farnham, thirteen feet high with at least sixteen different sorts of roses growing on it and all in full bloom at the same time. The Single Tree Rose is not so common, nor have we seen any large plants of it except two in the nursery of Mr. Sharles of Little Chelsea, which were about eight feet high and very bushy. The foliage of this rose is scented and although not so powerful as that of some of the Sweet Briars, yet it may certainly be regarded as nearly related to, if not one of the Eglantine family.'

Sweetest of all our wild roses, sweeter even than sweet-briar is *R. spinosissima*. We have the cultivated varieties of this rose, but why do we not grow the wild variety in the garden, where it deserves a place, not only for its beauty but for its fragrance? True, this dwarf rose never looks lovelier than when it is seen growing wild with its blush-white flowers and red tipped buds in close proximity to a tangle of undergrowth and wild flowers. It still grows wild in parts of England, it loves sandy, waste ground and chalk, and is the only British rose which may be found growing naturally near the sea-shore. By the sea, it is even more dwarf than inland, for inland it grows to a height of between two and four feet. It is the rose which grows farthest north, it being the only rose growing wild in Iceland. It is very widely spread, North and Central Europe, Italy, Spain, Northern China and Japan, but not the Himalayas. It has been known to botanists for quite four centuries. Gerard, in his cata-logue of 1596, calls it the Pimpernel Rose. Linnaeus adopted the name 'spinosissima' from Bauhin. Were some skilful catalogue-writer to set forth the virtues of this rose, its delicious fragrance, its floriferousness, its suitability for a dwarf hedge, etc., it would be grown in every garden. As it is, it remains one of our scarcer wild roses, and the places where it grows wild are, fortunately, not too well known.

The Scotch roses originated with hybrids raised by Robert Brown of Perth, from the native Burnet rose

98

crossed with some double roses. In 1793, Robert Brown
of Perth and his brother transplanted some of the wild
Scotch roses from the Hill of Kinnoul in the neighbourhood of Perth into their nursery garden ; one of these
bore flowers slightly tinged with red, from which a plant
was raised. By 1802 they had eight good double varieties
to dispose of, and from this stock the nurseries of Scotland
and England were first supplied. The French growers
were taken up with Bengals, Centifolias, etc., and left
the spinosissima hybrids to the English growers. Wm.
Paul, in his *Rose Garden*, names 76 in vogue about 1840.
Of these there are now only about 8. It is noteworthy
that Redouté figures no Scotch roses. A beautiful
variety is Stanwell Perpetual. This bright pink rose has a
fine rich scent. It opens cupped, and has no resemblance
to the Scotch roses ; the petals have an occasional stripe
of carmine like a carnation or York and Lancaster. The
centre is rather flesh colour, the outer petals are paler.
It blooms later than the Scotch roses.

It is during the long June evenings that there are, I
think, more fairies in the garden than at any other time
of the year :

> ' Lightly tread, 'tis hallow'd Ground ;
> Hark, above, below, around,
> Fairy bands their Vigils keep
> Whilst frail Mortals sink to sleep,
> And the moon with feeble rays
> Gilds the Brook that bubbling plays
> As in murmur soft it flows
> Musick meet for Lovers' Woes.'

Those tantalizing fairies ! How elusively they, the
elves and all their kin flit through the pages of our literature ! The veil which separates us from them is rarely

99

lifted and we are afforded glimpses, all too fleeting, of a busy, happy little people, as interested apparently in us as we are in them. It is a curious fact that in all ages there has been the belief that though fairies were seen in former days, they could no longer be seen by mortal eyes. Chaucer tells us that in King Arthur's days all this land was filled with fairy folk, and that the elf queen and her merry court danced often in our green meadows, but that was many hundred years ago and ' now can no man see non elves mo.' Yet nearly two hundred years later the same fairy queen and her train were known and loved by one greater than Chaucer.

Though immortal, the fairies have changed as the human race has changed. The fairies who dance in our meadows, disport themselves in our gardens and warm themselves by our firesides bear little resemblance to the elves who peopled the trackless wastes of heath and moor, the terror-infested bogs and the impenetrable forests of Saxon days. These elves were mighty of stature, fearsome and characteristic of an age when man fought with Nature, wresting from her the land, and when unseen powers resented this loss of their domains. Place-names in the more remote parts of Great Britain still recall the memory of the supernatural terror with which the water elves of the dark mere pools, ' the muckle mark-steppers ' of the lonely moors and the fiends of the mists inspired our ancestors. The sea-elves were impersonations of the fury of the waves, and the wolf-haunted mark was a resort of creatures, not of sun, but of darkness, akin to the Formon in Irish mythic history, and the Mallt-y-nos, the huge uncouth creatures immortalized by the Welsh bards. Yet even in those days there were elves of surpassing beauty, ' sheen bright elves ' of whom in later days Shakespeare and Shelley had rare visions. Indeed our Saxon ancestors would have understood Ariel as few of us understand him, for he is the old English ' bright elf.' As for that mischievous elf Puck, he and all his kind were continually about their ways.

Even before the twelfth century the dark monstrous elves had begun to disappear, for the learned Gervase of Tilbury tells us of creatures more akin to our Brownies, impish creatures, ' making sport of man's simplicity.' In mediaeval and Tudor days, the fairies we know and love disported themselves in our fields and gardens, tripped about in our houses and held their midnight revels with grasshopper, gnat and fly serving them for minstrelsy.

> ' Round about, round about in a fine ring-a :
> Thus we dance, thus we dance, and thus we sing-a :
> Trip and go, to and fro, over this green-a,
> All about, in and out, for our brave queen-a ! '

We have glimpses of fairy feasts, concerts and revels, and even of preparations for a fairy wedding, and the bride's gown of pansy, pink and primrose leaves embroidered with flowers of rosemary, her head-dress

> ' Of the yellows in the full-bloom rose
> Which in the top it doth enclose
> Like drops of gold ore shall be hung '

and the canopy to be borne aloft over her of ' moons from the peacock's tail ' and pheasant's head feathers ; we read of a dowry in fairyland, consisting of a house of mother-of-pearl, an ivory tennis court, a nutmeg parlour, a sapphire dairy, chambers of agate, kitchens all of

crystal, walks of amber, orchards bearing fruit throughout the year, groves filled with birds, fish ponds full of
nectar, and above all ' an abundance of lady-birds.'
Glimpses of Oberon and his queen enchant us. What
more attractive than the picture of the fairy king and
queen taking refuge from the rain under a mushroom,
' fretted overhead with glowwormes,' and giving such
glimmering light ' as stars doe in a frosty night,' their
supper furnished by their ' nimble footed trayne '
bringing the choicest dainties, one little fairy making his
way through the crowd loaded with an ear of wheat,
' the whitest and the fairest hee cann gett.' What more
appealing than the ' Beggar's Petition to the Fairy
Queen.' Yet even in those days there were people who
did not believe in fairies. For according to Bishop
Corbet ' since of late Elizabeth and later James came in '
the fairies had vanished, though one cannot help wondering whether the worthy Bishop really disbelieved in them,
when one reads the full title of the ballad in which he
deplored their departure—' A proper new ballad intituled
the Fairies Farewell, or God of mercy Will ! to be sung or
whistled to the tune of the Medow Brow by the learned,
by the unlearned to the tune of Fortune.'

Rarest of all are those glimpses of a race of beings more
beautiful even than the fairies to be found in all literature
and notably in ancient Celtic poetry, embodying folk-
memories of an age lost in the mists of antiquities and
possibly of beings who inhabited this planet before man.

> ' From thence we see, though we be not seen,
> We know what has been and shall be again,
> And the cloud that was raised by the first man's fall,
> Has concealed us from the eyes of men.'

Was 'La Belle Dame sans Merci' the last exquisite vision vouchsafed of this race?

I think the fairies we all love most are the flower fairies, the fairies who play about in the scent of the thyme and in and out of the foxgloves, swing themselves in the bluebells and ring the exquisite little bells of the wood-sorrel to summon Oberon and Titania's court to their midnight revels. The pixies use the tulip flowers as cradles, and there is a charming West Country tale of an old woman who grew tulips in her cottage garden and never allowed them to be gathered because of the pixies. They could be heard at night singing their babies to sleep, and these tulips lasted longer than any others and their scent was sweeter than the scent of roses. When the old woman died, the tulips were dug up and the garden left desolate, but the pixies tended her grave and in spring time planted it with wild flowers. And what of the fairies' sea gardens? The little rocks which they plant so lovingly with tiny seaweeds, anemones and coralline, and the green 'Mermaid's lace' we see in pools? What of St. Brandan's Fairy Isle, which on summer evenings on our western shores we behold bathed in the golden splendour of the sunset? And we all know the little fairy gardens, the tiny patches of greensward starred with minute sea-pinks in the sheltered pockets of our rocky coasts. It is easy to believe the old tales of the fairy music heard at night, the hundreds of little lights moving about and the sweet perfume wafted far out to sea from the small people's gardens. In our own gardens do we not, every summer morning, see the fairies' handiwork— the long hanging bridges and palaces we call cobwebs, and which are amongst the loveliest and least earthly of

103

earthly things ?   And who but the fairies deck the flowers
and leaves with dewdrops ?

> ' The light fairies danced upon the flowers
>   Hanging on every leaf an orient pearl,
>   Which struck together with the silken wind
>   Of their loose mantles made a silver chime.'

But alas ! the little people themselves we do not see.

> ' Methinks we walk in Dreams in Fairyland.'

There are many roads leading to Fairyland, and at first
the way seems as simple as the little people themselves, but
how soon mists arise and we find ourselves in a pathless
waste, for as Spenser told us long ago :

> ' None that breatheth living aire does know
>   Where is that happy land of Faerie.'

'… look at the old roses set in a crock on a cottage window sill.' *(See page 105)*

CHAPTER V

THE OLD ROSES

'SHE arayeth her thorn wyth fayr colour and good smell, among all floures of the worlde the floure of the rose is cheyf and beareth ye pryse. And by cause of vertues and swete smelle and savour. For by fairness they fede the syghte : and playseth the smell by odour, the touche by softe handling.'[1] I am writing in a rose garden ; filled with the beauty of the roses, which for centuries have reigned in the gardens of princes and peasants alike and whose very names are full of romance. For centuries, these roses have held the secret of all that is sweetest and best in the home life of our race. Small wonder that the rose is our national flower, for it is the symbol of the home.

What modern roses can compare for beauty or for fragrance with these queens of ancient lineage ? Look at a bowl of these roses in a room filled with treasures of art, and see how perfectly both in form and colour they are in keeping with pictures by the great masters, with priceless furniture and tapestries. Put the ' elegant ' long stalked pointed modern hybrid teas in the same room and see how out of place they look. Or again, look at the old roses set in a crock on a cottage window sill. The queens

---

[1] From Batman's translation (1582) of *De Proprietatibus Rerum*, by Bartholomaeus Anglicus. In the original—' Decore et odore nobilitant spinam suam. . . . Flos ros int' flores optinet principatū, et ió solet prīcipalis que homīs scz capitis rosarū floribus coronare ut dicit pli et hoc ratione decoris odoris suavitatis et virtutes. Nam sua pulcritudie aspectū reficit suo odore olfactū afficit suavitatis mollicie tactum delinit.'

are serenely and happily at home, whereas the modern upstarts would look even more ill at ease than before. The old roses blend perfectly not only with each other but with other flowers, even the humblest, but the modern roses do not blend even with each other. On the show table, however, the modern roses reign supreme. Those serried ranks of hybrid teas give one the impression that not only are they at home at a show, but that they enjoy it. I am always struck with the fact that their colours are so curiously like the more expensive materials displayed in the shop windows. And the leaves (and even the thorns) of many of the modern varieties look as though they had been rationed. There is always just enough and not a leaf nor a thorn to spare. What a contrast to the abundant healthy foliage (and the thorns !) of the old roses. No, those of us who love the old roses are not blind, nor do we suffer from the hallucination that modern roses are scentless. We see quite clearly that they are beautiful, but somehow their beauty fails to touch our hearts. The perfume of the scented varieties is sweet, but it is not the incomparable fragrance of the old roses. At most of the shows you will find one small table devoted to the old roses. They look like dowerless queens and portionless princesses flung into a wilderness. When I see them I am seized with an almost irresistible desire to gather them all up and take them away. They look so pitiful. The few one sees at the shows are but a small remnant of the ancient royal tribes. If you do not grow the old roses, look at their beauty as depicted in the paintings of the old Dutch flower painters ; or look at those glorious roses portrayed in the three great rose books of a century ago—Redouté, Andrews and Miss

Lawrence. In their masterpieces, the beauty and the glorious colouring of the living flowers of over a hundred years ago are immortalized. But best of all, see them as I see them now, loved and tended in a secluded enclosure. This garden is famed, yet only a minority of those who come to see the treasures it contains visit this rose garden, which is filled with the beauty and the fragrance of the old roses. This morning I got up very early to see what is surely one of the fairest sights in the world—the roses ' spreading themselves towards the sun-rising.'

The Red Provence, the old cabbage rose (*R. centifolia*) was for centuries the Queen of all roses. With what royal grace she wears her gloriously uneven petals, a thousand times lovelier than the faultless and almost distressingly ' tidy ' roses of to-day. How satisfying, too, are her generous broad down-curled leaves ' somewhat snipt about the edges,' to quote Gerard's description of them. She thoughtlessly fails to grow the long stalks which seem essential for modern ' indoor decoration,' she nearly always droops, although only slightly, her big, lovely head (another fault !), she does not bloom perpetually, and her leaves lack the delicacy admired in modern roses (consequently they are virtually immune from disease). Is it for these reasons that this queen, who once ruled with the lilies in every garden, great and small, has been deprived of her rightful place ? Yet this was the rose of Chaucer's day, the rose of Provence.

> ' Of Roses there were grete wone
> So faire were never in Rone '

which reminds us of the Rhone, the great river of Provence, and the tradition that this glorious rose was brought in some immemorial time from the Caucasus to France. This was 'the Provincial Rose on my razed shoes' of which Hamlet spoke. Whether or no it is the rose of Homer we do not know. But for centuries it has been grown in our gardens, and alas! that now it is so seldom seen. I love the old descriptions of the cabbage rose, and I quote the following from Andrews:

'This is the most fragrant of all Roses and therefore particularly desirable, for although it cannot be ranked among the rare, it is nevertheless one of the most beautiful. Its sweetness joined to the abundance of its blossom, has rendered it an object of culture, for the purpose of distillation, as it yields a much greater quantity of scented water than any other rose. It is generally denominated the Cabbage Provence, from the extreme complexity of its petals, which sometimes adhere so closely together as to prevent entirely their expansion without bursting, a circumstance that frequently occurs in the vegetable from which its specific distinction is derived, and which we regard to be unequivocally good as we should every similitude of equally easy reference.'

In Redouté's time there were about a hundred varieties of this glorious rose, and in the middle of the nineteenth century about seventy, but the majority of these have long since been lost. The famous Yellow Provence (*R. sulphurea* syn *R. hemispherica*) is very hard to get now. Mr. Courtney Page has it. Lindley describes it as a species and gives Persia and Constantinople as its origin. William Paul, writing in 1847, also refers to it as a separate species and gives Persia and Turkey as its origin. According to Parkinson, this rose 'was first procured to be brought into England by Master Nicholas Lete, a worthy merchant of London and a great lover of flowers ; from Constantinople, which (as we heare) was first brought thither from Syria ; but perished quickly both with him and with all others to whom he imparted it ; yet afterwards it was sent to Master John de Franqueille, a Merchant also of London, and a great lover of all rare plants, as well as flowers, from which is sprung the greatest store that is now flourishing in this Kingdom.' Parkinson also emphasizes its tenderness : ' The flower being faire blowne open doth scarce give place for largenesse, thicknesse and doublenesse unto the great Provence or Holland Rose. This Rose bush or plant is very tender with us here about London and will require some more care and keeping then the single of this kinde, which is hardly ever ; for I have lost many my selfe, and I know but a few about this towne that can nourse it up kindly, to beare or scarce to abide without perishing but abideth well in every free aire of all or the most parts of this Kingdome : but (as I heare) not so well in the North.' Andrews, writing in 1810, says of *R. sulphurea* that it was not to be met with in flower in any of the nursery grounds very near London. ' We have not seen it even in a budding state nearer than Brentford in the collection of the Duke of Northumberland at Sion House.' Writing fifty years ago, Dean Hole said it was almost extinct and that he had seen it only at Burleigh House. This rose, which is still there, was brought from France by a French cook and was formerly called either the Burghley rose or the Yellow Provence rose. This rose is difficult not only to propagate and grow, but, as Parkinson noted three hundred years ago, when in bloom the flowers are ruined by our moist atmosphere—' but a few of them abiding whole and

faire in our Countrey, the cause whereof wee doe imagine
to bee the much moisture of our Countrey, and the time
of flowring being subject to much raine and showers.'
The colour of this rose is very pure.

We still have the beautiful white Provence rose, the
'Rose Unique'—*R. provincialis alba*. According to
Andrews, the introduction of this rose in 1777 was
'entirely accidental through the medium of the late
Mr. Grimwood, nurseryman, who in an excursion, which
he usually made every summer, in passing the front
garden of Mr. Richmond, a baker near Needham in
Suffolk, there perceived the present charming plant,
where it had been placed by a carpenter, who found it
near a hedge on the contiguous premises of a Dutch
merchant, whose old mansion he was repairing. Mr.
Greenwood requesting a little cutting of it, received
from Mr. Richmond the whole plant ; when Mr. Greenwood in return for a plant so valuable presented him with
an elegant silver cup with the Rose engraved upon it ;
and which in conversation has furnished food for many
a convivial hour. It is of a dwarf growth and remains in
flower near six weeks longer than the other Provence
Roses which renders it still the more estimable.' Rivers,
writing in 1837, says of this rose, ' The Unique Provence
is a genuine English rose which I believe was found by
Mr. Greenwood, then of the Kensington Nursery, in
some cottage garden. . . . This variety was at first much
esteemed, and plants of it were sold at very high prices.
Most probably this was not a seedling from the old
cabbage rose, as that is too double to bear seed in this
country, but what is called by florists a Sporting branch
or Sucker.'

We have too the Rose des Peintres, the rose with incurving petals and raised centre, which figures in the old Dutch flower paintings. We still have the Spong and de Meaux roses. According to Andrews, the Spong rose (a hybrid between the cabbage rose and the Rose de Meaux) was so called from having been first raised in quantities by a gardener of that name. According to Rivers, the de Meaux rose (the *R. Pomponiana* of Redouté) originated in a garden near Taunton. This little rose, which is only about 18 inches high, has exquisitely incurved pink petals and is wonderfully fragrant. All the old diminutive roses have, I think, the same fascination as paintings of children by the old masters. They have the same quaint demure charm. According to tradition the de Meaux rose grows only

> ' Where the great of other days have been ;
> Left, like a noble deed, to grace
> The memory of an ancient race.'

The origin of the name ' de Meaux ' can only be conjectured. It seems probable that it may have come from the flower-loving Bishop of Meaux, Domenique Séguier, who devoted so much care and thought to his garden. He was above all interested in roses, of which he had eighteen kinds. He was Bishop of Auxerre from 1631 to 1637, when he was translated to the see of Meaux. One of the loveliest of the smaller members of the Provence family is *Petite de Hollande*. Not only does it bear masses of charming little shell-pink flowers, but its curious branching habit is so attractive. The flowers of *Königen von Denmark* rather resemble *Petite de Hollande*, but the former are not so attractive.

There was formerly a versicolour Provence rose (*R. centifolia versicolor*). This rose was introduced in 1823, and was known in France as Le Petit Sultan. Amongst other varieties of *R. centifolia* we have apparently lost are *R. centifolia purpurea*, whose petals were dark purple on the upper surface and light purple underneath. We have lost too the Blandford rose (*R. parviflora provincialis*), introduced in 1791 by Kingston, a nurseryman of Blandford near Dorset. It had ' everything in common with the Provence rose, with a specifically distinct small flower (whence our name) which, contrasted with the largeness of its leaves, gives a singularity to its appearance. In its blossom it approaches nearest to the Roses of Burgundy and de Meaux, in shape like the former but in colour more resembling the latter, but no affinity whatever to the leaves of either.'[1] Still more regrettable is the loss of the Tuscan rose (*R. centifolia varietatis subnigrae*). Andrews describes it as ' most esteemed for its rich and deep colour ; it may well compare with the finest velvet. The small particle of white on the edge of some of the petals, instead of blemishes, may be regarded as an enlivening contrast.' The knobbly leaved Provence rose (*R. provincialis bullata*) is an even greater loss. Its curious foliage had an attraction of its own and the rose had the same glorious scent as the cabbage rose. Redouté figures a beautiful specimen of this rose.

We still have a few of the Moss Roses—the Common Moss ; the Bath White ; the Crested Moss (formerly known in France as Chapeau de Napoléon), etc.—but how few they are compared to those (about seventy at least) which we have lost. The history of the moss rose

[1] H. C. Andrews. *Roses.* 1827.

is wrapped in obscurity. William Paul says, ' It was first introduced to England from Holland and it is generally believed that it was a sport from the Provence rose.' Miller says, ' This rose is known to us only in its double state, and we are ignorant of the country to which we are indebted for it.' By Furber's catalogue it appears that it was cultivated here in 1724. William Paul, writing when moss roses were at the height of their fame, i.e. between 1850 and 1860, gives no less than 55 summer flowering varieties and 21 ' perpetual,' the latter being a cross between the Moss and the Perpetual. In those days many varieties were grown as standards and pillars. He states : ' I have seen the White Moss bearing at the same time, and on the same plant, red, white and variegated flowers. I have also seen the Perpetual White Moss, whose flowers should be white, produce pink flowers, entirely destitute of moss. I am informed, and think it probable, that the Moss Unique was first obtained in this manner : a branch of the White Provence rose produced flowers enveloped in moss ; the branch was propagated from, and the plants so propagated produced flowers retaining their mossy characteristic.' He mentions some very interesting moss roses in his list, notable the Damask moss rose, raised at Tinwell in Rutlandshire and hence sometimes called the Tinwell Moss. He lists also :

Crimson French. Rose-crimson flowers, the wood has a reddish appearance from being densely covered with red spines.

Emperor. Reddish crimson flowers, shoots thickly covered with red spines.

Etna. Brilliant crimson flowers with purplish tinge and

very double. A beautiful rose. Raised at Angers and introduced in 1845.

Gloire des Mousseuses. Flowers pale rose margined with blush, very large, full and well mossed. One of the handsomest.

Panachée pleine. Flowers white or flesh-colour, occasionally beautifully streaked with rose. Very double, cupped form. Probably a sport from the White Bath Moss.

Nuits d'Young. Flowers dark velvety purple, very double.

Ma Ponctuée. Flowers rose-colour spotted with white.

According to Prévost, who was the first to describe *R. centifolia cristata*, this crested moss was found by a botanist, whose name is not recorded, growing on the top of a ruined tower. William Paul, in his *Rose Garden*, gives a convent garden near Berne as its habitat. Rivers, writing in 1840, says it was discovered growing from a crevice of a wall at Freiburg. It was introduced by Vibert in 1827. At one of the summer shows this year (1930) Mr. Bunyard had amongst the 'old' roses one named violaceae, which evidently came of moss rose parentage. The petals were deepest claret colour, the calyces were mossy and it was exquisitely fragrant. But we have lost the Pompon Moss which figures in Redouté. France has given us so many lovely roses that it is pleasant to remember that we sent her the moss rose. Parsons, writing in 1847, says, 'The first Moss rose known in France was said to have been introduced there by Madame de Genlis, who brought it with her on her return from England.'

The Damask rose, which ' casts fragrant smell amid fra golden graines,' came to us, according to tradition, through the Crusaders. Small wonder that they brought back with them this treasure from the gardens for which Damascus in those days was so famed. For the Damask rose is surely one of the loveliest flowers in the world. With its exquisite petals flung wide to the sun, its great golden eye and its atmosphere of a wondrously storied past, there is something so arresting about the beauty of this rose that familiarity only increases its hold on our affection.

According to Loiseleur-Deslongchamps this rose was grown in France centuries before Crusading days, and he says it was the rose extolled by Homer. There is no reason why this rose should not have been grown by the ancient Romans in their villas in Gaul, and if so, considering the continual intercourse between all parts of the Empire, it was quite possibly grown in England also in those far-off days. In the troublous days of the Saxon invasions it may have been lost. What roses, if not varieties of *R. centifolia*, *R. damascena*, *R. gallica* and *R. alba*, did they grow in the monastic gardens in early Norman days? What were the roses William II demanded to see in the convent garden of Romsey? Eadmer, who records this famous incident, was told it by Anselm, who had it direct from the Abbess Christina. According to Eadmer, William Rufus desired to see Maud (who was afterwards wife of Henry I) and went to the convent of Romsey, where she was being educated by her aunt, the Abbess Christina. On arriving at the convent, he gave as his pretext that he wished to see the roses and flowering herbs. Maud, veiled like the other nuns, passed with them through the garden and the King subsequently left peaceably. We have, alas! no records to tell us which were the roses grown in the numerous monastic gardens, but roses were so largely used for medicinal purposes that they must have been grown in abundance. The 'roser' in mediaeval days was part of the herb garden. Fortunately we have not yet lost the pleasant habit of growing roses in our kitchen gardens, and the 'old' roses always look at home there. As Chaucer wrote :

> 'For nothing liken me might more,
> Than dwelling by the Roser aye,
> And then never to pass away.'

It is impossible to say when the roses which have been famed for centuries were first grown in England. They may have been introduced and lost several times in the troublous days of old. Hakluyt tells us that the Damask rose was brought by 'Doctor Linaker, King Henry the seventh and King Henrie the eight's Physician.' Certainly no rose was more esteemed for fragrance in Tudor and Stuart days. Parkinson says of the Damask rose : 'The flowers are of a fine deep blush colour, as all know, with some pale yellow threads in the middle . . . of the most excellent sweet pleasant sent, far surpassing all other Roses as Flowers, being neyther heady nor too strong, nor stuffing or unpleasant sweet, as many other flowers.'

There are still many varieties of the Damask rose grown, their colours ranging from pure white to the deepest red. The most famous variety perhaps is the York and Lancaster. The true York and Lancaster rose is not striped red and white like Rosa Mundi and some other *Gallica* roses, but has an occasional red petal. The

116

variety of Damask rose grown in the Balkans for attar of roses is *R. trigenta petala*. This is very pink, double and very sweetly scented. They grow them in hedges, allowing six feet between each, wide enough for a team of oxen to plough. Miss Jekyll mentions as rare a very dark damask rose called the Velvet rose. I have never seen this rose, but my mother has often told me that when she was a child this rose was grown, and that she well remembers its deep velvet petals and wonderful fragrance. The favourite old variety, Hebe's Lip, fortunately still survives. Miss Willmott gives the characteristics which principally distinguish *R. damascena* from *R. gallica* and *R. centifolia*, as the long deciduous sepals, reflexing during flowering time, the tall arching stems, which are nearly always green in colour, the larger hooked prickles, thinner leaflets, softly pubescent beneath, flowers many in a corymb and elongated fruit, which turns bright red and pulpy in September.

R. gallica was one of the roses Gerard grew in his Holborn garden. It is listed in his catalogue (1596) as *R. rubra*. *R. gallica* and its numerous hybrids (in its wild state it hybridizes with *R. canina*, etc.) is a native of central and southern Europe, and eastward as far as the Caucasus. ' Its dominant characters are transmitted in a greater or lesser degree to all the hybrids. The rather thick wrinkled leaflets, generally five in number, **are** hoary below and smooth, rather pale green above, and the running roots throw up numerous stiff stems which rarely exceed three feet in height. The flowers are large in proportion, generally solitary, rarely exceeding three and very fragrant.'[1]   There are a large number of garden

[1] Ellen Willmott. *The Genus Rosa.*

hybrids, for during the first half of the eighteenth century the Dutch nurserymen devoted great attention to raising roses from seed, and they experimented first with the *gallicas*. Then in the early years of the nineteenth century the French rose growers, stimulated by the enthusiasm of the Empress Josephine, carried on the work. Dupont, who founded the rose garden of the Luxembourg, collected for her all the best varieties of roses then in existence. Paul, in his *Rose Garden*, states that Kennedy, who owned the vine nurseries at Hammersmith, was given a passport during the war to enable him to go to and from Paris to assist the Empress with her garden at Malmaison. One of the most famous French rose growers of this period was Vibert, who saved Descemets' collection of ten thousand seedlings by removing them all to his own nursery when the Allied troops entered Paris in 1815. Of the 250 varieties of roses grown by the Empress Josephine, the French Government, with the assistance of M. Jules Gravereaux, seconded by M. Thuilleaux, have now managed to reinstate 197 in the gardens of St. Cloud.

There are both a Gallica versicolour rose and a Damask versicolour. As Miss Willmott points out, ' this has led to a certain amount of confusion, which it is difficult to overcome. Both are occasionally spoken of as Rosa Mundi, and also as the York and Lancaster rose.' Rosa Mundi (*R. gallica* var. *versicolor*) has been grown in English gardens for centuries, and just possibly may be connected with the twelfth century Fair Rosamond, whose name the rose immortalizes. The earliest representation of this rose is to be found in Miss Lawrence's *Roses* (1799). In her book, in Andrews and Redouté, this variety of *R. gallica* is called Rosa Mundi. Some of the older writers, notably Crépin, regarded the Provins rose and its hybrids as members of the Gallica family. Of the relationship of the Provins rose to the Provence rose Miss Wilmott says : ' Botanists are not yet agreed upon the precise relationship of these two roses and their exact position still remains a vexed question.' The two names are certainly most confusing. The name of the Provins rose is supposed to have arisen from the picturesque legend related by Loiseleur-Deslongchamps (*La Rose*, 1844), that these roses were brought from Syria by Thibaut le Chansonnier, who cultivated them in his garden at Provins, the old capital of La Brie. Naturally the inhabitants of Provins clung to this legend, and the cultivation of roses was a great source of income to their district. In 1807 the inhabitants petitioned the Minister of the Interior to grant them the privilege of supplying the roses required by the military hospitals and pharmacies. Many of the varieties were striped. Striped roses were highly esteemed in France during the first half of the nineteenth century. Perle des Panachées, one of the loveliest, is, fortunately, still with us, and so is Oeillet Parfait. William Paul in his *Rose Garden* (1848) says this rose was raised at Angers, and introduced in 1845. *R. provincialis bullata*, the knobby-leaved Provins rose, was formerly universally grown. I have not seen it for many years. Its curious foliage had an attraction of its own, and the flowers were deliciously fragrant. Andrews says this rose was imported from Holland in 1815. Redouté describes it as a member of the Provence family, and says it was raised by Dupont.

The best known varieties of the Gallica family now

grown are the old blush Gallica, which, as Miss Jekyll long ago emphasized, thrives in the poorest soils, and will flourish even on dry banks. Of *R. gallica officinalis* Andrews says, ' This large grand rose is both useful as well as ornamental. The flowers are used in medicine in preference to many other restoratives. By the Arabian physicians they were held in great estimation for their mild astringent and corroborant virtues. The flowers cannot be too quickly dried, as slowly drying them impairs both their colour and quality. They are prepared as a conserve by an infusion of honey.' Another lovely little variety is Tuscany, a small rose with semi-double flowers of the deepest velvet and very fragrant. The fragrant little Burgundy rose (*R. burgundiaca* syn. *parvifolia*), according to Rivers, bears the same relationship to the Gallicas as the de Meaux to the Provence rose. This rose, sometimes known as *R. parvifolia*, was cultivated at least as early as 1664, for it is figured in Tabernaemontanus' *Kreuterbuch* of 1664. He calls it *Rosa provincialis minor*. According to de Candolle, this rose grew wild on the mountains near Dijon, but it is not included by recent writers amongst the indigenous roses of France.

In the stained-glass windows of cathedrals it is nearly always a variety of *R. gallica* which is depicted. Which rose was the red rose of the House of Lancaster we do not know for certain. Possibly it was one of the Provins roses, but it is equally possible that it was a Provence rose. The House of Lancaster adopted the badge of the red rose in 1277. Edmund, Earl of Lancaster, son of Henry III of England, was also Count of Champagne, and was sent by the French king to Provence to avenge

120

the murder of one of the royal officials. On his return to England he took the device of the red rose. The Gallica rose is very prolific in producing seed, and there were formerly innumerable varieties in cultivation. Of these we have unfortunately lost the Portland rose. According to Andrews, this rose was ' called after the late Duchess of Portland, a great lover of roses. A fine scarlet rose, in flower like the *gallica officinalis*, in foliage like the Provence, with seed buds more resembling the Damask species ; yet with all these affinities it has a perfectly distinct character in the fiery colour of its flowers, its stalks of a whiter green, and the foliage of a yellower green than roses in general. It continues in bloom from the middle of summer to late in autumn.'

No one knows the origin of the white rose of England (*R. alba*) and the red variety, the red rose of England. Parkinson, writing of them in 1629, describes them as ' the most ancient and knowne Roses to our Countrey, whether naturall or no I know not, but assumed by our precedent Kings of all others, to bee cognizances of their dignitie, the white rose and the red.' Is there not a tradition dating from time immemorial that England was called Albion from the beauty of these white roses ?[1] *R. alba* (according to some a cross between *R. canina* and *R. gallica*) was the white rose of the House of York. It is described by Gerard as having ' very faire double flowers of a white colour and very sweete smell.' Parkinson, in his *Theatrum Botanicum* (1640), refers to the old tradition

---

[1] Albion insula sic dicta ab albis rupibus quas mare alluit vel ob rosas albas quibus abundat.—PLINY. (The Isle of Albion is so called from its white cliffs washed by the sea or from the white roses with which it abounds.)

that before the Wars of the Roses a rose tree at Longleat
was observed to bear both white and red roses. ' It is too
lamentably knowne in this land, the civill warres betweene
the houses of the two brethren John of Gaunt, Duke of
Lancaster, and Edmond of Langley, Duke of Yorke,
the one making a red rose his cognizance for them and
their followers, the other a white : but it is said that
before this division, there was seene at Longleete a white
Rose tree to beare on the one side faire white Roses, and
on the other side red, prognosticating as it were both the
division and uniting of both their families.'

The white rose is often mentioned and figured by the sixteenth century botanists, and according to Bauhin this was
one of the roses mentioned by Pliny. The variety Maiden's
Blush (*R. alba* var. *rubicunda*) was formerly commonly
grown in every cottage garden, and Miss Willmott says
its origin is lost in the mists of antiquity. This is probably the ' Incarnation Rose ' mentioned by Turner in
1557, and it is certainly the ' Incarnation Rose ' described
by Parkinson, who says of it, that it is ' in most things like
unto the white rose, both for the growing of the stocke,
and bignesse of the flower, but that it is more spread
abroade when it is blown than the white is, and is of a pale
blush colour all the flower throughout. This kinde of
Rose is not very great but very thicke and double, and is
very variable in the flowers, in that they will be so different
one from another : some being paler than others, but
the best flowers (whereof there will bee still some) will
be of a bright pale murrey colour.' The very dark leaves
give great character to this lovely rose and the flowers
have a fragrance peculiarly their own. This rose, which
Redouté calls Le Rosier Blanc Royal, ' la grand Maiden's

Blush des Anglais,' is, I think, the rose Kneller depicted in his portrait of Queen Henrietta Maria, now at Munich. The Queen, who wears a beautiful silk robe, and has pearls round her neck and on her hair, holds this rose in her lap. A fitting symbol ; for was she not known as ' the rose and lily queen ' ?

The musk rose (*R. moschata*), immortalized by Bacon, Shakespeare and Keats, was apparently first introduced into England in the first half of the sixteenth century, for Hakluyt says, ' Of later times the Musk Rose was procured out of Italy.' Bacon describes the musk rose as flowering in July. ' In July come gilliflowers of all varieties ; musk roses ; the lime tree in blossom ; early pears and plums in fruit, genitings, codlins ' ; in *Midsummer Night's Dream* it was in bloom on that night, and Keats describes the rose as ' mid May's eldest child.' It was *R. moschata* crossed with *R. indica* which gave us the Noisette rose, named after M. Philippe Noisette, who raised it in America in 1817. Although of American origin the best known of the Noisette roses is the French rose, Aimée Vibert, raised at Angers by the famous French grower, J. P. Vibert, who named it after his daughter. *R. moschata* is also a parent, or rather, grandparent, of such famous roses as Cloth of Gold, and possibly of Maréchal Niel. According to some authorities, however, Maréchal Niel, which was first sent out by Pradel in 1864, was, like the Gloire de Dijon, a chance seedling. The late Mr. Pemberton used *R. moschata* in producing his hybrid musks. The true musk rose has single white blooms borne in large trusses. *R. moschata alba* (syn. *nivea*) has white flowers faintly tinted blush and a decided musk perfume. One of the most beautiful of the musk roses is *R. rubus,* which the late Mr. R. Farrer describes so enthusiastically as the 'snowdrift rose' in his book, *The Eaves of the World*.

The Cinnamon rose (*R. cinnamomea*), formerly called the Whitsuntide rose, has large flat pink flowers. Modern authorities assure us that the name is a misnomer, and certainly the very faint scent of this rose is not even suggestive of cinnamon. Gerard, who describes both the single and double cinnamon rose, tells us that its scent is in its leaves : ' The Cinnamon Rose, or the Rose smelling like Cinnamom hath shootes of a browne colour, four cubits high, beset with thorney prickles, and leaves like unto those of Eglantine, but smaller and greener of the savour or smell of Cinnamom, whereof it tooke his name and not of the smell of his flowers (as some have deemed) which have little or no savour at all : the flowers be exceeding double, and yellow in the middle, of a pale red colour, and sometimes of a carnation : the roote is of a wooden substance.' The old ' Rose without thorns' has also wellnigh disappeared. It was commonly grown in Elizabethan days, when it was also known as the ' Rose of Austrich, because it was first brought from Vienna, the Metropolitan citie of Austrich and given to that famous Herbarist, Carolus Clusius.' Gerard describes it as ' of a most sweete smell.' I quote his picturesque yet accurate description :

' The Rose without prickles hath many young shootes comming from the root, dividing themselves into divers branches, tough and of a woodie substance ; of the height of five or sixe cubites, smooth and plaine without any roughnesse or prickles at all ; whereon do growe leaves like those of the Holland Rose, of a shining deepe greene colour on the upper side, underneath somewhat hoarie and hairie. The flowers growe at the tops of the branches, consisting of an infinite number of leaves greater than those of the Damaske Rose, more double and of a colour betweene the Red and Damaske Roses, of a most sweete smell. The fruit is rounde, red when it is ripe, and stuffed with the like flockes and seedes of the Damaske Rose. The roote is great, woodie and far spreading.' Gerard also grew the Apple rose (*R. pomifera*), which grows wild in many parts of Europe but not Britain. Its chief beauty is its peculiarly vivid red fruit. The yellow, so-called Austrian briar (*R. Foetida*), which ranges in a wild state from the Crimea through Asia Minor and Persia to the Punjab, was well known in gardens in the sixteenth century. Gerard had both the type and the copper-coloured variety in his Holborn garden in 1596. The flowers have an unpleasant scent, but the leaves when crushed have a pleasant smell, faintly suggestive of apples.

The first American rose cultivated in Europe was *R. virginiana*. It must have been introduced fairly early in the seventeenth century, for Parkinson mentions it in his *Theatrum Botanicum* (1640). Of it he says : ' The Virginia Bryer Rose hath divers as great stemmes and branches as any other Rose, whose young are greene and the elder greyish, set with many small prickles and a few great thornes among them, the leaves are very greene and shining small and almost round, many set on a middle ribbe one against another somewhat like unto the single yellow Rose : the flowers stand at the toppes of the branches consisting of five small leaves, of a pale purple or deepe incarnate colour like unto those of the sweet brier, which fall away quickly as they and others doe.' Andrews calls the Virginian rose *R. lucida* and *R. pennsylvanica*. This rose with its deeply-toothed leaves is still a treasure in our gardens, and we have also the double-flowered variety, Rose d'Amour, which was introduced by Philip Miller in 1768. The leaves of both turn a brilliant yellow in autumn and the fruit is bright red. *R. foliolosa*, discovered by Nuttall about 1818 in Arkansas, is very similar in appearance to *R. virginiana*. It is dwarfer and produces its sweetly-scented pink flowers rather later.

As early as the closing years of the seventeenth century roses were sent from China. How much we are indebted to the flower lovers in the old East India Company's service. To them we owe the exquisite China Monthly rose (*R. indica*), cultivated in China from time immemorial. The whole atmosphere of this rose is that of an ancient civilization. What tales it could tell us of Chinese gardens of possibly two and three thousand years ago! The Dutch East India Company introduced the rose to Haarlem in 1781. In 1789 Sir Joseph Banks introduced it into England, and it is recorded to have flowered for the first time in Mr. Parson's garden at Rickmansworth. The wild species (discovered by Dr. Henry, in 1885, near Ichang in Central China) have solitary flowers and usually red.

Of the China Monthly roses the pink is the best rain resister, for as a class their petals are so fragile that they suffer badly in a wet season. The widely popular *R. chinensis* var. *semper florens*, which is rarely without flowers the year round, was introduced into England in 1789 by Gilbert Slater of Knots Green. *R. chinensis* var. *grandiflora*, with very large pink and white flowers, was

126

found growing in Canon Ellacombe's garden at Bitton in Gloucestershire. The most beautiful variety is the rich red Cramoisie Supérieure, raised in 1832 by an amateur living near Angers, and distributed by Vibert in 1835. This rose has transmitted its beautiful colour to many hybrids. The ash-leaved variety (*R. fraxinellaefolia*), with fragrant white flowers, was introduced from France in 1816. Through the East India Company the China Monthly rose was sent to India, where it became known as the Bengal rose. According to Rivers, the China Monthly rose and the Rose of the Four Seasons were the only roses grown in the Isle of Bourbon as hedges, and, indeed, the only roses grown at all in the island in the eighteenth century. He gives the following account of the origin of the Bourbon rose : ' At the Isle of Bourbon the inhabitants generally enclose their land with hedges made of two rows of roses ; one row of the common China rose, the other of the Red Four Seasons.' Monsieur Perichon, a proprietor at St. Benoist in the Isle, in planting one of these hedges, found amongst his young plants one very different from the others in its shoots and foliage. This induced him to plant it in his garden. It flowered the following year, and, as he anticipated, proved to be of quite a new race, and differing much from the above two roses, which, at the time, were the only sorts known on the island. Monsieur Bréon arrived at Bourbon in 1817 as botanical traveller for the Government of France and Curator of the Botanical and Naturalization Garden there. He propagated this rose very largely and sent plants and seeds of it in 1822 to Monsieur Jaques, gardener to the Duke of Orleans, at the Château de Neuilly, near Paris, who distributed them amongst the rose cultivators of France. M. Bréon named it Rose de l'Isle de Bourbon. Bréon was convinced that it was a hybrid from one of the above roses, i.e. either the Common China or the Red Four Seasons. Redouté painted this rose from those growing in the Duke of Orleans' garden at Neuilly, in 1824. In the text Thory says, ' This rose, according to His Highness the Duke of Orleans, grows naturally in the Island of Bourbon. Seeds brought from there some years ago have reproduced it in his garden at Neuilly, where our drawing for this work was made. Its appearance is very beautiful. The abundance of its flowers, which are sometimes nearly single, but more often semi-double, their beautiful colour and perfume, will no doubt make it much sought after for outdoor gardens.'

Of the hybrids reared later, Charles Desprez and Mme Desprez (both raised by Desprez of Guignes) were the first. In 1845, Deluze of Lyons raised the beautiful Souvenir de Malmaison, which fortunately we still have. Few, alas! remain of the true old Bourbon roses, but of those a few at least should find a place in every rose-garden, not only for their old-world beauty, but also for their exquisite fragrance. However small a garden I had, I should grow Souvenir de Malmaison and Zephyrine Drouhin. Zephyrine Drouhin, with its lovely deepish pink petals, its vigorous growth and abundance of bloom, its delicious perfume (it has the true old-rose perfume) is a rose for every garden. As a bush it is beautiful, but against a wall as a pillar rose it is at its glorious best. Grown against a house its masses of bloom give that homely cottage look which we all love. If I had to live in a newly built house, I should smother at least one wall

with Zephyrine Drouhin. Why is this glorious old rose
(perhaps it would be more correct to say ' oldish,' for it
was not introduced till 1868) not more grown in small
gardens ? One sees it in nearly every large garden, but it
is also one of the roses for the small garden. And what an
array of virtues this rose has ! It is very vigorous, it
blooms from June to October, its fragrance is delicious,
it is thornless, it will thrive on a chalk soil, and it is one
of the few roses which will grow near the smoky atmosphere of a large town. And if I could grow only one
other Bourbon rose, it would be the vivid Madame Isaac
Pereire. True, she is only at her best in autumn, but her
fragrance is supremely lovely. For it is as true now as
when Rivers wrote nearly a hundred years ago, that the
Bourbon roses are roses for every garden, ' For the Queen
of Flowers boasts no members of her court more beautiful, their fragrance is delicate and pleasing, more particularly in the autumn.'

The Fairy rose (*R. Lawrenciana*), a variant of the China
Monthly, was named after Miss Lawrence, of rose-book
fame. Sweet introduced this rose from Mauritius in
1810, and named it after Miss Lawrence, who was
then at the height of her fame. The origin of this rose
remains to this day unknown. It is a China rose, dwarfed
in all its parts, but at what date some skilful Chinese
grower produced this little Fairy rose we do not know.

The cultivated type of China Monthly crossed with
R. gallica gave us the Hybrid China Roses. The Hybrid
China and the Hybrid Bourbon roses crossed with
R. damascena gave us the Hybrid Perpetual. The first
real Hybrid Perpetuals were sent out by the French
breeder, M. Laffay. Between 1860 and 1900 the Hybrid

Perpetuals were at their zenith, but now few of them are grown. Ulrich Brunner and Mrs. John Laing (introduced 1885), both of which rejoice in heavy soils, still hold their own. Ulrich Brunner's lovely cherry-red colour, large perfect flowers, and great fragrance, combined with being mildew proof, ensure continued popularity. The Hybrid Tea, Dame Edith Helen (introduced 1926), will, it is said, supplant Mrs. John Laing, for the former has the true old-rose scent, her rich pink colour is very beautiful, she is of vigorous growth, with dark green leathery foliage, and free of mildew. But, personally, I prefer Mrs. John Laing, for I love her globular shape, whereas Dame Edith Helen has the high-pointed centre, of which I am not an admirer. Dame Edith Helen is sometimes described as being nearly the perfect rose. Yet she does not look well blended with other roses. Incidentally, how curious it is that few modern roses look well when associated with others, even of their own kind, whereas a large bowl containing as many as half a dozen of the old roses is a picture of satisfying, refreshing beauty. In my room there is a great bowl nearly two feet across of blush Gallicas, Red Damask, Cottage Maid, Rosa Mundi, Moss roses, the Carnation rose, Musk roses and Oeillet Parfait, utterly happy in each other's company, and glowing with the soft, beautiful colours one never sees in the modern roses.

The China tea-scented rose was first sent to this country late in the eighteenth century. *R. gigantea* is said to be the original of the tea rose. This rose, with its 5-inch wide flowers and glorious scent, is a treasure which presumably everyone would like to grow, but though first discovered as long ago as 1882, it has never yet been

flowered in this country. I quote the following description of this rose from *The New Flora and Silva*.[1]

'The solitary short pedunculate flowers, which are
from five to six inches across, are golden colour in the bud
stage, creamy white when open, finally becoming pure
white, the deep orange anthers standing out conspicuous
against the large imbricate-obovate petals, the flowers
being deliciously scented like the Tea Rose, of which it is
thought to be the origin. The smooth, fleshy hips, or fruit,
which are as large as a small apple, are said to be eaten by
the Nagas, and are sold in the bazaars in Manipur. The
leaves of from five to seven leaflets, are a rich, brownish-
green tint when young, becoming pale shining green when
mature. On the Riviera it flowers very freely, and has
been used with success for hybridizing; also in Australia
it is being used more and more as a parent, owing to its
foliage, the progeny being found practically immune
from mildew and die back.' The most favoured of the old
tea roses was Fortune's Yellow (or Beauty of Glazen-
wood), the buff yellow rose sent to this country by R.
Fortune in 1846. This rose is unfortunately tender in
this country, and needs a wall even in favoured parts.
It was Fortune also who found *R. sinica anemone* in the
gardens of Shanghai. Why this rose, which, as its name
implies, resembles an anemone, is not more commonly
grown it is hard to understand; for apart from its beauty
it is in full flower in April.

How swiftly the Hybrid Teas have become the favourite roses, for in Dean Hole's famous book they are not
even mentioned. The first list of Hybrid Teas was
published by Hugh Dickson of Belfast in 1884. The

[1] *The New Flora and Silva.* July, 1929.

131

lovely Hybrid Tea, La France, raised by Guillot in 1867, still happily survives. How beautiful one thought this rose when one was a child! Mr. Henry Bennet was the first English breeder of Hybrid Teas, his most notable success being Caroline Testout, 'the slave of the rose garden,' during the latter part of the nineteenth century. Caroline Testout has wellnigh disappeared now, but she has famous descendants: Madame Abel Chatenay, General McArthur, Antoine Rivoire and Madame Ravary being amongst the most notable. Why does one so seldom see now the splendid old Gloire de Dijon, introduced in 1853, for this rose is at home under any conditions, one of the earliest to bloom and the last to give out, and has in abundant measure the true tea perfume. It was of this rose that Dean Hole said he would choose it if he could have only one rose for the rest of his life. Hybrid Teas have long since ceased to be crosses between true Tea roses and Hybrid Perpetuals, for now there is a bewildering infusion of Austrian Briars, Rugosas, Persian Yellow, Polyanthas, etc. It is a pity that Colonel Leclerc (sent out by Pernet Ducher in 1909) has gone out of commerce, for this cherry-red rose had a remarkable fragrance. Of the Hybrid Teas, the three whose perfume I love most are Château de Clos Vougeot (of straggly growth in bush form, should be grown as a climber), Columbia, and General McArthur, the last-named being by general consent one of the roses for every garden, for it succeeds in almost every soil, and blooms continuously. Ophelia, Etoile de Hollande and Shot Silk, especially the last two, have also the true old rose scent. Of the newer roses Lady Helen Maglona and Bedford Crimson are deliciously scented. Both are vigorous growers.

The beautiful Macartney rose (*R. Bracteata*), introduced from China by Sir George Staunton, who accompanied Lord Macartney's embassy to China in 1792, has a most curiously unroselike scent. Those great star-like golden-eyed, white flowers, set in a wealth of shining green foliage, have a smell suggestive of some pleasing but by no means sweet fruit. That lovely modern rose, Mermaid, which is a hybrid, is sweetly scented, but the peculiar fascination of the scent of the Macartney rose is entirely lacking. The rugosa rose, which is a native of Japan, Korea and the extreme north-east of Asia, was introduced into England in 1796. These roses are not notable for their fragrance but many of the hybrids are very sweetly scented, notably the silvery rose-coloured Conrad F. Meyer, and best of all, Rose à parfum de l'Hay, a treasure indeed, for the scent of this rose is wellnigh incomparable. The double white-flowered Banksian rose (which is exquisitely scented) was sent from China in 1807 by William Kerr, and the yellow-flowered variety was sent in 1824. This rose likes a chalk soil and a warm wall. Everyone has remarked how wonderfully this rose has bloomed this year (1930), for the continuous baking sun of last summer ripened the wood as it is seldom ripened in this country. William Paul mentions a Banksian rose growing in the Jardin de la Marine at Toulon. ' In 1842 the trunk was 2 feet 4 inches in circumference at its base. Its branches covered a wall 75 feet broad and 15 to 18 feet high ; and were there greater space it could be covered, for the tree is subjected to severe pruning every alternate year to keep it within bounds. At the time that it is in full blossom it is calculated that there cannot be less than from 50,000 to 60,000 flowers on the tree.' He mentions also a yellow Banksian rose growing at Goodrent, Reading, the seat of Sir Jasper Nicholls, Bart. It produced one year ' about 2000 trusses of flowers and there were from six to nine expanded roses on each truss.'

The double flowered white and pink multiflora or polyantha roses were introduced as cultivated plants from Chinese gardens more than a hundred years ago, and were the parents of many of our popular rambling and climbing roses. The Lyons rose growers crossed the seed with various double roses, and produced a large number of new varieties, some tall-growing and some dwarf, the latter being the now widely popular polyantha roses. Of the tall-growing varieties one of the most popular was the Seven Sisters rose, which is still occasionally to be seen in old gardens. Loudon, in his *Arboretum* (1838), describes a plant of the Seven Sisters rose which he saw at the Goldworth Nursery in 1826. ' It covered about 100 square feet and had more than 100 corymbs of bloom, with about 30 to 50 flower buds in each corymb, so that the amount of flower buds was about 3000. The variety of colour produced by the buds at first opening was not less astonishing than their number. White, light blush, deeper blush, light red, darker red, scarlet and purple flowers, all appeared in the same corymb, and the production of these seven colours at once is said to be the reason why this plant is called the Seven Sisters rose.' *R. multiflora* with single flowers is a native of Japan, and was introduced in 1875. The origin of the Crimson Rambler, which has been grown in China for centuries, is doubtful. According to the late Mr. E. H. Wilson it may be a hybrid with China Monthly parentage, a sport probably from the common wild pink-flowered China Rambler. The Red Rambler was sent to this country in 1878. Messrs. Turner of Slough bought the stock and gave the name Crimson Rambler. Few roses produce flowers in such profusion, for one plant may produce quite 6000 in bloom at the same time. *R. microphylla*, a native of Japan and China, was introduced in 1824. This rose is known in France as Rose Chataigne, because of its thorny fruit. Unlike the fruit of most roses it is sweetly scented. *R. Wichuraiana*, named after the German botanist, Wichura, came to England by way of the U.S.A. It was sent to Brussels in 1886 from Japan. An American named Perkins crossed this rose with the old Hybrid Perpetual, Mme Gabriel Luizet, thereby producing the formerly popular but now much maligned Dorothy Perkins. *R. Wichuraiana* (the type) has the wild rose perfume, but many of the hybrids are unfortunately scentless.

In 1838 Sir H. Willock, Envoy Extraordinary and Minister Plenipotentiary at Teheran, brought from Persia *R. lutea*. In 1900 M. Pernet Ducher gave us Soleil d'Or (a cross between the Persian yellow rose and Antoine Ducher), by no means a notable rose, but interesting as the forerunner of the Pernetian roses. Rayon d'Or (also raised by M. Pernet Ducher in 1910) was the first good modern yellow rose, and the parent of many of the fine yellow roses now grown. The best of the Pernetian roses, however, is Juliet (1910), for she is a very vigorous grower, and her fragrance is exquisite. Unfortunately she inherits the tendency to black spot, characteristic of the Persian yellow rose. One is always told that in the city of Adelaide the Pernetian roses flourish exceedingly, on account of the dry atmosphere.

Of the history of the rose during the last century much has been written. Much too of the rose in art and its use as an emblem. The rose is indeed indissolubly linked with the history of the human race. Since 1461 it has been the emblem of this nation. In Henry VII's chapel, in Westminster Abbey, wherever one looks there is the Tudor Rose 'looking down from the balconies of heaven, companying with angels and archangels, token of perfect beauty.'

'Dry roses put to the nose to smell do comfort the brayne and the herte and quickeneth the spryte.' To those of us who love the old roses there is no fragrance to equal theirs. It is from their petals that the sweetest potpourris are made. We cannot improve on the old instructions for gathering and drying roses. 'In summer-time when roses blowe gather them ere they be full-spred or blowne out, and in drie weather pluck the leaves.'

They should be gathered before they are full-blown because full-blown flowers when dried retain neither their colour nor their perfume. They should be gathered on a sunny day when the dew has dried off them and spread out on sieves, for this ensures quicker drying than laying the petals out on tables or trays. No bought potpourri is so pleasant as that made from one's own garden, for the petals of the flowers one has gathered at home hold the sunshine and memories of summer days, and of past summers only the sunny days should be remembered.

It was formerly the custom also to dry flowers in sand. Sir Hugh Platt, in his *Delights for Ladies* (1594), says, 'You must in rose-time make choice of such roses as are

'The very word "herb-garden" ... conjures up a vision ... of a secluded pleasaunce full of sunlight and delicious scents, and radiant with colours and quiet charm.' *(See page 138)*

neither in the bud, nor full blowne which you must specially cull and chuse from the rest, then take sand and drie it thoroughly well, and having shallow boxes, make first an even lay of sand, upon which lay your rose-leaves one by one (so as none of them touch other). Set this box in some warme, sunny place in a hot sunny day (and commonly in two hot sunny dayes they will be thorow dry), and thus you may have rose-leaves and other flowers to lay about your basons, windows, etc., all the winter long.'

CHAPTER VII

THE AROMATIC HERBS

'THE garden by meanes of a path shall be devided into two equall parts ; the one shall contain the herbes and flowers used to make nosegaies and garlands of, as March violets, gilloflowers, small paunces, daisies, marigolds, daffodils, Canterburie bells, anemones, mugwort, lillies and such like, and it may be called the nosegaie garden. The other part shall have all other sweet smelling herbes, as sothern wood, wormewood, rosemarie, jesamin, balme, mints, penneroyall, hyssop, lavendar, basill, sage, rue, tansy, thyme, cammomill, mugwoort, nept, sweet balme, all-good, anis, horehound and others such like, and they may be called the garden for herbes of a good smell.'

The very word ' herb-garden ' suggests old-world peace and fragrance. It conjures up a vision, as remote and yet as familiar as memory, of a secluded pleasaunce full of sunlight and delicious scents and radiant with the colours and quiet charm of all the lovable old-fashioned plants one so rarely sees nowadays. From Saxon days until the end of the eighteenth century the herb-garden reigned supreme in England, and now that we are reviving so much that is old and pleasant, perhaps we shall be wise enough to restore the herb-garden with its beautiful colours and its fragrance to its former pride of place. And what plants have such beautiful and such ' comfortable ' names as the denizens of the herb-garden ? Comfrey, bergamot, melilot (how came so humble a

138

herb by a name so lovely and so musical?), marjoram, lovage, sweet Cicely, woodruff, mullein—those names were not ' made.' They grew. The herb-garden is never more lovable than in the full blaze of sunlight on a summer day, for then it is full of bees and fairies. We live in such a hurrying material age that even in our gardens we seem to have forgotten the elves and fairies who surely have the first claim on them. Their inheritance has been wrested from them, but create an old-world herbgarden, fill it with thyme, foxgloves, rosemary, lavender, marjoram, hyssop, bergamot, horehound and the like, and they return as to a familiar haunt.

I know a herb-garden where the tiny paths are stoneflagged (the stones came from a Cistercian monastery), and between the stones grow varieties of wild thyme whose purplish-mauve tints are beautiful against the weatherbeaten stones. There is bergamot with its quaint, glorious red flowers (I think it is the most beautiful red in the garden), masses of it near bushes of horehound ; beyond are the mellow tints of marjoram, catmint, sage and balm, blending happily with the lovely blues of hyssop, borage, succory and flax. There are spaces restful with the soft tones of lavender, not only the mauve but also the pearly white, which was Queen Henrietta Maria's favourite, lad's love, rue, chives, savory, tarragon, dill and lovage, and in between bright splashes of colour—marigolds, valerian, tansy and the like. Here are the stately elecampane with its beautiful golden flowers (the herb which Helen of Troy is said to have held in her hand when carried off by Paris), and angelica (whose virtues are said to have been revealed by an angel). As tall as angelica are the bushes of fennel with their curiously polished

stems and feathery tufts of leaves and reminding one of
the monastic herb-gardens where this herb was grown in
abundance to eat with fish on fast days. In one corner is
an elder tree, and one recalls that if one stands near
Mother Elder at midnight on midsummer's eve one sees
the King of the Elves and all his train go by. The hedge
enclosing this peaceful sanctuary is of rosemary, and at
the end of the broad centre-path is a sundial which looks
as though it had not only lived with the same family for
generations but as though it had also been loved by them
and shared their joys and sorrows. The kindly herbs have
long since made it welcome and with them it seems to
have some secret understanding.

Lavender holds pride of place amongst sweet-smelling
herbs, and what more pleasant than gathering armfuls
of its scented blooms on a sunny day? The dwarf
lavenders are charming for edging, but they have not the
same sweet scent. The beautiful white lavender with its
pearl-like flowers is, however, just as strongly scented as
the mauve. It is rather delicate and one rarely sees a
large bush of it. It cannot endure exposure to cold
winds, but in these parts it survived the bitterly cold
winter of 1928 when many 'hardy' plants succumbed. In olden days they made lavender-scented
sugar by pounding the lavender flowers with three times
their weight of sugar. The author of *The Queen's Closet
Opened* (1655), who was cook to Queen Henrietta Maria,
says that this ' conserve ' would keep a year. The same
author gives a recipe for lavender wine made by putting
two ounces of lavender flowers into a bottle of sack with
three ounces of sugar candy, ' and shake it oft, then run
it through a jelly bag, and give it for a great cordiall after

a week's standing.' I love seeing clumps of the old red bergamot growing near lavender. Bergamot (*Monarda didyma*) is one of the most gorgeous of the aromatic herbs, with its tufts of glorious red flowers rising tier above tier, and crowning every branch. No variety is quite so attractive as the old red, and a great bowl of them with horehound or lavender is a lovely sight. The Monarda family are one of the treasures we owe to the New World, and one of the first from that source to be introduced into our gardens. ' Monarda,' it is interesting to remember, takes its name from Nicolas Monarda, the sixteenth century physician of Seville, who wrote the first treatise on ' American ' plants, a book which raised so much interest that it was translated by no less a botanist than Charles de l'Escluse into Latin, and by less eminent authorities into Italian, Flemish, French and English. The English translation—*Joyfull Newes out of the newe founde worlde wherein is declared the rare and singular vertues of diuerse and sundrie Hearbes*, 1577, went through four editions before 1600. The original book was written nineteen years before the defeat of the Spanish Armada, and it is impossible to look at the old-fashioned scarlet bergamot, still a favourite in our cottage gardens, without thinking of the Spaniard after whom it is named and whose book is so full of the pride of a Spanish subject in the splendid overseas dominions of his country, then the first empire in the World. It was not till long after the Spanish Armada, however, that bergamot was first introduced into England, John Tradescant, the younger (son of John Tradescant, gardener to Charles I), being the first to grow it. During the eighteenth century a herb tea from this plant was commonly made in the American colonies, and hence the name Oswego tea, from Oswego, in the State of New York. Incidentally, the taste of this ' tea ' is as delicious as its fragrance.

Hyssop is one of the small shrubs but too seldom seen. Yet the blue-flowered variety has a most attractive old-fashioned look, and the leaves and flowers have a strong aromatic scent. When kept well clipped, hyssop makes an excellent dwarf hedge, but it does well only on a warm light soil, for it is a native of the south of Europe. It has been grown in Britain for centuries. Hyssop was used both in cookery and medicine even in our grand-mothers' days. The young tops and flowers were used to flavour pottage, they were a common ingredient in salads, and hyssop tea and syrup were accounted excellent cordials. An old receipt book recommends hyssop in warm ale, taken fasting in the morning, ' to cause an excellent colour and complexion.'

Winter savory (*Satureia montana*) has been grown in Britain for many centuries, the date of its intro-duction being unknown. There are about fourteen species of this highly aromatic herb, but only two are commonly grown in England—summer savory (*S. hortensis*), which is a hardy annual, and *S. montana*, a hardy sub-shrub. Virgil accounts them amongst the most fragrant of herbs, beloved by bees, and therefore to be set near their hives. In Shakespeare's time it was a familiar herb in this country :

' Here's flowers for you,
Hot Lavender, Mints, Savory, Marjoram.'

On a poor dry soil savory flourishes, but on a rich soil it frequently perishes in a severe winter. Both the summer and winter savorys have always been largely used for flavouring and we might do worse than revive the Elizabethan custom of using it when dried and rubbed to powder to add to grated bread-crumbs ' to breade their meate, be it fish or flesh, to give it a quicker relish.'

Few of the aromatic herbs are more loved than southernwood (*Artemisia abrotanum*), with its pretty old names, ' Lad's Love,' ' Old Man,' etc. It is a native of the Mediterranean, and does not flower often in Britain. It is generally supposed to have been introduced into this country in the sixteenth century, but quite possibly long before. It is mentioned in the earliest herbals (the *Grete Herball* 1526, etc.), and on the Continent it had evidently been in common use for centuries. Walafred Strabo, the German monk who lived in the ninth century, mentions it amongst the healing herbs he grew in his ' Little Garden,' and of it he says that its ' hair-like leaves ' are good for fevers and wounds, and that the plant has as many virtues as leaves. It was one of the earliest shrubs imported by the settlers in the New World, for it figures in the list of garden plants which the first New England colonists tried to grow. The list is pathetic reading, for many of the plants, such as rosemary, lavender and southernwood, survived the long sea journey (it took 3 months in those days) but succumbed to the rigours of the New England winter. The book in which this list figures—*New England's Rarities Discovered, by John Josselyn Gent,* 1672—is of peculiar interest, for it contains the first published lists of English garden plants that would thrive in America, also of weeds such as dandelion, plantain, etc., unknown before in that country. Of southernwood the writer sadly observes :

143

' Southernwood is no plant for this country.' Southern-wood was valued not only for its pleasant invigorating scent and its medicinal qualities, but also as a dried herb to strew in cupboards and drawers to keep away moths. The clothes-moth dislikes the scent, and hence the old French name for this herb, ' Garde-robe '—for it literally protected clothes. ' Sir ' John Hill gives a recipe for sleeplessness which sounds a most pleasing way of using southernwood : ' Clip four ounces of the leaves fine and beat them in a mortar with six ounces of loaf sugar till the whole is like a paste. Three times a day take the bignesse of a nutmeg of this. It is pleasant and one thing in it is particular, it is a composer and always disposes persons to sleep.'

There are many Artemisias for the scented garden— *Artemisia abrotanum,* the ' lad's love ' of cottage gardens ; *A. canescens,* with lovely finely-cut silver foliage ; *A. pede-montana,* like silver filigree, but only faintly scented ; *A. pontica,* very strongly scented ; *A. ludoviciana gna-phaloides,* charming on a rockery ; *A. Villarsi,* like a tiny grey cypress ; *A. argentea,* with silver-grey foliage and very fragrant ; *A. frigida,* a Californian species ; *A. valesiaca,* a small silver-leaved shrub, very strongly scented ; *A. palmieri ;* the stately *A. lactiflora,* a Chinese herbaceous variety with spiraea-like plumes of scented white flowers in August and September ; *A. stelleriana,* a handsome trailing variety ; *A. procera* grows quite 6 feet, but it is not very attractive. Best of all is *A. tridentata,* a treasure we owe to the western United States. Indeed, this curious looking species is one of the most fascinating of all the aromatic plants. It grows from 6 to 8 feet high, but even a young plant arrests attention owing to its queer wedge-shaped leaves, thickly crowded in clusters. The scent of these leaves when crushed is more pleasing than that of southernwood, for it is even more aromatic and sweeter, and after rain it scents the air for yards round. Its silvery sheen in spring is also most attractive. It must be wonderful to see this plant in masses in its native habitats in North-West America, for even a single specimen gives one an impression of primeval arid districts.

Two of the humblest members of the Artemisia family, wormwood and mugwort, are amongst the bitterest of herbs, but their scent though bitter is pleasingly aromatic. These herbs have been used medicinally in England for at least 2000 years and probably longer. The common wormwood (*A. absinthium*), which is a native of the greater part of Europe and these islands, is intensely bitter, but Roman wormwood (*A. pontica*), which is the most delicate of the wormwoods, is supposed to be the best and is the sort still grown by country-folk. I know an old farmer who ascribes his wonderful health to the fact that every spring he takes a course of wormwood tea, but I should imagine it is more likely the result of a healthy active life ! Wormwood was also used formerly to keep moths out of clothes and rooms free from fleas. For the month of July we find in Tusser's *Five Hundred Points* (1577) :

' While Wormwood hath seed get a handful or twaine,
To save against March, to make flea to refraine ;
Where chamber is sweeped and Wormwood is strowne,
What savour is better (if physick be true)
For places infected than Wormwood and Rue ?
It is a comfort for hart and the braine,
And therefore to have it, it is not in vaine.'

Queen Henrietta Maria's cook gives a recipe for wormwood wine, made by putting two pounds of dried wormwood in two gallons of Rhenish wine, leaving it to ' digest ' for three or four months, ' shaking the vessel often,' and then, when settled, decanting the clear tincture.

Mugwort (*A. vulgaris*) is one of our commonest weeds, and was highly valued by our Saxon ancestors. In a Saxon herbal it is described as ' eldest of worts,' and a powerful protection against evil spirits. In the *Grete Herball* (1526) we find, ' If this herbe be within a house there shall no wycked spyryte abyde.' It was formerly used not only medicinally but to flavour beer.

Santolina chamaecyparissus (Lavender Cotton) was also cultivated in England in the sixteenth century, and how long before we do not know. It is a native of the Mediterranean, but unlike southernwood it flowers freely in this country. It is so commonly grown that we scarcely appreciate its beauty. It is one of the best of the small shrubs, either for edging or for laying out the design in a ' Knot ' garden. In Elizabethan and Stuart times lavender cotton was commonly used for the making of the dwarf shrub mazes which were such a charming feature of gardens in those days. Thomas Hyll, in his *Profitable Arte of Gardening* (1568), gives two designs for these aromatic dwarf shrub mazes : ' And there be some whiche set their Mazes with Lavender Cotton, Spike, Marjerome and such lyke.' During the latter years of the seventeenth century, small gardens laid out in the form of a sundial, the numerals being set out in small shrubs, were a fashionable ' conceit.' Lavender cotton would certainly have been used for this purpose and possibly the ' living sundials,' depicted in Loggan's *Oxonia Illustrata* and *Cantabrigia Illustrata*, were made of this shrub. These sundials are shown in the gardens of New College, Oxford, and Queen's College and Pembroke College, Cambridge. We know from William Hughes' *Flower Garden* (1671) that these ' living sundials ' were much in favour in the West Indies, where they were laid out with myrtle. *S. incana nana*, the very dwarf form, is a fine little plant for edging. *S. viridis*, which was not introduced till the eighteenth century, is also a native of the south of Europe. It is not nearly so attractive as *S. chamaecyparissus*, being green, with longer and thinner leaves, less dense in growth and with less fragrance. Also, it is not so hardy. *S. pennata* and *S. rosmarinifolia* are both attractive.

The thymes are fascinating to collect and amongst the most attractive are, I think, *T. erectus*, the cypress thyme, which looks like a little juniper, a tiny pillar of green for the greater part of the year, but wreathed in summer in a thick cloud of purplish aromatic flowers, and *T. nitidus*, a compact fairy bush, like a miniature Irish yew. In May the latter has a profusion of pinkish flowers. We have about 30 kinds altogether—the common thyme (*T. vulgaris*), which is an improved variety of the wild thyme of the Mediterranean coast ; *T. aurea* (golden dwarf) ; *T. azoricus* (dwarf), with purple flowers ; *T. chamaedrys montana* (pink flowers) ; *T. carnosus erectus* (erect variety, about 9 inches, with white flowers in August and September) ; *T. citriodorus* (lemon scented) ; *T. c. coccineus* (magenta crimson flowers) ; *T. c. lanuginosa* (carpeting variety with downy foliage) ; *T. c. fol. arg.* var. Silver Queen ; *T. c. aur.* var. (golden variegated) ; *T. corsicus* syn. *Mentha requienii* ; *T. ericae folia* (golden

147

foliage) ; *T. herba barona* (a Corsican variety, caraway scented) ; *T. hyemalis*, *T. mecans* (carpeter) ; *T. serpyllum* and varieties ; *T. odoratus* (very fragrant) ; *T. pyrenaicus* (lilac flowers) ; *T. Marschallianus* (narrow foliage and pinkish flowers) ; *T. villosus* (purple crimson) ; *T. balearicus* (creamy mauve flowers) ; *T. pulciflorus* (very upright with cream-coloured flowers). Then there is *T. membranaceus*, which was shown by Mr. Ashton Lofthouse at one of the July shows. This delightful thyme, a hardy plant for the rock garden, was collected in Spain in 1924 and again in 1926, at an altitude of 6000 feet. The white flowers are long and tubular, and are set in membraneous cream-coloured bracts. The flowers smell strongly of sage and the leaves, when bruised, have a rich aromatic scent.

No thyme has the wonderful scent of the wild thyme (*T. serpyllum*) which grows on our downlands, and whose clean, delicious perfume has been beloved by fairies and bees from time immemorial. In the *Gardener's Labyrinth* (1577), we find that ' the owners of hives have a perfite forsight and knowledge what the increase or yeelde of honye will be everie yeare, by the plentiful or small number of flowres growing and appearing on the thyme about the Summer solstice. For this increaseth and yeeldeth most friendly floures for the bees, which render a coloure and savoure to the Honey.' ' Bee-alluring thyme,' as Spenser called it, in his *Muiopotmos*, was a favourite herb for paths in the days when they delighted in making sweet-scented walks. ' Those flowers which perfume the air most delightfully, not passed by as the rest, but being trodden upon and crushed, are three, that is Burnet, Wild Thyme and Watermints ; therefore

148

you are to set whole alleys of them, to have the pleasure when you walk or tread.' Thyme in old flower language is the symbol of courage, and in Lancastrian days ladies embroidered a bee hovering over a sprig of thyme on the scarves they gave their knights. In Elizabethan days thymes were used in many ways. Parkinson tells us : ' We preserve them with all the care wee can in our gardens, for the sweete and pleasant scents and varieties they yeeld. . . . There is no herbe almost of more use in the houses both of high and low, rich and poore, both for inward and outward occasions ; outwardly for bathings among other hot herbes, and among other sweete herbes for strewings ; inwardly in most sort of broths with Rosemary, as also with other farsing herbes, and to make sawce for divers sorts both fish and flesh. . . . It is held by divers to bee a speedy remedy against the sting of a Bee, being bruised and layd thereon.' And one recalls that quaint passage in Bullein's *Bulwarke of Defence*, *which Bulwarke is kepte with Hillarius the Gardiner* (1562), ' There be no flowers growing in fields or gardens better beloved of Bees than the flowers of Thyme. . . . And thus I do conclude of Time, desiring God that we may spende the tyme well to his glory, and profite of our neighbour : for tyme cannot be called againe, but by litle and litle slippes away ; they which godly observe the tyme, in tyme to come shall receive the fruictes of theyr owne labours, wyth happy lives, quiet mindes, and blessed endes : whereas the shamefull abuses of time, and mis-users of themselves, although evyll spent tyme seeme well unto them, yet theyr lives be wicked, their labor fruict-lesse, and their end horrible ; as once shall appeare when death doeth come, whych is the end of every tyme.'

149

And the prettiest recipe in the English language is, I think, one in which thyme, picked ' from the side of a fairy throne,' is the chief ingredient. 'To enable one to see the fairies. A pint of sallet oyle and put it into a vial glasse : and first wash it with rose-water and marigolde water ; the flowers to be gathered towards the east. Wash it till the oyle becomes white, then put into the glasse, and then put thereto the budds of hollyhocke, the flowers of marygolde, the flowers or toppes of wilde thyme, the budds of young hazel, and the thyme must be gathered near the side of a hill where fairies used to be ; and take the grasse of a fairy throne, then all these put into the oyle in the glasse and sette it to dissolve three dayes in the sun, and then keep it for thy use.'

Rue (*Ruta graveolens*) is at last coming back into favour. On a chalk soil it is one of the most pleasing of the small shrubs, especially the variegated kind, but it is invariably poor where chalk or lime is lacking. The tiny *R. padavina*, which grows only 6 inches high, is charming for the rock garden. The glaucous green leaves of *R. graveolens* are attractive at all times, and especially when set off by the corymbs of little yellow flowers. It flowers from July onwards. The variegated kind is especially attractive in early summer. Rue is one of those plants which give one an impression of age and mystery, and its scent is unlike any other leaf-scent. From time immemorial it has been used in medicine, and was probably introduced into this country in Roman days if not before. It is frequently mentioned by Shakespeare, and both Ophelia and the gardener in *King Richard II* speak of it as ' herb of grace.' According to some authorities it derived this name from the fact that the holy water was sprinkled with it, but this is doubtful. Rue has always been famed for its property of warding off infection, and even as late as the nineteenth century sprigs of rue were placed before the Judges at Assizes to counteract possible infection from the prisoners. It is still used by country folk to counteract the poison of bee and wasp stings. It was also used in spells to ward off evil spirits and as an amulet against the evil eye. From the earliest times it was regarded as of sovereign efficacy to preserve eyesight and to strengthen it when vision was becoming dim. It was with ' euphrasy and rue ' that the angel cleared Adam's eyes in *Paradise Lost*. Rue is one of the few ' herbs ' which figure in heraldry. Frederick Barbarossa in 1181 gave the first Duke of Saxony the right to bear a chaplet of rue on his arms, and six hundred years later the first King of Saxony created the Order of the Crown of Rue. This order was conferred on King George when he was Prince of Wales, in 1902.

The various aromatic sages make a delightful group in the scented garden, and some of them, particularly *Salvia sclarea* (the old ' Clary '), with its huge leaves and 4 feet high heads of pale pink and blue flowers, are handsome enough for the choicest herbaceous border. It remains in full beauty till cut down by the first frosts. Picked for indoor decoration it fades almost at once, but I have found that if one hammers the stalks (literally with a hammer, just as one does Christmas roses) they will usually last well, especially if one picks the young branches. A few days ago I filled a huge bowl with clary and the giant catmint, which grows to nearly the same height (incidentally, why is this lovely catmint so seldom grown?), and foxgloves, and the clary is still perfectly fresh. Another method is to dip the ends of the stalks in boiling water for about ten seconds. (This is the method used to make Oriental poppies, etc., last when exhibited at shows.) *S. virgata nemorosa* is an invaluable member of the sage family. *S. Grahami* is charming, and should certainly find a place in the scented garden, not only for the beauty of its bright red flowers and pale green leaves, but also for its delicious perfume. It is rather tender and likes the protection of a wall. It flowers from July to the end of October.

The humble member of the Salvia family, the common sage (*Salvia officinalis*), should find a place in the scented garden, especially the red-leaved variety, which looks so charming when its lavender-coloured heads of flowers are in full bloom. Sage is very variable in cultivation, and one of the most attractive ' sports ' is the variegated red-leaved variety, which has large cream-coloured blotches. These varieties always have a tendency to revert to type, and cuttings should be taken from the branches showing most variegation. The red-leaved variety seems a little less hardy than the green, and never flowers unless in a very dry, sunny place. Red sage was apparently more highly esteemed in olden times than the green sage. For instance, in the *Receipt Book of Joseph Cooper* (Joseph Cooper was cook to Charles I) it appears that he preferred to use red sage for the royal table. He gives a recipe for sage cream made by pounding red sage-leaves in a mortar, and then mixing them with a quart of cream, a quarter of a pint of canary, a quarter of a pint of rose-water and half a pound of sugar. Sage was very highly esteemed for its medicinal properties, and, indeed, the plant derives its name from *salveo*, I heal. John

Evelyn in his *Acetaria* wrote of it, ' 'Tis a plant indeed with so many and wonderful properties that the assiduous use of it is said to render men immortal.' And one recalls the old English proverb, ' He who would live for aye must eat sage in May.' ' Sir ' John Hill, who had a famous garden in Bayswater during the latter half of the eighteenth century, tells us in his *Vertues of British Herbs*, that the chief goodness of sage was to be found in the sage flowers when they begin to open. ' Just when the flowers of sage begin to open there is in their cups a fragrant resin, highly flavoured, balmy, delicate, and to the taste one of the most delicious cardials that can be thought, warm and aromatic. . . . Sage properly prepared will retard that rapid progress of decay that treads upon our heels so fast in the latter years of life, will preserve the faculties and memory, more valuable to the rational mind than life itself without them ; and will relieve that faintness, strengthen that weakness, and prevent absolutely that sad depression of spirits, which age often feels and always fears, which will long prevent the hands from trembling, and the eyes from dimness and make the lamp of life, so long as nature lets it burn, burn brightly.'

Sage tea, made either by pouring a pint of boiling water on to two large handfuls of the leaves or by putting the leaves into the same quantity of cold water, and bringing them to the boil, is an excellent tonic, and it was also used formerly as a gargle for sore throats. In the old cookery and still-room books one also finds more elaborate recipes for ' sage water ' (made with balm, lemon, etc.), cheeses were flavoured with this herb, and sage wine was very commonly made in the eighteenth

and nineteenth centuries. Gerard mentions ' sage ale.'
' No man need to doubt of the wholesomeness of Sage
Ale, being brewed as it should be with Sage, Betony,
Scabious, Spikenard, Squinnette and Fennell Seed.' An
old lady told me that in her youth saucers of sage leaves
were invariably handed with the glasses of medicinal
waters at Tunbridge Wells. They were used to rub one's
teeth after drinking the water, as they removed the iron
stains. Another old lady told me that when she was a
child, their old nurse invariably insisted on her charges
rubbing their teeth with sage leaves after cleaning them
with tooth powder. When they protested against this
additional cleaning, she would say, ' The tooth-powder
is to clean your teeth and the sage leaves are to make
them beautiful.'

Three old-fashioned herbs now rarely seen are lovage,
sweet Cicely and costmary. I do not know any catalogues
in which they are offered for sale. Lovage (*Ligusticum
scoticum*) is said to have been introduced by the Romans,
but formerly it grew wild near the coast of Scotland and
Northumberland. It is a handsome plant, and the scent
of the big succulent leaves is rather suggestive of parsley,
only sweeter. Hence, probably, the old Scotch name,
' Sea parsley.' In the Shetland Islands it was called
Siùnas. In olden days it was one of the herbs used for
scenting baths. Thomas Hyll, in *The Gardeners' Labyrinth* (1577), tells us ' This herbe for hys sweete savoure
is used in bathe.' Another old writer tells us, ' it joyeth
to growe by wayes and under the eaves of a house, it
prospers in shadowy places and loves running water.'
Sweet Cicely (*Myrrhis odorata*) is another rare native
plant which both for the beauty of its fern-like leaves and

154

its sweet scent is a treasure in the herb-garden. Old names for it were Sweet Bracken and Sweet Fern. Its big fleshy root is very sweet and aromatic, and the bright green aromatic leaves are still used in salads in Italy. Bee-hives were formerly smeared with it, balm being also commonly used for this purpose, for it was believed that the scent of both these herbs was particularly pleasing to bees. Costmary, or Maudeline (*Balsamita vulgaris*), is, I think, the only plant grown in our gardens called after Mary Magdalene. Gerard says, ' The whole plant is of a pleasant smell, savour or taste '; and Parkinson says it was much used ' with other sweet herbes to make sweete washing water : the flowers also are tyed up with small bundels of Lavender toppes, these being put in the middle of them, to lye upon the toppes of beds, presses, etc., for the sweete scent and savour it casteth.'

Where indeed shall we find scents to equal those in the herb-garden ? What bought perfumes can rival those of lavender, lad's love, rosemary, marjoram, thyme, lovage, sweet Cicely, bergamot and balm ? They are so full of sunshine and sweetness that it seems there can be no tonic like them. Small wonder that in former days herbs were so largely used to ward off black magic, and did we but know how to use them aright, who shall say they would not be as powerful to-day to dispel gloom and depression ? Anyone who is familiar with the fascinating old herbals knows how full they are of recipes, for potions concocted from herbs to cure melancholy and ' to make one merry.' We may laugh at these quaint recipes but is not this mere ignorance on our part ? We have neither the understanding hearts nor the wit to realize all the knowledge

155

handed down through the ages that lies behind these charmingly worded directions. I think what is most lovable in these old books is the spirit of reverence which pervades them. ' The principal delight is in the minde singularly enriched with the knowledge of these visible things, setting forth to us the invisible wisdome and admirable workmanship of almightie God.' Lawson, the author of those two fascinating books, *A New Orchard and Garden* (the first book written for North Country gardeners), and *The Countrie Housewife's Garden* (the first book written for women gardeners), was a gardener for forty-eight years before he wrote, and then, as he tells us, he only ventured to write ' lest I should hide the least talent given me of my Lord and Master in Heaven.'

I am writing this in a room filled with old books—a library in which I am in the atmosphere of the fifteenth century. Through the mullioned windows I see a Macartney rose nearly 20 feet high covering part of a wall with its polished leaves and exquisitely scented white flowers. Beyond is the Anemone rose (*R. sinica anemone*), which flowers in April. Near by are great bushes of rosemary and through the windows comes the scent of jasmine, both the white and the old-fashioned yellow (*R. revolutum*) and sweet-briar. The walls of this library are lined and the cupboards filled with the most remarkable collection I know of herbals and old gardening books. As a private collection it is probably unique and any adequate description of it would fill a large volume. If one were asked to name the most remarkable treasures in this room I think one would say the Herbal of Apuleius Barbarus (very few known copies), *Le Grand Herbier*,

Ortus Sanitatis (1515) and several later editions ; *The Grete Herball* (1526), the first and second editions of Fuchs (1542 and 1543), Gerard's Catalogue (very few known copies), *The Wilton Garden*, by Isaac de Caus (only two known copies), Walafred Strabo (first and second edition, Vienna 1510 and Nuremburg 1512), Bartholomaeus Anglicus (1483), Pliny's *Historia Naturalis* (1480), the first editions of both Colonna's books and twenty original drawings by Ehret.

Le Grand Herbier is amongst the rarest of herbals and during recent years very few copies have come into the market. It is far rarer than the earlier *Ortus Sanitatis*. The English translation, *The Grete Herball*, printed by Peter Treveris, was the earliest English-printed herbal, although no copies of the first two editions (1516 and 1525), mentioned by Ames and Hazlitt, are now to be found in any of the chief British libraries. The printer's device at the end of the English translation is fascinating. The woodcut represents a man and a woman on either side of a tree from which hangs a shield with Peter Treveris' initials. It is generally supposed that Peter Treveris was a member of the Cornish family of Treffry, sometimes spelt Treveris. A Sir John Treffry who fought at Poitiers took as supporters to his arms a wild man and woman, and his descendant perpetuated the memory of his ancestor by adopting the sign for his device.

Of the earliest German herbals this library contains Brunfels' *Herbarum vivae eicones* (1532), notable for its beautiful illustrations, Brunfels being the first to use naturalistic drawings ; the first edition of Hieronymus Bock's *Kreuterbuch* (1539), also the 1546 edition ; the first

and second edition (1542 and 1543) of Fuchs' magnificent
books, the finest in many respects of all the early herbals.
The beautiful woodcut illustrations were widely used—
by William Turner, 'the Father of English botany,' by
Lyte in his translation of Dodoens, by Bock (in the 1546
edition of his book), by Dodoens in his *Kruydeboeck* (1554),
by Bauhin in his *Historia plantarum universalis* (1651),
and some of the figures by Egenolph in his *Herbarum
Imagines vivoe* (1535), d'Aléchamps and others. Then
here are the splendid Low Country herbals, notably those
printed by Plantin. Even after seventeen years of work at
early garden literature I still cannot open a book with the
impressive inscription ' Antverpiae—Ex officina Christophori Plantini,' without a thrill. The Plantin Museum
is unique and presumably few who go to Antwerp fail to
make a pilgrimage there. It is interesting to remember
that this great printer only took up the work which made
him world famous owing to an accident to his arm, which
ruined his career as a bookbinder. (On a carnival night he
was, by mistake, run through the arm by a party of
masqued revellers.) In this library there are a large
number of the books published by Plantin—amongst
them Dodoen's *Stirpium historiae* (1583), *Florum et
Coronarium* (1569), *Historia Frumentorum* (1569), Clusius'
Rariorum aliquot stirpium, de l'Obel's *Plantarum seu stirpium icones* and the Flemish translation (dedicated to
William of Orange and the Burgomasters of Antwerp).

The treasures from the early Italian presses include
Acosta (Venice 1585), Prosper Alpini *De Balsamo Dialogus*
(Venice 1591), and *De Plantes exoticis*, Anguillara's
Semplici (Venice 1561), Marco Bussato's *Giardina d' Agri-
coltura* (Venice 1599) and the 1612 edition; Colonna's

two books, Castor Durante's *Herbario Novo* (Venice 1602) and *Il Tesoro della Sanita* (Venice 1593). The collection of old English gardening books and herbals is very fine, ranging from the earliest printed in the English language. Thomas Hyll's *Proffitable arte of gardening* (1577) is in the original binding. And the copy of Sir Hugh Platt's *Delights for Ladies* (1572), which is amongst the rarest English books of garden interest, has the bookplate of King James I. Here too are the most notable of the old rose books, now almost unobtainable.

I love the details in these old books—the quaint and sometimes very beautiful initial letters, the printers' devices, the epistles dedicatory and the occasional inscriptions both on the title page and at the end of the book. Even an insignificant little book of *Approved Receipts* delights one, for the title page shows that it was printed on old London Bridge, at the ' Three Bibles,' in the reign of Charles II. At the end there is this inscription, ' God save the King and likewise our loving and gratious Queen Katherine, his Majesties Royal Consort.' In one's imagination one sees old London Bridge with its street of gabled houses, the jostling crowds, and at the sign of the ' Three Bibles ' a cart being loaded with the little calf-bound volumes of the newly printed *Approved Receipts*, to be distributed to the booksellers' shops in the City. One of the most charming epistles dedicatory is to be found in *A greene Forest* (1567). It concludes thus—' And thus I make an end : desiring God to blesse you in all his giftes, both ghostlye and bodilye : and to continue you in long life and true Honour, to his glory : the helpe and assistance of others : and your owne, and endlesse comfort. Amen.'

The Epistle dedicatory I like most I have put at the beginning of this book—a wish for the friend to whom the book is inscribed. As brief as it is beautiful is the inscription at the end of *The vertuose boke of Distyllacyon of the waters of all maner of Herbes* (1527):

' Goddes grace shall ever endure.'

'... the scent of the Madonna lily is the scent of ages yet to come and of beauties and splendours yet unrevealed.' *(See page 163)*

CHAPTER VII

THE rose, though a queen, is a friendly queen ; but about her rival, the lily, there is always an atmosphere of isolation. Lilies do not reign like the roses, they live apart. There is some indefinable enchantment which puts the whole lily tribe in an altitude so far above other flowers that they are more than regal. How conscious one was in childhood of this strange sweet aloofness of the lilies ! One could pick a basketful of roses, but I do not think any child would voluntarily pick lilies. It would seem like sacrilege.

The rose sleeps in her beauty, but the lily seems unaware of her own exceeding loveliness. The rose is never so glorious as in cultivation and fares sumptuously, with every care lavished on her, but, given rich food instead of the sharp drainage and leaf mould to which she is accustomed, the lily withdraws her gracious presence. The purity of the lily is not only in her outward form, but it is characteristic of the food she requires. No members of the lily family tolerate manure, artificial or otherwise. The lily is at her fairest in the waste places of the earth, where human eyes rarely see her in her beauty. Think of the splendour of *Lilium regale* in her native haunts where her discoverer, the late Mr. E. H. Wilson, found her, in that little-known, wild territory which separates China proper from mysterious Thibet. In narrow valleys bordering on the roof of the world, in a region dominated by lofty peaks crowned with eternal snows, subjected to

161

intense cold in winter and terrific heat in summer, in solitudes where only a few intrepid explorers and wild tribesmen venture, the regal lily reigns. Both in summer and winter these regions are swept by storms of awe-inspiring violence, yet in June the precipitous, arid mountain-sides blossom with countless thousands of these glorious lilies filling the air with their wondrous perfume. And from her mountainous fastnesses this radiant queen has been transported to our gardens. When one looks at her with the rich wine-colour shining through the snow-white inner surface of her petals and her golden anthers in this exquisite setting, and bearing sometimes as many as fifteen flowers on each slender stalk, it seems as though one so gorgeously apparelled must live delicately in Kings' courts, yet her dwelling is amidst the bleakest solitudes of this planet. Still stranger is it that this lily ripens seed freely in this country, the seeds germinate in a few weeks and the plants flower after their second year.

We have not only caught and tamed the rose and changed her character, but like the human race she differs through the centuries. The roses depicted in the old missals and books of hours in the pictures by the great masters and the stained glass windows in our Cathedrals resemble the roses of to-day as little as the mediaeval mystic's outlook on life resembles that of the modern scientist. But the lily remains unchanged, and hybridists, hybridize they never so wisely, have (mercifully) succeeded in doing virtually nothing. The Nankeen Lily (*L. testaceum*) is supposed to be a hybrid of *L. candidum* and *L. chalcedonicum*, although this is not certain, and it is generally regarded as the best hybrid in cultivation. But hybrid lilies are few and usually poor. To quote Mr.

A. Grove : ' It is not perhaps so generally known as it might be, that no hybrid Lily seems definitely fixed, not even *Lilium testaceum*—by far the oldest hybrid known. None of those which have come into the writer's hands can be trusted to breed true from seed and all must be raised by offsets, scale bulbs or stem cuttings.'[1]

On the lilies cultivation produces but little effect. The Madonna lily which our Anglo-Saxon ancestors knew and loved is the same to-day, unchanged through centuries. What lily is so fair as the beloved Madonna lily, with her ' holy garments fit for beauty and for use ' like Aaron's robe ? Never lovelier than in cottage gardens, yet what can compare with ' the plant and flower of light,' as Ben Jonson called her, or to what can she be likened ? Upborne on a slender stem, arrayed in lustrous sheen whiter than snow, and with only her delicate orange-golden stamens for a crown, what other flower offers so rare a vision of royal glory and even more royal humility ? And her scent, though of surpassing sweetness, is like the radiance of the flower, elusive and not of this world. The scent of roses is the scent of summer in all its beauty, but the scent of the Madonna lily is the scent of ages yet to come and of beauties and splendours yet unrevealed. From those glorious trumpets float melodies at one with the music of the spheres, and which must surely have ascended in unison with the morning stars when they sang together. Although the Madonna lily lives apart and on a wholly different plane from the other denizens of the garden, yet the characteristic we love more than her beauty, her purity and aloofness is the most royal of all her attributes—her humility. Unconscious

[1] *Gardeners' Chronicle*, October 22, 1927.

of her own serene loveliness and ' apartness ' she is at home with the lowliest, both human beings and flowers. This attribute the two sovereigns of the flower world have in common. One has only to look at the lilies and the roses to know that between these queens and the humblest inhabitants of the garden there is a bond of mutual love and understanding. Whereas some flowers— begonias for instance—look as though they had never even heard of daisies ! The rose is intolerant of other flowers being too near her, but the lily welcomes the kindly ministrations of plants which afford shade to her roots. The rose reigns, but the presence of the lily is a benediction. The rose speaks of the beauty of this earth but the lily dreams of a new heaven and a new earth.

Small wonder that our mediaeval ancestors with their deep love and understanding of flowers placed the Madonna lily as a symbol of their lives in the hands of the saints. Above all the lily is the flower of the Annunciation. In the earliest representations of the Annunciation the Angel Gabriel holds a herald's wand, and in later Byzantine art the wand terminates in a fleur-de-lis, a symbol of royalty since the days of ancient Assyria. But by the great masters the Angel Gabriel is almost invariably represented carrying a lily. The lily has always been the symbol of purity. One recalls Chaucer's derivation of Saint Cecilia's name—' Heaven's lily.'

> ' First wol I you the name of Sainte Cecilie
> Expoune as men may in hire storie see :
> It is to sayn in English, Heven's lilie,
> For pure chasteness of virginitee,
> Or for the whitenesse had of honestie,
> And grene of conscience, and of good fame
> The swote savour, lilie was her name.'

Saint Catherine is almost invariably represented with a lily, and the lily is also the symbol of the austere St. Dominic. One recalls also the words of the ninth century monk and garden-lover, Walafred Strabo.

' Who can describe the exceeding whiteness of the lily ? The rose, it should be crowned with pearls of Arabis and Lydian gold. Better and sweeter are these flowers than all other plants and rightly called the flower of flowers.

' Yes, roses and lilies, the one for virginity with no sordid toil, no warmth of love, but the glow of their own sweet scent, which spreads further than the rival roses. . . . Therefore roses and lilies for our church, one for the martyrs' blood, the other for the symbol in his hand. Pluck them, O maiden, roses for war and lilies for peace, and think of that Flower of the stem of Jesse. Lilies His words were, and the hallowed acts of His pleasant life, but His death redyed the roses.'

Who can say when these lilies were first grown in England ? For all we know, it may have been before even the Roman occupation. Druid colleges in these islands were so famous that youths were sent to them from all parts of the Continent, and many plants which we ascribe to Roman days may well have been introduced long before. The Madonna lily is a native of Southern Europe, Palestine, Turkey, and the Caucasus. Our Anglo-Saxon ancestors loved it for its beauty, and valued it for its wound-healing qualities. In an eleventh-century Saxon herbal there is a drawing of the whole plant with the stamens standing out beyond the petals so that they look like rays of light emanating from the flowers and as it were crowning them. In a miniature in the Benedictional of Saint Ethelwold of Winchester

165

(tenth century) the Saxon queen Ethelreda, the foundress of Ely Cathedral, is depicted holding in one hand a book of the Gospels, and in the other a Madonna lily.

Throughout mediaeval days the Madonna lily was 'the lily.' One of the most beautiful word-pictures of the Madonna lily is that given by Bartholomaeus Anglicus, the great thirteenth-century scholar, in his *De Proprietatibus Rerum*. Of the lily he writes : ' The lily is an herbe with a white flower : and though the leaves of the floure be white yet within shineth the likenesse of gold. The Lily is next to the Rose in worthiness and nobleness. Nothing is more gracious than the Lily in fairness of colour, in sweetnesse of smell, and in effect of workng and vertue.' ' Though the leaves of the floure be white yet within shineth the likenessse of gold '—one feels that this description could have been written only by a child or a great scholar, for it describes not only the lily but the atmosphere of the lily with inimitable simplicity. Bartholomaeus Anglicus, who ranks with Roger Bacon and Thomas Aquinas, was one of the greatest theologians of the thirteenth century and his book was the source of common information on Natural History throughout the Middle Ages. We do not know whether he was a gardener, but his writings about flowers and fruits and woodlands give the impression that he possessed a garden and worked in it. His descriptions do not savour of a study, for there is fresh air and the beauty of the living flowers in them. I love also the description in Lyte's *Herbal* (1578) of the Madonna lily and especially of the stamens. ' The white Lilly, his leaves be long and broad, and somewhat thicke or fat, amongst the which springeth up a straight stem or stalke of three foot long or more, set and garnished

166

with leaves from the root to the top, which by little and little as they grow up towards the top, do waxe smaller and smaller. In the top of the said garnished stem grow the pleasant, beautiful, white and sweet smelling Lillies divided into six small, long and narrow leaves, which have in the outside of every leafe a certaine strake or rib, but within they are altogether of an excellent showing and pure white colour, bending somewhat backwards at the top : in the middle amongst these leaves, there hang up six very small stems, six small yellow points, or little markes, as it were tongues : in the middle amongst these also, there groweth another long upright and triangled stem, thicker than the rest, and like to the clapper of a bell.'

There is a considerable amount of truth in the statement that Madonna lilies flourish best in cottage gardens. For cottagers plant them amongst other flowers (thereby giving them shade at their roots) and in small gardens they are usually protected from the cutting winds which they abhor. Lastly, but very far from least, they are left undisturbed for years. These lilies never seem to flower so well as when their bulbs have worked themselves half out of the soil. Madonna lilies, so far from disliking lime, are lime lovers. On sandy soils, which otherwise they like, these lilies do very poorly indeed until they are given lime. At Kew it was found that they usually died out after two years, and then they were planted in ground which had been given a good dressing of lime. This has kept them in perfect health and every November they are given basic slag (6 ozs. to the square yard).

Our florists call *Lilium auratum* ' the golden-rayed lily of Japan,' and it is frequently described as the most beautiful of lilies, but the Japanese themselves, so far from appreciating its beauty, eat the bulbs as placidly as we eat potatoes. It is strange that to such a flower-loving nation lilies make little or no appeal. Plum and cherry blossom, the wistaria, and the chrysanthemum are to the Japanese the most lovely of flowers, but both in their art and in their literature the lily is conspicuous by its absence. *L. auratum* is the commonest wild lily in Japan and grows abundantly, notably on the slopes of Fuji, and on the volcanic deposits of the province of Idzu. The Western demand has created the industry of farming these bulbs, and on rich moist land they quickly attain the large size demanded by the trade and incidentally makes the bulbs fall a prey to disease. Hence the difficulty of getting healthy bulbs of this beautiful lily, which when first introduced was easily grown. Lily experts are notoriously shy of laying down any hard and fast rules on the subject of lily culture, but they do not cease to emphasize that the craze for large bulbs is death to the lily. For instance, extra large bulbs of the magnificent Himalayan lily *L. giganteum* make wonderful growth the first year, but not enough roots to sustain the towering twelve feet of stature which they should attain ; unless given exceptional conditions they usually fail miserably. Yet these superb lilies are not difficult to grow if moderate sized bulbs are planted in half-shade and given the well-drained, extensive root-run in leaf mould which they require. *L. giganteum* dies after flowering, but it usually produces a few small bulbs round the parent bulb, and these can be grown on.

Second only to the rose for beauty of scent is the carnation, and, above all, the old clove carnation, the ' clove

Sweet Williams and hybrid pinks including the old 'Mrs Sinkins'. *(See pages 171, 292-3)*

gilly flower,' beloved in Chaucer's day. In the sixteenth and seventeenth centuries carnations vied with roses. Bullein, in his *Bulwarke of Defence* (1562), calls the gilliflower ' a domesticall flower,' which is, I think, not only a delightful phrase but an apt description, for, like roses, carnations are homely flowers. ' They are no less profitable then pleasante,' says Bullein, ' they do not only preserve the bodies of men, but also doth kepe the minde and spirituall partes, from terable and fearefull dreames, through their heavenly savour, and moste sweete pleasant odor . . . there is no Apothicarie can by any naturall Arte, make any confection so pleasant as this, which nature hath wrought most wonderous in pleasying of the sences, both of seeing and smellyng.'

Gerard expresses astonishment that so beautiful a flower was not mentioned by the ancient Greek and Roman writers. ' It is marvell,' he says, ' that such a famous flower, so pleasant and sweete, should lie hid and not be made knowen by the olde writers, which may be thought not inferior to the Rose in beautie, smell and varietie.' And Parkinson writes with equal enthusiasm. ' But what shall I say to the Queene of delight and of flowers, Carnations, Gilloflowers, whose bravery, variety, and sweete smell joyned together, tyeth every ones affection with great earnestnesse, both to like and to have them.' The most famous grower of carnations in Queen Elizabeth's reign was ' Master Tuggie ' of Westminster, and perhaps he was responsible for at least some of those enchanting names in the *Paradisus*—Master Tuggie's Princesse, Ruffling Robin, Lustie Gallant, Master Bradshawe his daintie Ladie, Fair Maid of Kent, John Witte his great tawny gillow flower, The Red

169

Hulo, The Fragrant, The Speckled Tawny, etc. If he were alive now and issued a catalogue, we should all fall victims and Master Tuggie would wax fabulously rich. But I don't think even riches would cloud either the happiness or the intelligence of anyone with so pleasant a name as 'Master Tuggie.' In the *Paradisus* he is described as 'the most industrious preserver of nature's beauties.' After his death his widow evidently kept up his collection of carnations, for Johnson, in his enlarged edition of Gerard's *Herball* (1633), advises carnation lovers to 'repaire to the garden of Mistress Tuggie (the wife of my late deceased friend Mr. Ralph Tuggie) in Westminster, which in the excellencie and varietie of these delights exceedeth all that I have seene, as also he himself, whilst he lived exceeded most, if not all, of his time in his care, industry, and skill, in raising, increasing, and preserving of these plants.' That great Yorkshire gardener, William Lawson, was also an enthusiastic carnation grower, and in his *New Orchard and Garden* (1618) he writes charmingly of them. 'July flowers,' he says, 'commonly called Gilly-flowers or Clove July-flowers (I call them so because they flowre in July) they have the name of Cloves of their scent and the best sort of them are called Queen-July-flowres. I have of them nine or ten severall colours and divers of them as bigge as Roses : of all flowres (save the Damask Rose) they are the most pleasant to sight and smell.'

The petals of Clove gillyflowers were used in as many ways as rose petals. Wine was flavoured with them (hence the popular name 'Sops in wine ') ; they were candied and made into conserves and pickled ; they were served as a sauce with mutton. Queen Henrietta Maria's cook, in his book, *The Queen's Closet Opened*, gives recipes for Clove gillyflower syrup and wine, and of gillyflower vinegar John Evelyn, in his *Acetaria*, says, 'Gillyflowers infused in Vinegar and set in the Sun for certaine dayes, as we do for Rose Vinegar, do make a very pleasant and comfortable vinegar, good to be used in time of contagious sickness, and very profitable at all times for such as have feeble spirits.' The use of the flowers in medicine was manifold. William Coles, in *Adam in Eden* (1657), says, 'The conserve made of the flowers and sugar is exceeding cordiall and wonderfully above measure doth comfort the heart, being eaten now and then, which is very good also against the plague or any kind of venome. It is likewise good not only for the falling sicknesse, palsy, giddiness and the cramp, but for the pestilence. . . . The syrup of the said flowers strengthens the heart, refresheth the vital spirits and is a good cordial in feavers, expelling the poyson and fury of the disease, and greatly comforting those that are sick of any other disease, where the heart hath need of relief. Moreover, the leaves of the flowers put into a glasse of vinegar, and set in the sun for certain dayes, do make a pleasant vinegar and very good to revive one of a swoon, the nostrils and temples being washed therewith.'

Sweet-williams were called *Caryophyllus Carthusianorum*, or *Lychnis Monachorum hortensis*, in the sixteenth century, and they are supposed to have been introduced into this country by the Carthusian monks in the twelfth century. According to another tradition they took their name from William the Conqueror. The varieties of sweet-williams with narrow leaves were formerly called sweet-johns, and as such are described in the *Paradisus*.

When the year is at its zenith the scents in the garden
are surely more varied than at any other time of the year.
Apart from the exquisite scents of the lilies and the
warm sweet scents of the carnations, there are the gorgeous scents of the magnolia and philadelphus, the
alluring, far-reaching perfume of the jasmines, the
homely sweet scent of the honeysuckles, the honey
scent of *Buddleia variabilis* (beloved by the autumn
butterflies, notably the peacocks, tortoiseshells and
admirals), the even more honey-like scent of *Cassinia
fulvida* (syn. *Diplopappus chrysophyllus*), the vanilla perfume of *Clematis flammula*, the lily of the valley-like
scent of the clethras (particularly *Clethra alnifolia pani-
culata*), the aromatic fragrance of the allspices (*Caly-
canthus floridus* and *C. occidentalis*), the cypress-like smell
of *Veronica cupressoides*, the pleasant hot scent of *Cistus
ladaniferus*, the sweet scents of the myrtles (particularly
M. luma), the lemon scent of lemon verbena, the delicious and indescribable scent of ' cherry pie,' the exquisitely
varied scents of the numerous sweet-scented geraniums,
the sweet, refreshing scents of lavender and marjoram,
the varied cordial scents of the other aromatic herbs and
the homely warm scents of the phloxes and marigolds.
And these are but a few of the scents in the garden in
' the afternoon of the year.'

Richest and sweetest are the scents of the magnolia
and the philadelphus. If I were a millionaire, I should
grow magnolias by the acre, for their beauty and scent
have held me captive nearly all my life. Possibly this is
owing to the fact that part of my childhood was spent in
an old house, one wall of which was completely covered
with a magnificent specimen of the old laurel magnolia

(*M. grandiflora*). I can remember gazing in silent fascination at the beauty of the milk-white flowers which grew low enough to come within my range of vision. Then (as now) I felt I was looking at flowers which did not seem to belong to this world, but to some big, splendid planet such as Saturn. A few days ago I was looking at a *Magnolia Watsonii* in flower, and the effect on my mnid was just the same, only intensified a thousand-fold. The primeval splendour of those great blooms, shining amid the dark foliage, held me spellbound. And the scent of magnolias literally goes to my head. The effect is such that for a moment I do not see the flower, but instead a fairyland of incredible splendour—cloud-capped towers and palaces of overwhelming magnificence —far remote from our own little friendly fairies.

How different is the homely sweet scent of honeysuckle. ' Oh how swete and pleasaunte is Woodbinde, in Woodes or Arbours, after a tender soft rain : and how friendly doe this herbe if I maie so name it, imbrace the bodies, armes and branches of trees, with his long windyng stalkes, and tender leaves, openyng or spreding forthe his swete Lilles, like ladies fingers, among the thornes or bushes. Is this Woodbinde so profitable as pleasaunt I praie you tell me ? ' ' Honeysuckle ' is one of our very oldest English flower names, going back to at least the early years of the eighth century, for the name occurs in the *Epinal Glossary*. As sweet as any garden honey-suckle is the honeysuckle of our hedgerows. ' The Honeysuckle that groweth wild in every hedge, although it be very sweete, yet doe I not bring it into my garden, but let it rest in his owne place, to serve their senses that travell by it, or have no garden.'

173

Who can picture an English lane at this time of year
without the beauty of honeysuckle flowers and their
exquisite scent ? Who can dissociate either from the
scent of fields of red clover and the golden splendour of
harvest ? Like apple blossom, the scent of honeysuckle
is at its sweetest in the early morning. Best of all
for the garden are the early and late Dutch varieties
—*Lonicera belgica* and *L. serotina.* The showiest of
the hardy honeysuckles, *L. tragophylla* (Chinese Woodbine), is scentless. *L. caprifolium,* so called because goats
are fond of eating its leaves, is exceedingly sweet of smell.
It is a very strong grower, often reaching 20 feet ; it
loves a chalky soil, and is a honeysuckle one frequently
sees growing rampantly over porches and arbours in
cottage gardens near the sea. We love the scent and
beauty of honeysuckle in the late summer, but I think
we love it just as much in winter, for honeysuckle is one
of our earliest plants in leaf. By the end of February
its red-green leaves are tiny inch-long heralds of spring,
long before any other leaves, save the pale green shoots
of the elder, show more than a faint sign. Honeysuckle,
or woodbine, has always been the symbol of faithful love.
Chaucer tells us that those that

> ' Wore chapelets on hir hede
> Of fresh wodebind, be such as never were
> To love untrue, in word ne thought, ne dede,
> But ay steadfast : ne for pleasance, ne fere
> Tho' that they shoulde hir hertes all to tere,
> Would never flit, but ever were stedfast
> Till that hir lives theie asunder brust.'

The scent of Jasmine has the richness of flowers such as
hyacinths, the sweetness of the lily of the valley, and,

above all, an elusive quality which gives its perfume a
fascination peculiarly its own.

> ' Nor knows he well to make his Garden shine
> With all delights, Who fragrant Jassamine
> Neglects to cherish.'

The Common Jasmine (*Jasminum officinale*) has been
grown in England from time immemorial, yet there
is still an aroma of mystery in the scent of these Eastern
flowers. Various authorities on the composition of scent,
ranging from Piesse to Dr. Hampton, have commented
on the curious characteristics of the scent of jasmine.
In spite of the skill of modern chemists, it remains the
mysterious scent. ' Is Jasmine then the mystical Morn—
the centre, the Delphi, the Omphalos of the floral
world ? Is it the point of departure, the one unapproach-
able and indivisible unit of fragrance ? Is Jasmine the
Isis of flowers, with veiled face and covered feet to be
loved of all yet discovered by none ? '

What a thousand pities it is that the sweet-scented
geraniums have been allowed wellnigh to disappear from
our gardens. When they were introduced, about 1795,
from the Cape they became universally popular, and were
soon grown on every cottage window-sill as well as in
palatial greenhouses. But the introduction of the showy
zonal pelargoniums soon diminished the popularity of
the humble sweet-scented geraniums, and we are only
beginning to appreciate them again at their true worth.
The finest collection of sweet-scented geraniums is at
Aldenham House. One could easily spend two hours
looking at that wonderful array, and nowhere else have I
seen standards quite ten years old and measuring roughly
5 feet round. To mention but a few—there are the old

favourites such as Lady Plymouth, 'Purple Unique,' etc.;
aristocrats such as the variegated 'Prince of Orange,' which
is so difficult to grow, all the charming *crispums* (*varie-
gatum*, *maximum*, and *minimum*). Sweetest scented of
all is the well-namèd 'attar of roses.' *Scabrum* also is
peculiarly sweet scented. (The gardener told me that the
original plant at Aldenham came from the Cape in an
ordinary parcel). Then there are *Ionidifolium*, the
attractive greyish *Blanfordianum*, *artemisifolium betu-
linum*, Lady Scarborough, Lady Mary, Schotte (tuberous
rooted and difficult to propagate), *terebintha*, saxa-
fragoides, Fair Emily, Joan (a sport from Clorinda),
tetragonum, *abrotanifolium*, *rapaceum*, and the enchanting, well-named Curly. And these are but a few of these
old-fashioned scented treasures in this collection.

A friend told me that in Greece they make delicious
apple jelly flavoured with sweet-scented geranium leaves.
One leaf is sufficient for an ordinary preserving pan, and
it has to be put in for the last three minutes the jelly is
boiling and of course taken out before the jelly is put
into pots. It is certainly excellent and gives the apple
jelly a suggestion of Turkish Delight flavour.

Some months ago I read an article[1] in the Bulletin of
the Garden Club of America which delighted me, for it
was by a lover of sweet-scented geraniums, and I felt
that if I met the writer we should be friends at once,
because in our childhood we had both loved these sweet-
leaved plants. There must be thousands of folk who
associate the scent with their childhood, for with the
exception of lemon-scented verbena, and 'cherry pie,'
there are, I suppose, no scents which attract one more

[1] *Sweet-leaved Geraniums* by L. B. Wilder.

'Like apple blossom, the scent of honeysuckle is at its sweetest in the early morning.' *(See page 174)*

Great-aunt Lancilla's summer border was full of scent and colour. *(See page 179)*

when one is very young. I think this must be because, although sweet, yet they are so pungent and vigorous and surprisingly unexpected from such delicately cut leaves. The writer of the article in question described how, when a child, she used to go with her father on winter Sunday afternoons to see a friend who was renowned for his collection of sweet-leaved geraniums. She used to follow ' the two flower-lovers, the one so tall and straight, the other old and bent, up and down the narrow aisles between the benches of plants, pausing when they paused, moving slowly forward when they advanced, filled with beatitude by the warm, sweet odours given off by the moist earth and the growing green things. No notice was taken of me, and so, left to my own devices, I would snip as I went, a leaf here, a leaf there, until finally with my hands and pockets full of aromatic leaves I would subside on an upturned tub in a corner and sniff and compare the different scents to my heart's content. It was a very good game indeed, as well as valuable nose training. It always seemed amazing that just leaves could have such a variety of odours. Some had the scents of oranges or lemons, some were spicy, others had a rose-like fragrance, and many were vaguely familiar but tantalizingly illusive. One that especially ravished my youthful nose smelled exactly like the pennyroyal that grew in our woods. The leaves of this kind were large and soft, and the bush was lax and ungainly in habit. I know it now for *Pelargonium tomentosum*, usually called the peppermint geranium.[1]

---

[1] In her delightful *Kitchen Essays*, Lady Jekyll gives a recipe for peppermint jelly flavoured with these leaves. With her kind permission I quote this recipe :—' Make a quart of good lemon jelly in the approved way, preferably with calves' feet, more probably with best

But my favourite was a little slender plant with small much-cut leaves that had the sharp refreshing scent of lemon, with something sweet behind it. It had the charm of lemon drops—acid and sweet—and always made my mouth water ecstatically. It was probably *P. citriodorum*.'

My own first recollections of sweet-leaved geraniums go back to the days when as a child I used to stay with my great-aunt Lancilla. And whenever I smell those leaves I am instantly transported to her house, and in particular to the broad, sunny passage which led to the kitchen. The sun came pouring through the sloping glass roof, and there was a whole bank of the sweet-leaved geraniums, reaching well above my head. Pinching the leaves was always a joy, for the scents were so rich and so varied. And those scents now never fail to remind me of a gracious old lady who looked well to the ways of her placid, well-ordered household and was loved by every one who served her, and every man, woman and child in the village.

When I think of scented gardens I remember hers first and foremost, for though since those days I have seen many gardens, I do not think I have ever seen a pleasanter, homelier one. The house was Georgian, and the short drive to it was flanked on both sides by pollarded lime trees. (I have only to shut my eyes to hear the hum of the bees now.) The drive was never used by the household

leaf gelatine—but not—oh not!—with jelly powders. Whilst warm, add a handful of those large green peppermint geranium leaves, thick as a fairy's blanket, soft as a vicuna robe, and to be found in most old-fashioned gardens, and let them flavour your blend; or you can use 3 or 4 drops of essence of peppermint, ½ teaspoonful of apple green to colour, or home-made spinach greening for a substitute. Pass through your jelly bag and serve very cold. A glass of crème de menthe might well improve this but it is by no means indispensable.'

nor indeed by anyone who came on foot, for the shortest way from the village was through a gate leading from the road to a side door. The path was perfectly straight, and bordered on either side by very broad beds, and except in midwinter they were full of scent and colour. I can see the big bushes of the pale pink China roses and smell their delicate perfume ; I see the tall old-fashioned delphiniums and the big red peonies and the clumps of borage, the sweet-williams, the Madonna and tiger lilies and the well-clipped bushes of lad's love. Before the time of roses I remember chiefly the Canterbury bells and pyrethrums, and earlier still the edge nearest the path was thick with wallflowers and daffodils. I have never seen hollyhocks grow as they grew at the back of those borders, and they were all single ones, ranging from pale yellow to the deepest claret. Beyond this path, on one side was the big lawn with four large and very old mulberry trees. As a child it frequently struck me that considering how small mulberries were compared to apples, plums and so forth, it was really little short of a miracle what a glorious mess one could get into with them in next to no time. Amongst the flowers great-aunt Lancilla loved most were evening primroses. I have never since then seen a large border, as she had, entirely given to them. She used to pick the flowers to float in finger bowls at dinner.

I can see the kitchen garden too, with its long paths and espalier fruit trees and the sweet peas grown in clumps, and they *were* sweet peas then, for they were deliciously scented. And big clumps of gypsophila and mignonette, which everyone in those days grew to mix with the sweet peas. There were great rows of clove carnations for picking, and never have I smelt any like them. Nor have

I since tasted the like of the greengages which grew against the old wall. Is there anything quite so good as both the smell and the taste of a ripe greengage picked hot in the sun? I can see the orderly rows of broad beans, lettuces, peas and scarlet runners and stout cabbages. The onions and ' sparrer grass ' were the special pride of the old gardener's heart. I can see the well and hear the pleasant clanking sound of the bucket as it was let down. I see old Gregory attending to the bee-hives with the calm gentle movements which characterize all experienced bee-keepers. He invariably talked to the bees when he was attending to them, and one day when, as a small child, I was watching him, I asked him, ' Do the bees understand what you are saying to them, Gregory ? ' ' Understan', Missie ? ' he replied, ' Just as much as horses an' dogs an' cattle ; it stands to sense and reason they do. An' sometimes I thinks they understan' more nor we do.' And the raspberries and gooseberries ! My great-aunt had a favourite Aberdeen, who, incredible though it may seem, loved ripe gooseberries. He used to sit up, as though he were begging, and eat them and wail aloud every few minutes whenever his nose was pricked. I love to think of the huge bed of lilies of the valley, where one could gather and gather to one's heart's content for one's friends in the village. But my chief recollection of that kitchen garden is of roses. Cabbage roses and La France and Gloire de Dijon and Maiden's Blush, and if one gathered armfuls it seemed to make no difference. Those were the days when people filled their rooms with innumerable small vases of flowers, but my great-aunt, who went her own way entirely, loved to have big bowls of flowers everywhere, even in the passages of her house.

And how well I remember the sweet, subdued scent of pot-pourri, for as well as flowers there were in every room big open bowls of the pot-pourri she loved to have about her. In many of the bowls there were oranges stuck with cloves. Everyone loves picking these up and sniffing them, yet few people make them nowadays.[1]

My great-aunt only allowed candles for lighting purposes, for she always declared she could smell gas in any house where it was laid on, and ' that ill-considered invention,' as I once heard her describe a gas-cooker, she would not tolerate. I remember so well the burnished silver candlesticks set out on a side-table in the hall every evening to take up to the bedrooms. Making paper spills (especially very long ones) for lighting the candles was a pleasant occupation when she read aloud to one. She had a wonderful collection of children's books, and though she had read them to two generations of children, she enjoyed them with as much zest as one did oneself. The books one loved in one's childhood are, I think, the books one loves most all through one's life. If I live to be ninety I know I shall still be reading Hans Andersen, Mrs. Ewing, Charlotte Yonge and the four bound volumes of the delightful *S. Nicholas' Magazine*, which my father and mother gave me as they came out. (I have many American friends now, both personal friends and those I know only through correspondence with them, but my first American friends were amongst the contributors to the Letter-Box pages of *S. Nicholas' Magazine*.) Of the many books my great-aunt read to me, I remember amongst others a dumpy calf-bound volume of stories translated from the Hungarian original, and one tale in

---

[1] For recipe see p. 219.

particular about a small boy, a little prince (whose name was quite half a line long, but I can only recall it began with K) who, as my great-aunt and I enviously agreed, thought of more naughty things to do in a day than either of us could contrive in a whole week. In the art of telling the old fairy stories and Hans Andersen's immortal tales she excelled. We all remember the type of kindly grown-up who was ready enough to tell one stories but seemed to be unable to tell the same story exactly the same again. Out of consideration for their feelings one tried not to show how unsatisfactory this was, but all the time one had the unpleasant sensation that the ground was slipping away from under one's feet. Whether it was due to her love of the old stories, or because years of practice had taught her (and I fancy it was the former), my great-aunt could tell favourite stories over and over again with never a word wrong. Most soothing those tales were, and how gratefully those of us to whom she so generously gave much of her valuable time remember those happy hours.

And I account it one of the privileges of my life to have heard her read aloud from the Bible. Prayers were before breakfast, but after breakfast it was her unfailing custom, however busy she might be, and her life was a very busy one indeed, to read some part of the Bible aloud. I can see her reverently placing the Book on the small table by her special chair and then when she had found the part she wanted, she either read it, or, as frequently as not, she removed her spectacles and with her hands clasped before her, she would repeat by heart a chapter or so. It was my firm belief in those days that she knew the whole Bible by heart, and she certainly knew very large portions by heart. As to countless others the Word of God was indeed a lantern unto her feet and a light unto her paths. By that unfailing source of light she ruled herself, her household and the village. She had in full measure that deep-rooted love of the Bible which is so characteristic of our race, and I often heard her repeating passages to herself as she went about the house and garden. Small wonder that her ways were ways of pleasantness and all her paths were peace. I remember standing one evening with her by the side of the great pond at the further end of the lawn and watching a singularly beautiful sunset. She looked at it in silence for a few minutes, and then almost unconsciously she repeated the whole of the Psalm ' The heavens declare the glory of God and the firmament sheweth his handiwork.' To this day I can never read or hear that Psalm without thinking of her.

In appearance great-aunt Lancilla was a very impressive old lady. In the days when everyone of her age wore long skirts she invariably wore skirts quite four inches off the ground, both during the day and in the evening. The colour she most affected was a certain soft cinnamon brown one rarely sees nowadays. Others wore bonnets, but summer and winter she wore wide-brimmed hats, almost devoid of trimming and tied under her chin with a large flat bow. She rarely wore jewellery, but instead enchanting strings of beads which she had acquired in various parts of the world, and that was quite a generation before Paris or Chelsea had even dreamt of beads. No one loved pretty things more than she did, but I think she was almost unconscious of passing fashions. Under her skirt and fastened like an apron she wore a Pocket. Only a capital letter can give an idea of the size and importance of this curious garment, which consisted of a whole array of flat, envelope-like receptacles, into which she slipped anything and everything she needed. A trowel and a small hand-fork, for instance, disappeared easily into those capacious depths, to say nothing of such trifles as stale bread for the ducks, corn for the pigeons, etc. Most people would find it difficult to walk gracefully with trowels and such knocking their ankles, but these impedimenta never seemed to interfere with her quick, yet dignified movements. I never remember her carrying anything in her hands except flowers, fruit, or the candle lantern she took to light her way to church on winter evenings.

The process of furnishing her Pocket was usually done in the garden-room. Like most garden-rooms, that was a wholly delightful place. Comfortable, worn old chairs, a long table used for arranging flowers and countless other processes, a rocking chair which rocked to such a pitch that it was a joy for ever, a large desk containing many treasured recipes, and all those fascinating odds and ends which seem to collect themselves in old desks, and which are so much more attractive to childhood than any toys. I wonder what manner of folk invented those entrancing fittings in the desks and work-boxes of Victorian days. Amongst my great-aunt's numerous gifts to me was a work-box, a treasure indeed, for it had belonged to her mother. The outside and all the trays and lids, etc., are entirely inlaid with ebony, silver and ivory in a tiny intricate pattern, and inside the partitions are fitted with those little ivory objects of which no one nowadays seems to know the use. What, for instance, are these little ivory barrels with tops which screw on

Great-aunt Lancilla's kitchen garden, with its flowers and fruit, much loved by child and Aberdeen Terrier. *(See pages 179, 180)*

and with slender ivory sticks thrust into them ? In those
days I never thought of asking, for I only wanted to play
with these smooth lovely little toys.

And there was a store-cupboard in the garden-room,
which was an overflow from the store-room proper. That
was a store-cupboard ! Apart from the home-candied
rose-petals, violets, carnation-petals, cowslips, rosemary
and borage flowers, the damson cheeses and so forth, to
be found in every well-regulated store-room in those
days, that cupboard contained triumphs of the culinary
art not to be bought nowadays. Great-aunt Lancilla
candied oranges whole, and when done they were like
semi-transparent globes of orange gold. Before being
candied a tiny hole was made in the place where the stalk
was and every bit of the pulp was scraped out with a salt-
spoon, a slow and delicate process. Then the oranges
were steeped in a strong salt and water pickle for a week,
then soaked in fresh water for two or three days, the
water being changed every day. The oranges were then
boiled in syrup till they cleared. (This recipe has been
used for at least six generations in our family.) In candle-
light, or indeed any artificial light, these candied oranges
look exquisite.

And do you know whortleberry jam and jelly? Whortle-
berries have many different names in Britain. Scotch
folk call them blaeberries, and in Surrey we call them
' hurts.' They are, I fancy, the only fruit one cannot
buy in London, and so far as I know whortleberry jelly
and jam are also not to be bought. I suppose the process
of picking the tiny berries being so slow, added to the
cost of transit, and the fact that they travel badly account
for this. But is there a more delicate, delicious fruit,

whether plainly stewed or made into a conserve ? And I remember also the bunches of white and red currants candied whole. These were very attractive, for they looked as though they were made of glass. They seemed very 'superior' to the rose leaves, but the latter were sweet and the former very acid, in spite of their deceptive coating of sugar. Both rose and carnation petals were preserved by coating them on both sides with white of egg well beaten. It was a fascinating process, done with a tiny brush like a paint-brush. Then the petals were spread out on very large dishes, and castor sugar carefully and evenly shaken over them. Then they were turned over, and the other side was sugared. My great-aunt invariably dried these rose petals *in the sun*, and perhaps that is why they were so sweet. When dry they were beautifully crisp and put away in layers with paper between each layer in air-tight boxes. Primroses done like this look very pretty, for the flowers are done whole. And such syrups ! Elder syrup, which was very pungent and luscious, clove carnation syrup (the best of all), mint syrup (quince juice strongly flavoured with mint), and saffron syrup, of which I only remember that one of the ingredients was Canary wine. The name ' Canary wine ' made an impression on me, for as a child I thought it must have something to do with canary birds, and I vaguely wondered why ! The cupboard also contained many homely medicines in which in those days I took no interest at all. But I remember how often the village women came for these remedies. For great-aunt Lancilla was the trusted friend of every soul in the place. She had known all the young generation from their birth upwards, and for the scapegraces, of whom the village had quite its normal share, she had a very understanding heart. One of the scapegraces was the garden boy. Even as a child I was conscious that between such a luminary as, for instance, the coachman, and the garden boy there was a great gulf fixed, but I was equally conscious that between my great-aunt and ' the young limb ' (the cook's epithet for him, not mine) there was a solid bond of comradeship. She understood him perfectly, and I think he would cheerfully have gone to the stake for her.

It was my great-aunt who first introduced me to the joys of a water-garden. I think it is the small water-garden which fascinates one most. Even in the most diminutive scented-garden one could have a little pool, measuring only a few feet each way, holding *N. Laydeckeri fulgens* and *N. Odorata alba*. A cement-lined pool 12 inches deep would allow for 5 inches of loam at the bottom and 7 inches of water. To keep the pool sweet golden orfe are perhaps the best, for they are so greedy ! Their principal food is the larvae of the mosquito and the daphne of the water midge and other animalculae. Mr. Amos Perry told me that the right proportion of fish is to allow ' one inch of fish to a gallon of water.' An eighth of an inch of very coarse bonemeal is excellent manure. For larger water-gardens there are deliciously scented hardy nymphaeas, amongst the most beautiful being *N. odorata maxima, Caroliniana* and *James Brydon*.

And what of the night-scented flowers ? To many of us there is no time when the scents in the garden are more exquisite than at twilight. The scents of the roses and the lilies then seem sweeter than at any other hour. The scent of honeysuckle is richer, and lured by it the hawk-moths fly to extract the honey which lies too deep for the bees or wasps to reach. Nor do the jasmines exhale their richest perfumes until darkness falls and the bells of the yuccas turn to stars. The scents of those old favourites, the night-scented stock (*Hesperis tristis*) and the old double white Rocket (*H. matronalis*) and *Nicotiana affinis*, have rejoiced generations of scent-lovers with the sweetness of their perfumes in the evening. The old double white Rocket was formerly known as Dames Violets, for in the evening it exhales a violet-like fragrance, whereas as Parkinson noted three hundred years ago this 'pretty sweet scent' is almost absent during the day. One of the sweetest of all evening scents is that of one of our native catchflies, *Silene nutans*, sometimes called the Nottingham catchfly, because it formerly grew in such abundance near that town, and in still older days it was called the Dover catchfly, because the cliffs there for miles were starred in the evening with its fragrant flowers. It is, alas! not a common wild flower now, and for those who love its rich scent it is well worth growing in a garden where there is chalky soil. But the scent is never so strong as when in its wild state. Even when gathered and brought indoors this catchfly opens only in the evening, and the scent in a room is overpowering. The wild evening campion (*Lychnis Vespertina*) opens its flowers during the day, but as its name implies it is only in the evening that it breathes forth its incense. The humble little *Linnaea borealis*, which grows wild in parts of Norway and Scotland, scents the air round with its delicious fragrance in the evening. Sowerby gives the following account of this plant : ' For this most interesting addition to the British Flora we are indebted to Professor James Beattie, junior, of Aberdeen, who discovered it in an old fir wood at Mearns in that neighbourhood and communicated wild specimens, along with an accurate coloured drawing, to the Linnaean Society, June 2nd, 1795. The *Linnaea* grows in dry, stony, mossy woods. The flowers are said to be very fragrant at night, smelling like the meadowsweet. Linnaeus in *Critica Botanica*, p. 80, has traced a pretty fanciful analogy between his own early fate and this " little northern plant, long overlooked, depressed, abject, flowering early," and we may now add more honoured in its name than any other.'

No evening scents, I think, have the fascination of the delicate fragrance of the evening primroses, especially that of the commonest variety. Those pale moons irradiate the twilight with their sweet elusive perfumes. Like the flowers themselves their scent as night draws in becomes full of mystery and holds our imagination captive. And the scent of limes, what an exquisite scent this is—as exquisite as the music of the trees. To me the loveliest music in the world is the music of the evening breeze in the lime trees on a July evening. Each one of us, I suppose, dreams their own dreams and reads their own thoughts in the wondrously varied music of trees. Just as with the music of bells. ' He that hears bells will make them sound what he list ; as the soul thinketh, so the bell clinketh.' The sound of the wind amongst beeches is a glorious sound, deep, rich and full. It is magnificent, but it is a song of this earth. The music of limes is a faraway melody reaching to the stars, a music which sweeps our thoughts to those stupendous flowers set by Almighty God in the gardens of space. Are other worlds wrapped in mantles of beauty like this earth ? Sometimes one wonders whether there is, so to speak, a pattern in the robe of flower and leaf wherewith this old earth is adorned, a pattern so grand and yet so intricate that only the angels can apprehend it in its beauty. Are those other vast worlds—so vast that beside them this earth is almost negligible—but the larger flowers which adorn the paths of the angels? Is even their stupendous grandeur but a minute example of the perfection of Divine workmanship, whose endless perfections aeons of time will not be sufficient to reveal? What melodies and what fragrance must rejoice the angels in those far-flung gardens of space? Whilst we on this earth cannot yet understand or even know very much about a petal of a flower or a blade of grass, in themselves worlds of beauty, setting forth, no less than the greatest stars, the perfect workmanship of God.

'The night has made a nosegay of the stars
Bound with a straying fragrance from the South:
Of wax white Jasmine, and of that dark Rose—
That sombre Rose—to whom the fountains sing—
(She seems so like a wild heart listening),
From Night's faint hold it drops down to the Sea;
Slowly the radiant flowers—one by one—
Are freed, and float in silence out of sight.
The sea stirs—as a child stirs half asleep—
Gathers them to invest her wistful dream
With beauty; for who else knows loneliness
Wraith-bound—close and forever—like the Sea?

Across the fair pavilion of the Moon
A shadow passes—in swift ordered flight
Wild geese, miles high, whose echoed trumpet call
Soars eastward—sweeping to the port of dawn.'

CHAPTER VIII

SWEET BAGS

To make little cusshins of parfumed Roses.

TAKE buddes of redde Roses, their heades and toppes
cut awaye, drie them in the shadowe upon a
table, or a linnen cloath : water and sprinkle the sayde
buddes with Rose water, and let them drie, doynge this
five or sixe times, turning them alwayes, to the end
they waxe not mouldy : than take the poudre of Cipre,
Muske & Amber, made into a pouder according as you
woulde make them excellent, for the more you put in
of it the better they shal be : put to it also Lignum
aloes well beaten in pouder. Let the saide pouder be
put wth the budds wete with rose water, mixing well
the budds together with the pouder, to thend al may be
wel incorporated, so shal you leave them so al a night,
covering them wth som linnen cloth or Taffeta that the
musk may not breath or rise out. The whiche thing done,
take finallye lyttle bagges of Taffeta of what bignesse
you wil, and according to the quantitie of the buddes
that you would put among all the pouder. Then close
up the bagges, and for to stop up the seames, you must
have your mixion of Muske, Amber, & Civette, made as
it were to seare with, wherewith you shall rubbe all a
longe the seames, to stoppe the holes made with the needle
in sowinge : you may also sowe ribande (of gold or silke,

191

or what you will) over the said seames. These be the best that a man can make : and (as I have sayed) the more Musk, Amber, Civet & Aloe you put in the better thei will be. If you wyll make them with lesse cost, take such buddes as are spoken of before, prepared and ordered in the same sort, and in steede of Muske and Amber, put in the pouder of Cloves, Synamom, & a little Mace, observing such a manner of parfuming the buddes as before.

The secretes of the reverent Maister Alexis of Piemont.

To make an especiall sweet Powder for sweet Bags.

Take of the purest Orris one pound, of Red and Damask Rose-leaves, of each two ounces, of Cloves three drams, Coriander seed one dram, Cyprus and Calamus of each halfe an ounce, Benzoin and Storax of each three drams ; beat them all save the Benzoin and the Storax, and powder them by themselves, and mix it with the rest of the powder ; then take of Muske and Civet, of each twentie graines, mix these with a little of the foresaid powder with a warm Pestle and so by little and little you may mix it with all the rest, and so with Rose-leaves dried you may put it up into your sweet Bags and so keepe them seven yeares.

Sir Hugh Platt. *Delights for Ladies* (1594).

For a sweet bag.

Take of Orris six ounces, of Damask Rose-leaves as much, of Marjerom and sweet Basil of each an ounce, of Cloves two ounces, yellow Sanders two ounces, of Citron pills seven drams, of Lignum Aloes one ounce, of Benjamin one ounce, of Storax one ounce, of Musk one

192

dram ; bruise all these, and put them into a bag of Silk or Linnen, but silk is the best.

Gervase Markham. *The English Housewife* (1625).

To make sweet powder for bags.

Take of Orris four ounces, of Rose leaves dryed two handfuls, of dryed Marjerom one handful, of Spike one handful, Cloves one ounce, Benjamin two ounces, of white Sanders and yellow of each one ounce, beat all these into a gross powder, then put to it of Musk a dram, of Civet half a dram, and of Ambergreece half a dram, then put them into a Taffety Bag and use it.   *Ibid.*

A sweet bag.

Take half a pound of Benjamin and half a pound of storacks, half a pound of orris, an ounce of cloves, and a few orange peels dryed, a little sweet marjerrum dryed ; beat all these pretty gross.

Take half a bushell of Damask Roses, and a gentle fire under a Still : fill the Still with roses, first damp them, then take them out and put them into a large dish and pull them all to pieces while they be hot. Strew these, powders being mixt, on the roses, work all these together so that the powder may stick on the roses, and thus till all the roses be done ; then take a great preserveing glass or 2 that will more than hold it and lay in a lay of roses and strew in some powder ; so do till all be in the glasses. Then bind it up close with a double white paper and leather on the top. Then set it as hot as you can in the sun every day. Shake the glasses very well if you find it do cake in the middle, put your hand in the glasses and stir

193

it very well and when tis very dry put some amber grease pounded and some civet ; rub it about the leaves what quantity you please ; so you may keep it in bags as long as you please.　　　*A Book of Simples (circa* 1650).

A perfume for a sweet bagg.

Take half a pound of Cypress Roots, a pound of Orris, 3 quarters of a pound of Rhodium, a pound of Coriander Seed, 3 quarters of a pound of Calamus, 3 oranges stuck with cloves, 2 ounces of Benjamin, and an ounce of Storax and 4 pecks of Damask Rose leaves, a peck of dryed sweet Marjerum, a pretty stick of Juniper shaved very thin, some lemon pele dryed; let all these be powdered very grosely for the first year and immediately put into your baggs ; the next year pound and work it and it will be very good again.

MARY DOGGETT : *Her Book of Receipts* (1682).

Our great-grandmother's sweet bags.

Equal quantities of dried lavender, verbena and sweet geranium leaves.

For Ordinary Linnen.

Take of orrice 8 pound, callamase 2 pound, damaske powder a pound, cloves a pound, gallingall half a pound, benjamin half a pound, storax half a pound, lavender a pound : to every pound of rose leaves you must put a pound of powder.　　　*A Book of Simples (circa* 1650).

194

For Fine Linnen.

Take of orrice 4 pounds, callamase half a pound, benjamin a pound, storax a pound, cloves a quarter of a pound, civet half an ounce, muske an ounce, ointment of oringe flowers 2 ounces, lignum alloes 2 ounces, ambergreese half an ounce, rose wood half a pound ; the amber, civet, musk and ointment of oringes must be mingled together and melt'd and you must either rub the roses with it or else some wool : the wool will keep the smell longest. To every pound of roses a pound of powder.

Ibid.

The best way to break Sweet Powder.

Take of Orrice one pound, Calamus a quarter of a pound, Benjamin one half pound, Storax half a pound, Civet a quarter of an ounce, Cloves a quarter of a pound, Musk one half ounce, Oyl of Orange flowers one ounce, Lignum Aloes one ounce, Rose wood a quarter of a pound, Ambergreece a quarter of an ounce. To every pound of Roses put a pound of powder ; the bag must be of Taffety, or else the Powder will run through.

A Queen's Delight (1664).

Sweet-scented Bags to lay with Linen.

Eight ounces of coriander-seeds, eight ounces of sweet orris-root, eight ounces of damask rose leaves, eight ounces of calamus aromaticus, one ounce of mace, one ounce of cinnamon, half an ounce of cloves, four drachms of musk-powder, two drachms of white loaf sugar, three ounces of lavender flowers, and some of

195

Rhodium wood, beat them well together and make them in small silk bags.

Mrs. Glasse. *The Art of Cookery* (1784).

An agreeable sweet-scented Composition.

Take Florentine Orrice, a pound and a half; Rose Wood, six ounces; Calamus Aromaticus, half a pound; Gum Benjamin, five ounces; Cloves, half an ounce, and Cinnamon an ounce; beat the whole into powder and fill your bags with it. *The Toilet of Flora.*

Bags to scent Linen.

Take Rose Leaves dried in the shade, Cloves beat to a gross powder, and Mace scraped; mix them together, and put the composition into little bags. *Ibid.*

Ingredients for various Sorts of these little Bags or Satchels.

For this purpose may be used different parts of the Aromatic Plants; as Leaves of Southernwood, Dragon-wort, Balm, Mint, both garden and wild, Dittany, Ground-ivy, Bay, Hyssop, Lovage, Sweet Marjoram, Origanum, Pennyroyal, Thyme, Rosemary, Savory, Scordium, and Wild Thyme. The Flowers of the Orange, Lemon, Lime, and Citron Tree, Saffron, Lavender, Roses, Lily of the Valley, Clove-july flower, Wall-flower, Jonquil, and Mace. Fruits, as Aniseeds, etc. The Rinds of Lemons, Oranges, &c. Small green Oranges, Juniper-berries, Nutmegs, and Cloves, Roots of Acorus, Bohemian Angelice, Oriental Costus, Sweet Flag, Orrice, Zedoary, &c. The Woods of Rhodium, Juniper, Cassia, St. Lucia,

Sanders, &c. Gums, as Frankincense, Myrrh, Storax, Benjamin, Labdanum, Ambergrise, and Amber. Barks, as Canella Alba, Cinnamon, &c.

Care must be taken that all these ingredients are perfectly dry, and kept in a dry place. To prevent their turning black, add a little common Salt. When you choose to have any particular Flower predominant, a greater quantity of that plant must be used in proportion to the other ingredients.

Ibid.

A Perfumed Basket.

Place a layer of perfumed Cotton extremely thin and even on a piece of Taffety stretched in a frame ; strew on it some Violet Powder, and then some Cypress Powder ; cover the whole with another piece of Taffety : nothing more remains to complete the work, but to quilt it, and cut it of the size of the basket, trimming the edges with ribband.

Ibid.

SCENTED POWDERS

Powder of Violets.

Take Treos Root of Florence halfe a pound, Roses foure ounces, Ciprus roots, Marjoram, Cloves of each an ounce, yellow Sanders, Benjamin of each foure ounces, Storax an ounce, beat them into powder.

The Charitable Physitian by PHILIBERT GUIBERT,
Physitian Regent in Paris (1639).

Another Powder of Violets.

Take Treos root of Florence foure pound, dry Marjoram foure ounces, Calamus Aromaticus three ounces, Roses and Violets of each five ounces, Cloves halfe a dramme, Muske a dramme, make them into a very fine powder.

Ibid.

To dry Roses for Sweet Powder.

Take your Roses after they have layen 2 or 3 days on a Table, then put them into a dish and sett them on a chafering dish of Charcole, keeping them stirred, and as you stir them strew in some powder of orris, and when you see them pretty dry put them into a gally pot till you use them.

MARY DOGGETT : *Her Book of Receipts* (1682).

Jasmine Powder.

Powder French Chalk, sift it through a fine sieve, put it in a box, and strew on it a quantity of Jasmine Flowers ; shut down the lid close, and add fresh Flowers every four and twenty hours. When the Powder is well impregnated with the scent of Jasmine, rub together a few grains of Civet, Ambergrise, and a little white Sugar Candy, and mix them with the Powder. *The Toilet of Flora.*

Coarse Violet Powder.

Beat separately into coarse Powder the following ingredients, viz. half a pound of dried Orange Flowers ; of Lemon-peel dried, Yellow Sanders, Musk Roses, and Gum Benjamin, each a quarter of a pound ; Lavender Tops dried, three ounces ; of Rose Wood, Calamus Aromaticus and Storax, each two ounces ; an ounce of Sweet Marjoram, half an ounce of Cloves, two pounds of Florentine Orrice-root, and a pound of dried Provence Roses ; mix the whole together. When you want to fill bags with this powder, mix a drachm of Musk and half a drachm of Civet, with a little Mucilage of Gum Tragacanth made with Angelic Water, and rub the inside of the bags over with the composition, before you fill it with the Violet Powder.

Ibid.

Orange-Flower Powder.

Put half a pound of Orange Flowers into a box that contains twelve pounds and a half of powdered Starch, and stir the mixture at intervals, to prevent the Flowers from heating. At the expiration of twenty-four hours remove the old flowers, and mix with the Starch the same quantity of fresh Orange Flowers. Continue acting in this manner for three days together, and if you think the perfume not sufficiently strong, add fresh Flowers once or twice more. The box must be kept close shut, as well after as during the operation.

Ibid.

Jonquil Powder.

Take of Starch Powder, and Jonquil Flowers, in the same proportion as in the preceding article ; strew the Flowers among the Powder, and at the expiration of twenty hours, sift it through a coarse sieve. Then throw away the Flowers, and add to the Powder the same quantity of fresh Flowers. Continue this method four or five days, observing never to touch the Powder while the

199

Flowers lie mixed with it ; and the former will hence acquire a very agreeable perfume.

In the same manner are prepared, Hyacinth, Musk Rose, and Damask Rose Powders, &c.

Ibid.

To make Mosse Powder.

Take two pound of Mosse of a sweet Apple tree, gathered between the two Lady-dayes, and infuse it in a quart of Damask rose-water, four and twentie houres ; then take it out, and dry it in an oven upon a sive's bottome, and beat it to a powder ; put to it an ounce of Lignum Aloes, beaten and searced, two ounces of Orris, a dramme of Musk, half a dram of amber-greece, a quarter of a dram of Civet ; put all these into a hot Mortar and Pestle, and beat them together : then searce them thorow a coorse haire searce, and put it into a bag and lay it among your clothes.

Sir Hugh Platt. *Delights for Ladies* (1594).

Damask Powder.

Take five ounces of Orace, two ounces of Cypresse, two ounces of Calamus, halfe an ounce of Cloves, one ounce of Benjamin, one ounce of rose leaves, one ounce of Storax calamitum, half an ounce of Spike flowers ; mix them well together.

Ibid.

Perfumed Powder.

Take a pound of Florentine Orrice-root, two ounces of Gum Benjamin, a pound of dried Roses, an ounce of Storax, an ounce and a half of Yellow Sanders, a quarter of an ounce of Cloves, and a small quantity of Lemon-peel; beat the whole together into fine powder, and then add twenty pounds of Starch-powder. Sift through a lawn sieve; and colour the powder according to your fancy.

The Toilet of Flora.

How to make Sweet Powder for Clothes.

Take orris roots two pounds and a half, of lignum rodium six ounces, of scraped cypress roots three ounces, of damask roses carefully dried a pound and a half, of storax two ounces and a half, of sweet marjoram three ounces, of labdanum one ounce and a drachm of calamus aromaticus and one drachm of musk cods, six drachms of lavender and flowers and melilot flowers if you please.

MRS. GLASSE. *The Art of Cookery* (1784).

POT-POURRI

Pot-pourri.

Preparations of spices to half a Peck of Rose petals.

1½ lbs. Bay Salt.
3 oz. bruised Allspice.
1 ,, ,, Cinnamon.
1½ ,, ,, Cloves.
2 ,, ,, nutmegs.
½ ,, Anise seed.
10 grains musk.
½ lb. Lavender flowers.
2 oz. Powdered orris root.

½ oz. oil of jasmine.

¼ ,, each of oils of Rose geranium, Lavender, Lemon.

½ drachm oil of musk.

10 drops ,, neroli.

5 ,, ,, Patchouli.

¼ drachm ,, Rosemary.

Gather Rose petals in dry weather, and dry in shade by spreading out well on paper. Damask roses are best. When quite dry make in a covered crock, 1 handful of Bay salt to three of Rose leaves. Let it remain by 5 days turning twice a day. Then add allspice and cinnamon. Let it remain a week turning from bottom to top. Then add everything else including oils. You can add fresh dried leaves of Marjoram, Sweet balm, Verbena, Tuber rose, Orange blossom, Gardenia, Clove Carnation, Violets, etc.

Stir with a wooden spoon at intervals.

Pot-pourri.

Gather the roses on a dry day only, and lay them on sheets of newspaper to dry in the sun, then sprinkle them freely with finely powdered bay-salt. Pound smoothly together a small quantity of musk, storax, gum benjamin, dried Seville orange peel, angelica root, cloves, Jamaica pepper, coriander seed, and spirits of wine. Now take sun-dried rose leaves, clove carnations, lavender, woodruff, rosemary, and any fragrant flowers, such as orange blossom, violets, &c., and place them in layers in a china or earthenware jar, alternately with salt and the pounded spices mentioned above. Or, pound very fine 1 lb. bay-salt, 2 oz. saltpetre, ½ oz. each of cloves and allspice, and

mix these thoroughly with a grated nutmeg, the very
finely pared rind of four lemons (being careful to omit
all white pith), 1 dr. of musk, 1 oz. of bergamot, 6 dr.
powdered orris root, and 1 dr. each of spirits of lavender,
essence of lemon, and storax. Have ready minced a handful each of bay leaves, rosemary, myrtle, lemon thyme,
and sweet verbena. Place these all, when well hand-mixed,
into a jar with a close-fitting lid, adding to them, as you
can get them, six handfuls of sweet-smelling and dried
rose leaves, three of orange blossom, three of clove pinks,
and two each of rosemary flowers, lavender flowers,
jasmine flowers, and violets. The roses must be gathered
on a perfectly dry day, and may then, if liked, be placed
in the jar at once—and the same applies to the other
blossoms, for all sweet-scented flowers (as long as they are
not succulent) can be used for pot-pourri—stirring them
all well into the mixture, for pot-pourri cannot be too
much stirred, especially at first. But remember no flowers
must be added while the least damp, either from rain or
dew. If the pot-pourri appears to become too dry, add
more bay-salt and saltpetre ; if too moist, add more spice
and orris root ; but always start your beau-pot (as our
grandmothers called it) with the quantities given above,
adding more flowers from time to time, as the spice
retains its strength for years. As to the best flowers for
the purpose, the old cabbage roses are really the most
fragrant, but any kinds will do as long as they are dry ;
still, to have the scent perfect, there should be a strong
proportion of the old-fashioned blooms ; the more
modern tea-roses are almost too faint to be entirely relied
on. The question of drying simply depends on how long
it takes to remove any moisture from the rose leaves.

If gathered on a hot, sunny day, when absolutely dry, they need little, if any, exposure to the sun.

Recipe dated 1890.

Pot-pourri.

Put into a large China jar the following ingredients in layers, with bay-salt strewed between the layers : two pecks of damask-roses, part in bud and part blown ; violets, orange-flowers, and jasmine, a handful of each ; orris-root sliced, benjamin and storax, two ounces of each ; a quarter of an ounce of musk ; a quarter of a pound of angelica-root sliced ; two handsful of lavender-flowers ; half a handful of rosemary-flowers ; bay and laurel leaves, half a handful of each ; three Seville oranges, stuck as full of cloves as possible, dried in a cool oven, and pounded ; half a handful of knotted marjoram ; and two handsful of balm of Gilead dried. Cover all quite close. When the pot is uncovered, the perfume is very fine.

Domestic Cookery (1834).

A quicker sort of Sweet Pot.

Take three handsful of orange-flowers, three of clove-gillyflowers, three of damask roses, one of knotted marjoram, one of lemon-thyme, six bay-leaves, a handful of rosemary, one of myrtle, half one of mint, one of lavender, the rind of a lemon, and a quarter of an ounce of cloves. Chop all ; and put them in layers, with pounded bay-salt between, up to the top of the jar.

If all the ingredients cannot be got at once, put them in as you get them ; always throwing in salt with every new article.

Ibid.

A sweet smelling Perfume.

Take a pound of fresh-gathered Orange Flowers, of common Roses, Lavender Seeds, and Musk Roses, each half a pound ; of Sweet Marjoram Leaves, and Clove-july-flowers picked, each a quarter of a pound ; of Thyme, three ounces ; of Myrtle Leaves, and Melilot Stalks stripped of their Leaves, each two ounces ; of Rosemary Leaves, and Cloves bruised, each an ounce ; of Bay Leaves, half an ounce.

Let these ingredients be mixed in a large pan covered with parchment, and be exposed to the heat of the sun during the whole summer ; for the first month stirring them every other day with a stick, and taking them within doors in rainy weather. Towards the end of the season they will afford an excellent composition for a perfume ; which may be rendered yet more fragrant, by adding a little scented Cypress-powder, mixed with coarse Violet-powder.

The Toilet of Flora.

SWEET WATERS

Divers sorts of sweet handwaters made suddenly or extem-pore with extracted oyles of spices.

First you shall understand, that whensoever you shall draw any of the Oyles of Cynamon, Cloves, Mace, Nut-megs or such like, that you shall have also a pottle or a gallon more or lesse, according to the quantity which you draw at once, of excellent sweet washing water for your table ; yea some doe keepe the same for their broths, wherein otherwise they should use some of the same kinds of spice.

But if you take three or foure drops only of the oyle of Cloves, Mace or Nutmegs (for Cinamon oyle is too costly to spend this way) and mingle the same with a pinte of faire water, making agitation of them a pretty while together in a glasse having a narrow mouth, till they have in some measure incorporated themselves together, you shall find a very pleasing and delightful water to wash with and so you may alwaies furnish yourself of sweete water of severall kinds, before such time as your guests shal be ready to sit downe. I speake not of the oyle of Spike (which will extend very far this way) both because every Gentlewoman doth not like so strong a scent and for that the same is elsewhere already commended by another Author. Yet I must needs acknowledge it to be the cheaper way, for that I assure myself there may be five or six gallons of sweet water made with one ounce of the oyle, which you may buy ordinarily for a groat at the most. Sir Hugh Platt. *Delights for Ladies* (1594).

An excellent sweet water for a casting bottle.

Take three drammes of oyle of Spyke, one dram of oyle of Thyme, one dram of oyle of Lemmons ; one dram of oyle of Cloves, then take one graine of Civet, and three graines of the aforesaid composition well wrought together. Temper them well in a silver spoon with your finger ; then put the same into a silver bowl, washing it out by little and little into the bowle with a little Rose-water at once, till all the oyle be washed out of the spoon into the bowl ; and then do the like by washing the same out of the bowle with a little Rose-water at once, till all the scent be gotten out, putting the Rose-water still in a glasse, when you have tempered the same in the bowl sufficiently. A pint of Rose-water will be sufficient to mingle with the said proportion : and if you finde the same not strong enough put one graine and a halfe, or two graines of Civet to the weight of three graines of the aforesaid composition of oyles.

Ibid.

Water for the castyng glasse

Put into some little vessell of Silver, a little Rose water made with Muske, and a little Civet, and Cloves, and Styrax. Mix them and perfume any clothes with the vapour or the smoke thereof, it is a marvellous sweet savoure, if thou wilt kepe close the vessell diligently, and when thou thinkest good, put more Rose water unto it, that it maie be renewed.

Bulleins Bulwarke of defence . . . which Bulwarke is kepte with Hillarius the Gardiner (1562).

Another.

Thou shalt put into fower pounds of Rose water, somewhat gross beaten Styrax and Cloves, Camphire, Muske, Civet, putte these together in a glasse, shutte with a Parchment, prickte through with tenne or twelve smalle holles, and let the vessell boile fower howers in a kettell full of cleane water, as though it were in Balneo Maria, after when it is colde, strain it through a fine linnen clothe, and kepe it in a glasse in which graines XII of Muske shal be put, whiche beyng moisted, and steped with water, thou shalt stoppe the glasse, and sette it in the

Sunne VIII daies, so shalt thou have a wonderfull well smellyng water, a sweete water and a secrete, whereof one parte mixte with ten partes of pure water, maketh the whole most sweete.

Ibid.

Rose water.

Some do put rose water in a glass and they put roses with their dew thereto and they make it to boile in water thā thei set it in the sune tyll it be readde and this water is beste.

Also drye roses put to the nose to smell do comforte the braine and the harte and quencheth spirits.

Askham's Herbal (1550).

A very rare and pleasant Damask-water.

Take a quart of Malmsey lees, or a quart of Malmsey simply, one handful of Marjerom, of Basil as much, of Lavender four handfuls, Bay-leaves one good handful, Damask Rose-leaves four handfuls, and as many of Red, the Peels of six Oranges, or for want of them one handful of the tender leaves of Wallnut leaves, of Benjamin half an ounce, of Calamus Aromaticus as much, of Camphire four drams, of Cloves one ounce, then take a Pottle of running water and put in all these spices bruised into your water and Malmsey together, in a close stopped pot with a good handful of Rosemary, and let them stand for the space of six dayes : then distill it with a soft fire : then set it in the Sun sixteen dayes with four grains of Musk bruised. This quantity will make three quarts of Water. *Probatum est.*

GERVASE MARKHAM. *The English House-Wife* (1625).

Jessemain Water.

Take two handfuls of Jeseme flowers and put them into a flagon or earthen pot, put to them about a quart of fair water and a quarter of a pound of Sugar, let this stand and steep about half an hour, then take your water and flowers and pour them ouṭ of one vessell into another till such time as the water hath taken the scent and tast of the flowers, then set it in a cool place a cooling and you will find it a most excellent scented water.

A Perfect School of Instructions for the Officers of the Month by Giles Rose, one of the Master Cooks to Charles II, 1682.

To make a speciall sweet water to perfume clothes in the folding being washed.

Take a quart of Damaske-Rose-Water and put it into a glasse, put unto it a handfull of Lavender Flowers, two ounces of Orris, a dram of Muske, the weight of four pence of Amber-greece, as much Civet, foure drops of Oyle of Cloves, stop this close, and set it in the Sunne a fortnight : put one spoonfull of this Water into a bason of common water and put it into a glasse and so sprinkle your clothes therewith in your folding : the dregs, left in the bottome (when the water is spent) will make as much more, if you keepe them, and put fresh Rose-water to it. Sir Hugh Platt. *Delights for Ladies* (1594).

Sweet water for linnen.

Three poundes of Rose water, Cloves, Cinamon, Saunders, two handfull of the flowers of Lavender, lette it stand a moneth to still in the Sonne, well closed in a Glasse; then destill it in Balneo Mariae. It is marvellous pleasant in savour, a water of a wondrous swetenes, for the perfumyng the shetes of a bedde, whereby the whole place, shall have a most pleasaunt scent.

Bulleins Bulwarke of defence . . . which Bulwarke is kepte with Hillarius the Gardiner (1562).

An excellent hand water or washing water.

Take a gallon of faire water, one handfull of Lavender flowers, a few Cloves and some Orace powder and foure ounces of Benjamin; distill the water in an ordinary leaden Still. You may distill a second Water by a new infusion of water upon the leaves; a little of this will sweeten a bason of faire water for your table.

SIR HUGH PLATT. *Delights for Ladies* (1594).

How to make Sweet Water.

Take of Bay-leaves one handful, of red Roses two handfuls, of Damask-roses three handfuls, of Lavender four handfuls, of Basil one handful, Marjerom two handfuls, of Camomile one handful, of the young tops of Sweet bryer two handfuls, of Dandelion, Tansy, two handfuls, of Orange peels six or seven ounces, of Cloves and Mace a groats worth : put all these together in a Pottle of new Ale in corns, for the space of three dayes, shaking it every day three or four times; then distill it the fourth day in a Still with a continual soft fire, and after it is distilled, put into it a grain or two of Musk.

T. HALL. *The Queen's Royal Cookery* (1719).

An excellent Water for Perfume.

To make an excellent sweet water for perfume, you shall take of Basil, Mints, Marjerom, Cornflay-roots, Hyssop, Savory, Saje, Balme, Lavender and Rosemary, of each one handfull ; of Cloves, Cinnamon and Nutmegs, of each half an ounce ; then three or four Pine-citrons cut into slices, infuse all these into Damask Rose-water, the space of three dayes, and then distill it with a gentle fire of char-coal, then when you have put it into a very clean glass, take of fat Musk, Civet, and Amber-greece, of each the quantity of a Scruple, and put it into a rag of fine lawn, and then hang it within the water. This being burnt either upon a hot pan, or else boyled in perfuming-pans with Cloves, Bay-leaves and Lemon pills, will make the most delicate perfume that may be, without any offence, and will last the longest of all other perfumes, as hath been found by experience.

GERVASE MARKHAM. *The English House-wife* (1625).

A Sweet Water.

Take a gallon of Spring water, a handfull of Lavender flowers, as many pinks, 3 handfulls of roses, as much sweet marjoram, the peeling of 6 oringes, 12 cloves : bruise all these and put to them one ounce of orrice powder, 4 ounces of benjamin. Put all these into a rose still and draw off the first quart by itselfe and then a pint, you may draw after that another water from the leefe which will serve for present use but not keep, put into your quart bottle 12 pennyworth of musk, and in the pint bottle 6 pennyworth tied in bags and a little juniper sliced very thin as much as will lay on half crown, 2 or 3 spoon-fulls will sweeten a bason of water : keep it stop't very close : it will keep a year or 2.

The Book of Simples (*circa* 1650).

To make a rare Sweet Water.

Take sweet Marjoram, Lavender, Rosemary, Muscovy, Mandlin, Balm, Thyme, Walnut Leaves, Damask Roses, Pinks, of all a like quantity, enough to fill your Still, then take of the best Orrice Powder, Damask Rose Powder, and Storax, of each two Ounces ; strew one handful or two of your Powders upon the Herbs, then distill them with a soft fire ; tie a little musk in a piece of lawn, and hang it in the Glass wherein it drops, and when it is all drawn out, take your sweet Cakes and mix them with the powders which are left, and lay them among your Clothes, or with sweet Oyls, and burn them for perfume. *A Queen's Delight* (1662).

To make sweet water of the best kind.

Take a thousand Damask Roses, two good handfuls of Lavender tops, a three-penny weight of Mace, two ounces of Cloves bruised, a quart of running water : put a little water into the bottom of an earthen pot, and then put in your Roses and Lavender, with the Spices by little and little, and in the putting in, always knead them down with your fist, and so continue it untill you have wrought up all your Roses and Lavender, and in the working put in always a little of your water : then stop your pot close, and let it stand in four dayes, in which time every morning and evening put in your hand

212

and pull from the bottom of your pot the said Roses, working it for a time, and then distill it, and having in the glass of water a grain or two of Musk wrapt up in a piece of Sarcenet or fine cloth.

GERVASE MARKHAM. *The English House-Wife* (1625).

A Perfumed Water.

Take a gallon of Spring water, a handfull of lavender flowers and as many pinks, 3 handfulls of damaske roses, as much sweet marjeram, the peels of 6 oranges, 12 cloves ; bruise all these and put to them one ounce of orrise powder, 4 ounces of benjamin powdered : put all in a rose stille and draw off the first quart by its self and then a pint you may draw after another water from the lees which will serve for present use but not keep ; put into your quart bottle 12 penny worth of muske and into your pint bottle six penny worth tyed up in a piece of sersnet and a little ginger sliced very thin, about as much as will lay on a half crown, 2 or 3 spoonfulls will sweeten a bason of water, stop it close.

The Book of Simples (*circa* 1650).

To make Sweet Water.

Take Rose leafs, Bay leafs, Lavender, Sweet Marjoram, Eglantine, Pinks, of each Two handfuls, Cloves, Cinamon, *ana* one ounce ; bruise all these ; and pour upon them two quarts of strong Ale (that is neer the grounds) let them infuse twenty four hours, then distil it, and draw it till the Ingredients remain almost dry.

SIR KENELM DIGBY. *Choice and Experimented
Receipts* (1668).

213

Another.

Take Damask Roses at discretion, Basil, sweet Majoram, Lavender, Wall-nut leafs, of each two handfuls, Rosemary one handful, a little Balm, Cloves, Cinamon, Bay-leafs, Rosemary tops, Limon and Orange Pills of each a few ; pour upon these as much white wine as will conveniently wet them, and let them infuse ten or twelve days ; then distill it off.

Ibid.

To make the Sweet water, the best, called in French L'eau d'ange.

Take three pints of Rose-water, half a pint of Orange-flower-water, Musk, *Ambirgris, Lignum Aloes,* twenty five grains, Civet fifteen grains, Benjamin four ounces, Storax one ounce, all in fine powder ; mix all these well together, and put them in a Brass-pot, covering it very close with Linen, and set it to boil in a kettle full of water the space of three hours ; then pour off the clear, and put upon the remaining matter the same quantity of fresh Rose and Orange-flower water, and five or six grains of Civet, then of the rest you may make Pastils or Cassolettes.

The Closet of Sir Kenelm Digby Opened (1669).

To make Rose-Water.

To make an excellent Rose-water, let the Flowers be gathered two or three hours after sun-rising in very fine weather ; beat them in a marble mortar into a paste, and leave them in the mortar soaking in their juice, for five or six hours ; then put the mass into a coarse canvas bag, and press out the juice; to every quart of which add a pound of fresh Damask Roses, and let them stand in infusion for twenty-four hours. Then put the whole into a glass alembic, lute on a head and receiver, and place it on a sand heat. Distil at first with a gentle fire, which is to be encreased gradually till the drops follow each other as quick as possible; draw off the water as long as it continues to run clear, then put out the fire, and let the alembic stand till cold. The distilled water at first will have very little fragrancy, but after being exposed to the heat of the sun about eight days, in a bottle lightly stopped with a bit of paper, it acquires an admirable scent.

The Toilet of Flora.

A curious Water, known by the Name of the Spring Nosegay.

Take six ounces of Hyacinths, a quarter of a pound of Picked Violets, the same quantity of Wall Flowers picked, and Jonquils; an ounce of Florentine Orrice bruised; half an ounce of Mace grossly powdered; and two ounces of Quintessence of Orange. Put the whole (the Jonquils, Wall Flowers, and Lilies of the Valley excepted) about the end of March, into a glass body, with a gallon of strong Spirit of Wine; bruise the Hyacinths, Violets, Orrice, and Mace; and towards the end of April, add the Jonquils, when in their perfection, that is to say, when full blown. A few days after, put in the Wall Flowers, the Petals only; then add the Lilies of the Valley, carefully picked and shake all the ingredients well; Eight days after having put in this last Flower, empty the infusion into an alembic, lute on a head and receiver, which must be placed in cold water, and distil in a water bath, with a gentle fire. From the above quantity three quarts of excellent Spirit may be drawn off, that justly deserves the appellation of the Spring Nosegay.

The Toilet of Flora.

Odoriferous Water.

Take sweet Basil, Mint, sweet Marjoram, Florentine Orrice-root, Hyssop, Balm, Savory, Lavender, and Rosemary, of each a handful; Cloves, Cinnamon, and Nutmegs, of each half an ounce; three or four Lemons, cut in thick slices; infuse them three days in a good quantity of Rose-water; distil in a water bath with a gentle fire, and add to the distilled water a scruple of Musk.

Ibid.

Angelic Water, of a most agreeable Scent.

Put into a large alembic the following ingredients, Benjamin, four ounces; Storax, two ounces; Yellow Sanders, an ounce; Cloves, two drachms; two or three bits of Florentine Orrice, half the Peel of a Lemon, Two Nutmegs, half an ounce of Cinnamon, two quarts of Rose-water, a pint of Orange Flower-water, and a pint of Magisterial Balm-water. Put the whole into an alembic well luted; distil in a water bath; and what you draw off will prove an exquisite Angelic Water.

Ibid.

Nosegay or Toilet Water.

Take Honey-water, an ounce; Eau sans Pareille, two ounces; Jasmine-water, not quite five drachms; Clove-water, and Violet-water, of each half an ounce;

Cyprus-water, sweet Calamus-water, and Lavender-water, of each two drachms; Spirit of Neroli, or Oranges, ten drops; mix all these Waters together, and keep the mixture in a vial close corked.

This water has a delightful scent; but its use is only for the toilet.   *Ibid.*

Orange-Flower Water.

Take four pounds of unpicked Orange Flowers, bruise them in a marble mortar, and pour on them nine quarts of clear Water. Distil in a cold still, and draw off five or six quarts, which will be exquisitely fragrant. If you are desirous of having it still higher flavoured, draw off at first full seven quarts, unlute the still and throw away the residuum; empty back the water already distilled, and add to it two pounds of fresh Orange Flowers bruised. Again luting the still, repeat the distillation, and draw off five or six quarts. Then stop, being careful not to draw off too much water, lest the Flowers should become dry and burn-to.

The use of Orange-Flower Water is very extensive. It is high in esteem for its aromatic perfume; and it is used with success for hysteric complaints.   *Ibid.*

An excellent water to clear Hands and Face.

Take a quart of fair water, a pint of white wine, the juice of 4 lemons: put into these bean blossoms, elder blossoms, white lily blossoms, a handfull of them all: put them amongst the wine and water and put into 4 wild dasie roots, 4 marsh mallow roots and 2 or 3 bunches of wild tansie, as much of fumitary, the weight of 2 pence in camphere : put all these together in an earthen pot, set the pot in warm aishes all night, then in the morning strain it through a piece of white cotton clean wash'd and put it into a narrow mouth glass : sit the glass in the sun 3 or 4 days in the heat of the sun. Wash your face with this water evening and morning. If you wash your hands with any of this water put thereto 3 or 4 bruised almonds, this is the most excellent water that ever was made to clear hands and face withall. *Probatum est.*   *The Book of Simples (circa* 1650).

Lavender Water.

Take a pint of highly rectified spirit of wine, essential oil of lavender one ounce, essence of ambergris two drachms ; put all into a quart bottle, and shake it extremely well.   *Domestic Cookery* (1834).

Lavender Water without Distillation.

If you would have speedily, without the trouble of distillation, a water impregnated with the flavour of Lavender, put two or three drops of Oil of Spike, and a lump of Sugar, into a pint of clear Water, or Spirit of Wine, and shake them well together in a glass phial, with a narrow neck. This Water, though not distilled, is very fragrant.   *The Toilet of Flora.*

POMANDERS, Etc.

Orange stuck with cloves.

Choose an orange that is (*a*) thin-skinned and (*b*) small. Stick it all over with cloves as thickly as possible. When done no particle of skin should be visible. If the skin is rather tough use a bodkin to make each hole. Then roll the orange in a powder consisting of equal parts of orris root and powdered cinnamon. Rub the powder well in all over the orange and leave it wrapped up in paper with this powder for about a week. The orange is then ready and will scent a drawer deliciously for well over a year. In time it will shrink considerably. (We have one many years old which is about the size of a walnut now.)

A Pomander.

Take Storax an ounce, Cloves two drammes, Benjamin halfe an ounce, Ambergreece halfe a dram, Muske fifteen graines, powder of Violets a little, incorporate them all together with Rose water.

A Pomander against Pestilentiall Aire.

Take Labdanum, Storax of each a dram, Cloves halfe a dram, Camphor, Spikenard, Nutmeg, of each seven graines, beat them into fine powder and make them into bullets with gum Fragrant dissolved in Rose water.

The Charitable Physitian by Philbert Guibert
Esqre and Physician Regent in Paris (1639).

219

A Pomander.

Take a quarter of an ounce of Civit, a quarter and a half-quarter of an ounce of Ambergreese, not half a quarter of an ounce of ye spiritt of Roses, 7 ounces of Benjamin, allmost a pound of Damask Rose buds cutt. Lay gumdragon in rose water and with it make up your Pomander, with beads as big as nutmegs and color them with Lamb (*sic*) black; when you make them up wash your hands with oyle of Jasmin to smooth them, then make them have a gloss, this quantity will make seaven Braceletes.

MARY DOGGETT: Her Book of Receipts (1682).

An excellent Pomander.

Take half an ounce of benjamin, half an ounce of Damask rose leaves, a quarter of an ounce of Storax: beat these very small severally, then sift them and mingle the powder : then take some gumdragon steep'd in rose water 24 hours and make it into a stiff paste ; then take 4 grains of ambergreese, 4 grains of musk and 2 of civit : grind these together with a little juice of Lemon till they are dissolved : then anoint the hand with essence of jessamie or roses and work the past well with the musk and amber : if it be too limber put in powder of roses, if too stiff, a little rose water, then weigh them of an equal weight and rowle them up in your hand, but while they are wet make holes through them with a bodkin : Dry them betwixt 2 papers.

The Book of Simples (circa 1650).

To make a Pomander.

Take of Beazon one dram and a halfe, of Storax halfe a dram, of Lignum Aloes in fine powder halfe a scruple, of Labdanum halfe an ounce : powder all these verie fine, and searce them thorow Lawne : and then take of Muske a dram, Ambergreece ten graines, Civet ten graines, and dissolve them in an hot mortar with a little Rose-water, and so make them into a Pomander, putting into it six graines of Civet.

SIR HUGH PLATT. *Delights for Ladies* (1594).

A sweet and delicate Pomander.

Take two ounces of Labdanum, of Benjamin and Storax, one ounce : musk, six grains ; civet, six graines ; Amber-grease, six graines ; of Calamus Aromaticus and Lignum Aloes, of each the weight of a groat ; beat all these in a hot mortar, and with an hot pestall till they come to paste ; then wet your hand with Rose-water and rowle up the paste suddenly. *Ibid.*

To renew the scent of a Pomander.

Take one grain of Civet, and two of Musk, or if you double the Proportion it will be so much the sweeter : grinde them upon a stone with a little Rose-water, and after, wetting your hands with Rose water, you may worke the same in your Pomander. This is a sleight to pass away an old Pomander : but my intention is honest.

Ibid.

To make Pomanders.

To make Pomanders, take two penny-worth of Labdanum, two penny-worth of Storax liquid, one penny-worth of *Calamus Aromaticus*, as much balm, half a quarter of a pound of fine wax, of Cloves, Mace two penny-worth, of liquid Aloes three penny-worth, of Nutmegs eight penny-worth, and of Musk four grains : beat all these exceedingly together, till they come to a perfect substance, then mould it in any fashion you please, and dry it.

Gervase Markham. *The English House-Wife* (1625).

To make a Pomander.

Take Benjamine, Storax, Labdanum, of each half an ounce : Muske, Civet, of each six grains, 2 grains of ambergreese, a dram of sweet balmesum : beat all these together in a hot morter : then rowle it up in beads as big or as little as you will have it while it is hot, and so make holes in them and so use them.

The Book of Simples (*circa* 1650).

To make a Pomos. *like those that are made in Spain.*

Take Benjamin half a pound, steep it in Rose-water, expose it to the Sun the space of six weeks, stirring it three or four times a day ; and when you see that it groweth dry add still more Rose-water to it. Then grinde it well with four Cloves and a little Cinamon in powder, and one ounce of storax, half an ounce of the thin rind of Limon shred very small, half an ounce of *Ambergris*, a quarter of an ounce of Civet, half an ounce of the perfumed *Italian* powder, one ounce of *Rose* powder, a dram of Musk: boyle this together in as much Rose-water as will just cover it till it be well incorporated together. This proportion will serve for Eight *Pomos*. In using it you must keep it always coverd with Rose-water.

Sir KENELM DIGBY. *Choice and experimented Receipts* (1668).

Cassolettes.

Take Benjamin four ounces, Storax two ounces, *Lignum Aloes* half an ounce, *Ambergris* two drams, Musk twenty four grains, Civet one dram, twenty Cloves, Cinamon in powder two drams, the Pills of two Limons (cut small without touching them with your hands). Mix all these together with Rose-water, and make a paste of it with your hands; and never use it without Rose-water or other Sweet waters. You may steep gum Tragaganth in Rose-water till it become a Mucilage, and with that work the other Ingredients into a paste, and form it to Cakes for use.

Ibid.

To make a familiar and cheap Pomo upon a sudden, which smelleth very well.

Smear the bottom of the *Cassolette* Pot with a little Civet, as much as you take upon the point of a knife: and pour upon it a pretty quantity of Orange-flower-water, and strew upon that some of buceanous, about as much as a thimble holds. Then kindle the Lamp under it. Be sure to supply it with fresh Sweet water, before what you put in be consumed.

Ibid.

To make an Odoriferant Ball.

Take Benjamin two drams, Storax, pure fine *Ladanum*, one dram, Bark of Cedar, the thin rind of Orange and Limon, Violets, Odoriferant Roses, Rosemary, red Sanders, *Calamus Aromaticus*, 2 scruples. Reduce all these into powder, and make Paste of it with gum Tragaganth steeped in Orange-flower or Rose-water. Then, heat a little the inside of a Mortar, and put a spoonful or two of Orange-flower or Rose-water in it, and upon that put one scruple of Civet, and half a dram of *Ambergris*, and grind it well together with a warm Pestil. When it is well incorporated, put half a scruple of good Musk to it : which incorporate also ; dropping into the Composition thirty drops of Oyl of Lilly Convally, when it is all cold. Then mix this Composition with the first Paste, working them well together ; and lastly, add to it ten drops of perfect Oyl or Quintessence of Cinamon made by Distillation. Then form this into Balls of such a bignesse as you will have them and dry them in the shadow.

Ibid.

SCENTS

Hungary Water.

To one pint of highly rectified spirit of wine, put an ounce of oil of rosemary, and two drachms of essence of ambergris ; shake the bottle several times, than let the cork remain out twenty-four hours. After a month, during which time shake it daily, put the water into small bottles.

Domestic Cookery (1834).

Eau sans Pareil.

One quart of spirits of wine, one ounce of essence of bergamot, two drachms of tincture of musk, add to them half a pint of water, and bottle them for use.

MRS. GLASSE. *The Art of Cookery* (1784).

Eau de Bouquet.

Take one quart of spirits of wine, half an ounce of musk, two drachms of tincture of saffron, mix them well together, and let them stand one day ; then filter it with any water. *Ibid.*

The Ambrosia Nosegay.

Take one pint of spirits of wine, one drachm of oil of cloves, one ounce of oil of nutmegs ; mix them and filter it as you please. *Ibid.*

Eau de Luce.

Two ounces of the best rectified spirits of wine, one drachm of oil of amber, two drachms of salt of tartar, prepared powder of amber two drachms, twenty drops of oil of nutmegs, put them all into a bottle and shake it well ; let it stand five hours, then filter it and always keep it by you, and when you would make Eau de Luce put it into the strongest spirits of sal-ammoniac. *Ibid.*

Miss in her Teens.

One quart of spirits of wine ; essence of bergamot one ounce ; oil of Rhodium two drachms, tincture of musk half a drachm, and half a pint of water ; mix them well together, and put them into bottles for use. *Ibid.*

225

An excellent Water for the Head and for Sleep called ye Emperour Charleses Water.

When roses are blown, take a quart of good aquavitae in a glass with a narrow neck and when the roses are half blown take a handfull of the leaves without ye seed, put them into the glass and when the marioran bloweth and the Apiastrum, take then a handfull of their buds, chop them small and put them into the glass. Take also Cloves, Nutmegs, Cinnamon, Mace, Cardamum, of each an ounce and a half : bruise all these grossly and put it in the glass and when the lavender and rosemary are blown add a handfull of each flowers, also, shake them well together and stop it close : let it stand 10 days in a hot sun : it must be used by anointing the temples and nostrells ; it fortifieth and corroborateth the head and memory. *The Book of Simples (circa* 1650).

A curious Perfume.

Boil, in two quarts of Rose-water, an ounce of Storax, and two ounces of Gum Benjamin ; to which add, tied up in a piece of gauze or thin muslin, six Cloves bruised, half a drachm of Labdanum, as much Calamus Aromaticus, and a little Lemon-peel. Cover the vessel up close, and keep the ingredients boiling a great while : strain off the liquor without strong pressure, and let it stand till it deposit the sediment, which keep for use in a box.

The Toilet of Flora.

Compound Balm-Water, commonly called Eau de Carmes.

Take of the fresh Leaves of Balm, a quarter of a pound ; Yellow Rind of Lemons, two ounces ; Nutmegs and

226

Coriander-seeds, of each one ounce ; Cloves, Cinnamon, and Angelica Root ; of each half an ounce ; having pounded the spices and seeds, and bruised the leaves and roots, put them with a quart of Brandy into a glass cucurbit, of which stop the mouth, and set it in a warm place, where let it remain two or three days. Then add a pint of simple Balm-water, and shake the whole well together ; after which distil in a vapour bath till the ingredients are left almost dry ; and preserve the water thus obtained, in bottles well stopped.

This water has been long famous at Paris and London, and carried thence to most parts of Europe.

Toilet of Flora.

All Flower Water.

Pour into a large vessel five quarts of strong Spirit of Wine, and infuse in it the following Flowers, as they come in season ; Violets, Hyacinths, and Wall Flowers, of each a quarter of a pound ; single and double Jonquils, of each two ounces ; a quarter of a pound of Lilies of the Valley, and the same quantity of Spanish Jasmine ; half an ounce of Rosemary Flowers ; an ounce of Elder Flowers ; two ounces of Wild, Damask, and White Roses, bruised ; three ounces of Orange Flowers ; a quarter of a pound of Clove-july Flowers, Syringo Blossoms, Tuberoses, and Tops of Mint in Flower ; and thirty drops of Quintessence of Musk-seed. The latter, however, need not be added till the close of distillation, which must not be till three days after the last Flowers have been infused. Perform the operation in a warm bath, and having carefully luted the head and receiver, which must be placed in a tub of cold water, to preserve the scent, draw off about

three quarts and a pint with a moderate fire, then change
the receiver, fix on another, and draw off another pint,
which, though of an inferior quality, is well worth preserving.   *The Toilet of Flora.*

Imperial Water.

Put into a gallon of Brandy, a quarter of a pound of
Picked Violets, an ounce of Florentine Orrice, a quarter
of a pound of Double Jonquils, two ounces of picked
Orange Flowers, two Ounces of White Musk-Roses, three
ounces of Tuberoses, a drachm of Mace, half a drachm
of Cloves, an ounce of Quintessence of Bergamot, and
an ounce of Quintessence of Oranges. All the Flowers
must be gathered in their proper season. Observe to put
into the Brandy at the same time with the Violets, the
Orrice, Mace and Cloves, in gross powder, then add
the different Flowers as they come in season, remembering
not to add the quintessences, till after the Tuberoses,
which are the last Flower. Every time you put in a fresh
Flower, shake the vessel, and cork it very tight. Eight
days after the Tuberoses have been infused, put the whole
into a glass body, lute on the head carefully, and place
under the receiver an earthen vessel filled with cold water,
that the Spirit may cool as fast as it comes over, by which
means its scent will be the better preserved. You may
draw off two quarts of a rectified Spirit, that will give
perfect satisfaction to the most delicate judge.   *Ibid.*

To make Spirit of Lilley of the Valley (from Norway).

N.B.—This serves in the room of *Orange-Flower-Water*
in Puddings, and to perfume Cakes ; though it is drank as
a Dram in Norway.

Gather your Lilley-of-the-Valley Flowers, when they are dry, and pick them from the Stalks; then put a Quarter of a Pint of them into a Quart of Brandy, and so in proportion, to infuse six or eight Days; then distil it in a cold still, marking the Bottles, as they are drawn off, which is first, second, and third, etc. When you have distill'd them, take the first, and so on to the third or fourth and mix them together, till you have as strong as you desire; and then bottle them and cork them well, putting a lump of Loaf-Sugar into each Bottle.

The Country Lady's Director (1732).

The Divine Cordial.

To make this, take, in the beginning of the month of March, two ounces of the Roots of the true Acorus, Betony, Florentine Orrice-roots, Cyprus, Gentian, and sweet Scabious; an ounce of Cinnamon, and as much Yellow Sanders; two drachms of Mace; an ounce of Juniper-berries; and six drachms of Coriander-seeds; beat these ingredients, in a mortar, to a coarse powder, and add thereto the outer Peel of six fine China Oranges; put them all into a large vessel, with a gallon and a half of Spirit of Wine; shake them well, and then cork the vessel tight till the season for Flowers. When these are in full vigour, add half a handful of the following; viz. Violets, Hyacinths, Jonquils, Wall Flowers, Red, Damask, White and Musk Roses, Clove-july-flowers, Orange-Flowers, Jasmine, Tuberoses, Rosemary, Sage, Thyme, Lavender, sweet Marjoram, Broom, Elder, St. John's-wort, Marigold, Chamomile, Lilies of the Valley, Narcissuses, Honeysuckle, Borage, and Bugloss.

229

Three seasons are required to procure all these Flowers
in perfection; Spring, Summer, and Autumn. Every
time you gather any of these Flowers, add them immediately to the infusion, mixing them thoroughly with
the other ingredients; and three days after you have put
in the last Flowers, put the whole into a glass cucurbit,
lute on the head carefully, place it in a water bath over a
slow fire, keep the receiver cool, and draw off five quarts
of Spirit, which will prove of rare quality. As a medicine,
it is far more efficacious than Balm-water; and for its
fine scent, one of the best perfumes.

The Toilet of Flora.

The Oil commonly called the Spirit of Roses.

Take of Damask, or red Roses, being fresh, as many as
you please, infuse them in as much warm water as is
sufficient for the space of twenty four houres: Then
strain, and press them, and repeat the infusion severall
times with pressing, untill the liquor become fully impregnated, which then must be distilled in an Alembick
with a refrigerator, let the Spirit which swims on the
Water be separated, and the water kept for a new infusion.

This kind of Spirit may be made by bruising the Roses
with Salt, or laying a lave of Roses, and another of Salt,
and so keeping them half a year or more, which then
must be distilled in as much Common water, or Rose-
water as is sufficient.

JOHN FRENCH. *The Art of Distillation* (1652).

PERFUMES.

Queen Elizabeth's Perfume.

Take eight spoonfuls of Compound water, the weight of two pence, a fine powder of Sugar, and boil it on hot Embers and Coals softly, and half an ounce of sweet Marjoram dried in the Sun, the weight of two pence of the powder of Benjamin. This Perfume is very sweet and good for the time.   *A Queen's Delight* (1664).

A very good Perfume to burn.

Take two Ounces of the Powder of Juniper Wood, one Ounce of Benjamin, one Ounce of Storax, six drops of oil of Limons, as much oil of Cloves, ten grains of Musk, six of Civet, mould them up with a little gum-Dragon steeped in Rosewater, make them in little Cakes and dry them between Rose leaves, your Juniper wood must be well dried, beaten and searced.

The Queen's Closet Opened (1662).

To make a Perfume to burn in a Chamber.

Take Benjamine, Storax and Labdanum, of each a little ; a little damaske powder, orace powder, a little, a little frankincense and mirr, powder of Jniper ; beat all these together to a paste in a hot morter and so make it up in the fashion of great black cloves and so burn them when you please, it's a pleasant smell.

The Book of Simples (*circa* 1650).

231

An odoriferous parfume for chambers.

Take a glasseful of Rose water, Cloves well beaten in pouder, a penny weight : than take the fire panne, and make it reede hote in the fyre, and put thereon of the saied Rose water wyth the sayd pouder of Cloves, making it so consume, by little and little, but the rose water must be muskt, and you shall make a parfume of excellent good odour.   *A Queen's Delight* (1662).

Rose Pastills to burn.

Take Benjamin three ounces, storax two ounces, Alexandrine or Damask Rose-buds one ounce ; grind the Roses by themselves, and the rest also : Then take *Lignum Aloes*, Amber, fine Sugar, Civet, powder of Cypress, half a quarter of a pound ; grind all these well together. Then mix it with gum Tragaganth dissolved in Orange-flowers or Rose-water, and make them up.

Sir Kenelm Digby. *Choice and Experimented*
Receipts (1668).

King Edward VI's Perfume.

Take twelve spoonfuls of right red Rose-water, the weight of six pence in fine powder of Sugar, and boil it on hot Embers and Coals softly, and the house will smell as though it were full of Roses ; but you must burn the sweet Cypress wood before, to take away the gross air.

The Queen's Closet Opened (1662).

A plesent and delicate perfume.

Lay two or three drops of liquid Amber upon a glowing coale, or a peece of Lignum Aloes, Lignum Rhodium or Storax. Sir Hugh Platt. *Delights for Ladies* (1594).

232

To perfume a House, and purify the Air.

Take a root of Angelica, dry it in an oven, or before the fire, then bruise it well and infuse it four or five days in White Wine Vinegar. When you use it, lay it upon a brick made red hot, and repeat the operation several times.

The Toilet of Flora.

To make Court perfumes.

Take three Ounces of Benjamin, lay it all night in Damask Rose Buds clean cut from the white, beat them very fine in a stone Mortar till it come to a Paste, then take it out and mix it with a dram of Musk finely beaten, as much Civet, mould them up with a little seazced Sugar, and dry them very well and keep them to burn, one at a time is sufficient.

Ibid.

A very good perfume.

Six spoonfuls of Rosewater, Musk, Ambergreece and Civet, of each two grams, a little Sugar beaten fine, mould them together with Gum-Dragon steeped in Rosewater, make them in little Cakes and dry them.

Ibid.

Perfumes to burn.

Take Damaske rose buds and cut off the whites, then beat them very small; take half a pound of them when they are beaten and put to them 3 ounces of benjamine, half a quarter of an ounce of Muske, as much of civet and as much ambergreese : then mingle it all well together and make it up in little thin cakes and lay them upon rose leaves and dry them in the sun till they be very dry.

The Book of Simples (circa 1650).

A Perfume to burn.

To make a good Perfume to burn, take Benjamin one ounce, Storax, Calamint two ounces, of Mastick white, Ambergreece, of each one ounce; Seeds, *Calamus Aromaticus*, Cypress wood, of each half an ounce, of Camphire one scruple, Labdanum one ounce; beat all these to powder, then take of Sallow Charcole six ounces, of liquid Storax two ounces, beat them all with *Aqua vitae*, and then you shall rowl them into long round Rowls.

SIR KENELM DIGBY. *Choice and Experimented Receipts* (1668).

To make Perfumes to Burn.

Take half a pound of Damask Rose-buds (the whites cut off) Benjamin three ounces beaten to powder, half a quarter of an ounce of Musk, and as much of *Ambergris*, the like of Civet. Beat all these together in a stone-morter. Then put in an ounce of Sugar, and make it up in cakes, and dry them in the Sun, or by the fire, there is no difference in making the Bags, but that they must be red Roses.

The Closet of Sir Kenelm Digby Opened (1669).

A Perfume against the corruption of the Aire.

Take red Roses, Spikenard, wood of Aloes, Costus, Rosemary, Masticks, red Saunders, Bdellium, Labdanum, Olibanum, Saffron, of each a dramme and a halfe, Dock roots, Pepper, yellow Sanders of each three drammes, Cardamomes, Cubibes, Camphor, of each halfe a dramme,

234

five grains of Muske, put them into powder, and make little Trochis ; with Rose water.

> *The Charitable Physitian*, by PHILIBERT GUIBERT,
> Physitian Regent in Paris (1639).

CORDIAL PERFUMES

A Perfume againste griefe and paine.

Take leaves of Wormwood, Rosemary, Staechados, Cammomill of each two ounces, Mirrh, Storax, Benzoin of each three drammes, make them into Trochisques, and perfume Cotton, and apply the Cotton very warme.

Ibid.

To make all Manner of Fumes and Perfumes.

A Suffumigation to stay and dry Catarhes. Take Coriander seeds, Roses, Nigilla infused in Vineger, of each an ounce and a halfe, Masticks, Frankincense, of each halfe an ounce, gumme of Juniper two ounces. Make them into a powder, the which strow upon a chafing dish of coales, and perfume the cap and clothes for the head. You may make them into Trochisques with Rosewater and gumme Dragant if you please.

Ibid.

Another perfume of the same.

Take Frankincense, Masticke, Labdanum, Storax, of each halfe a dramme, beat them together and make them into Trochisques with gumme Dragant dissolved in Rose water.

Ibid.

SCENTED BATHS

A Cosmetic Bath.

Take two pounds of Barley or Bean-meal, eight pounds of Bran, and a few handfuls of Borage leaves. Boil these ingredients in a sufficient quantity of spring water. Nothing cleanses and softens the skin like this bath.

The Toilet of Flora.

An Aromatic Bath.

Boil, for the space of two or three minutes, in a sufficient quantity of river-water, one or more of the following plants ; viz. Laurel, Thyme, Rosemary, Wild Thyme, Sweet-Marjoram, Bastard-Marjoram, Lavender, Southernwood, Wormwood, Sage, Pennyroyal, Sweet-Basil, Balm, Wild Mint, Hyssop, Clove-july-flowers, Anise, Fennel, or any other herbs that have an agreeable scent. Having strained off the liquor from the herbs, add to it a little Brandy, or camphorated Spirits of Wine.

To make a bath for Melancholy.

Take Mallowes, pellitory of the wall, of each three handfulls ; Camomell flowers, Mellilot flowers, of each one handfull ; hollyhocks, two handfulls ; Isop one greate handfull, senerick seede one ounce, and boil them in nine gallons of Water untill they come to three, then put in a quart of new milke and go into it bloud warm or something warmer.

Arcana Fairfaxiana.

WASH BALLS AND SCENTED SOAPS

Musked Sope.

Take foure pound of Castle Sope, cut it into small pieces ; then take powder of Cloves and white Sanders of each two ounces, Benjamin an ounce, Muske twenty graines ; incorporate them all together, and put to them two or three drops of Oyle of Cloves or Nutmegs.

The Charitable Physitian, by PHILIBERT GUIBERT, Physitian Regent in Paris (1639).

To make an Ipswich Ball.

Take a pound of fine white Castill Sope, shave it thin in a pinte of Rose-water, and let it stand two or three days, then pour all the water from it, and put to it half a pinte of fresh water, and so let it stand one whole day, then pour out that, and put half a pinte more, and let it stand a night more, then put to it half an ounce of powder called sweet Marjoram, a quarter of an ounce of powder of Winter Savoury, two or three drops of the Oyl of Spike, and the Oyl of Cloves, three grains of Musk, and as much Ambergris, work all these together in a fair Mortar, with the powder of an Almond Cake dryed, and beaten as small as fine flowre, so rowl it round in your hands in Rose-water.

The Queen's Closet Opened, by W. M., Cook to Queen Henrietta Maria (1655).

To make a Musk-ball.

To make Musk-balls, take Nutmegs, Mace, Cloves, Saffron and Cinnamon, of each the weight of two pence,

237

and beat it to fine powder, of Mastick the weight of
two pence half-penny, of Storax the weight of six-pence,
of Labdanum the weight of ten-pence; of Ambergreece
the weight of six pence; and of Musk four grains,
dissolve and work all these in hard sweet Sope till it
come to a stiff Paste, and then make Balls thereof.

GERVASE MARKHAM. *The English Housewife* (1625).

Balles for the face.

Take greate Allecant reasons (raisins) a quarter of a
pounde, stone them but wash them not and beate them in
a morter very fine, take as many almonds, not Jordans,
but of ye common sort and blanch them and drye them
in a cloth very well and beate them in a stone morter
also very fine, when you have done thus to them bothe,
mingle them bothe together and beate them againe, and
putt to it half a quarter of a pounde of browne leavened
bread, wheaten breade, and beate them altogeather and
mingle them well togeather and then take it and make
it in little balles and then wash yor face at night with one
of them in fayre water. Yf you have this only to wash
yor hands, put in a little Venice Soape but putt none of
that in for youre face. *Arcana Fairfaxiana.*

Honey Soap.

Take four ounces of White Soap, and as much Honey,
half an ounce of Salt of Tartar, and two or three drachms
of the distilled Water of Fumitory; mix the whole
together. This Soap cleanses the skin well, and renders
it delicately white and smooth. It is also used advantage-
ously to efface the marks of burns and scalds.

The Toilet of Flora.

A Wash-ball, an excellent Cosmetic for the Face and Hands.

Take a pound of Florentine Orrice, a quarter of a pound of Storax, two ounces of Yellow Sanders, half an ounce of Cloves, as much fine Cinnamon, a Nutmeg, and twelve grains of Ambergrise; beat the whole into very fine powder, and sift them through a lawn sieve, all except the Ambergrise, which is to be added afterwards. Then take two pounds of the finest White Soap, shaved small, and infuse it in three pints of Brandy, four or five days. When it is dissolved, add a little Orange Flower-water, and knead the whole into a very stiff Paste with the best Starch finely powdered. Then mix the Ambergrise, with a little Gum Tragacanth liquified in sweet-scented Water. Of this Paste make Wash-balls; dry them in the shade, and polish them with a pasteboard or Lignum Vitae cup.

Ibid.

A perfumed Soap.

Take four ounces of Mash-mallow Roots skinned and dried in the shade, powder them, and add an ounce of Starch, the same quantity of Wheaten Flour, six drachms of fresh Pine-nut Kernels, two ounces of blanched Almonds, an ounce and a half of Orange Kernels husked, two ounces of Oil of Tartar, the same quantity of Oil of Sweet Almonds, and thirty grains of Musk; thoroughly incorporate the whole, and add to every ounce, half an ounce of Florentine Orrice-root in fine powder. Then steep half a pound of fresh Marsh-mallow Roots bruised in the distilled Water of Mallows, or Orange Flowers, for twelve hours, and forcibly squeezing out the liquor, make, with this mucilage, and the preceding Powders and Oils, a stiff Paste, which is to be dried in the shade, and formed into round balls. Nothing exceeds this Soap for smoothing the skin, or rendering the hands delicately white.

Ibid.

To make Wash-Balls.

Shave thin two pounds of new white soap into about a tea-cupful of rose-water, then pour as much boiling-water on as will soften it. Put into a brass pan a pint of sweet oil, four-pennyworth of oil of almonds, half a pound of spermaceti, and set all over the fire till dissolved ; then add the soap, and half an ounce of camphor that has first been reduced to powder by rubbing it in a mortar with a few drops of spirit of wine, or lavender-water, or any other scent. Boil ten minutes, then pour it into a basin, and stir it till it is quite thick enough to roll up into hard balls, which must then be done as soon as possible. If essence is used, stir it in quick after it is taken off the fire, that the flavour may not fly off.

Domestic Cookery (1834).

A delicate Washing Ball.

Take three ounces of Orace, halfe an ounce of Cypres, two ounces of Calamus Aromaticus, one ounce of Rose leaves, two ounces of Lavender flowers : beat all these together in a mortar searcing them thorow a fine Searce ; then scrape some castill sope, and dissolve it with some Rose-water, then incorporate all your powders therewith by labouring them well in a mortar.

SIR HUGH PLATT. *Delights for Ladies* (1594).

To make Washing-balls.

To make very good washing-balls, take Storax of both kinds, Benjamin, *Calamus Aromaticus*, Labdanum, of each alike, and bray them to powder with Cloves and Orris ; then beat them all with a sufficient quantity of Sope till it be stiff, then with your hand you shall work it like paste, and make round balls thereof.

GERVASE MARKHAM. *The English House-Wife* (1625).

Lady Lilleys Ball.

Take twelve ounces of oil-soap shaved very fine, sper-maceti three ounces, melt them together ; two ounces of bismuth dissolved in rose-water for the space of three hours, one ounce of oil of thyme, one ounce of the oil of carraways, one ounce of essence of lemons, mix all well together. MRS. GLASSE. *The Art of Cookery* (1784).

Fine scented Wash-ball.

Take of the best White Soap, half a pound, and shave it into thin slices with a knife ; then take two ounces and a half of Florentine Orrice, three quarters of an ounce of Calamus Aromaticus, and the same quantity of Elder Flowers ; of Cloves, and dried Rose Leaves, each half an ounce ; Coriander-seeds, Lavender, and Bay Leaves, of each a drachm, with three drachms of Storax. Reduce the whole to fine powder, which knead into a paste with the Soap ; adding a few grains of Musk or Ambergrise. When you make this Paste into Wash-balls, soften it with a little Oil of Almonds, to render the composition more

241

lenient. Too much cannot be said in favour of this Wash-ball, with regard to its cleansing and cosmetic property.

The Toilet of Flora.

To make Blue, Red or Purple Wash-Balls.

Get some white soap and cut it into square pieces about the bigness of dice ; let it lie in a band-box or a sieve on the top of an oven to dry, beat it in a mortar to a powder, and put it into a pan ; damp it with rose water, mix it well with your hands, put in some hair-powder to make it stiff, then scent it with oil of thyme, and oil of carraway.

If you would have them blue, put in some powder-blue, if red, some vermilion, if purple, some rose-pink ; mix them well together with your hands, and squeeze them as close as possible ; make them very round, of a size agreable to your mind ; put them into a sieve two or three days ; then scrape them a little with a wash-ball scraper and let them lie in the sieve eight or nine days. After-wards scrape them very smooth, and agreable to your mind.

Mrs. Glasse. *The Art of Cookery* (1784).

White Almond Wash-Balls.

Take some white soap and slice it thin and put it in a band-box on the top of an oven to dry, three weeks or more ; when it is dry beat it in a mortar till it is a powder ; to every four ounces of soap add one ounce of hair-powder, half an ounce of white-lead, put them into a pan, and damp them with rose-water to make it of a proper consistency; make them into balls as hard and close

242

as possible, scrape them with a ball-scraper letting them lie three weeks in a sieve to dry; then finish them with a ball-scraper to your mind.

Ibid.

AROMATIC VINEGARS

Aromatic Vinegar for the Toilet and the Sick room.

Put a handful of rosemary, of wormwood, lavender and mint into a stone jar and cover with a gallon of strong vinegar. Keep near a fire for 4 days and then strain, add one ounce of powdered camphor. Bottle for use.

The Toilet of Flora.

Distilled Lavender Vinegar.

Put into a stone cucurbit any quantity of fresh-gathered Lavender Flowers picked clean from the Stalks; pour on them as much distilled Vinegar as is requisite to make the Flowers float; distil in a vapour-bath, and draw off about three fourths of the Vinegar.

In the same manner are prepared the Vinegars from all other vegetable substances. Compound Vinegars are made by mixing several aromatic substances together; observing only to bruise all hard woody ingredients, and to let them infuse a sufficient time in the Vinegar before you proceed to distillation.

Ibid.

Vinegar of the Four Thieves.

Take of the tops of Sea and Roman Wormwood, Rosemary, Sage, Mint, and Rue, of each an ounce and a half; Lavender Flowers two ounces, Calamus Aromaticus,

243

Cinnamon, Cloves, Nutmeg, and Garlic, of each a quarter of an ounce; Camphire, half an ounce; Red Wine Vinegar, a gallon. Choose all the foregoing ingredients dry, except the Garlic and Camphire; beat them into grose powder, and cut the Garlic into thin slices; put the whole into a matrass; pour the Vinegar on them, and digest the mixture in the sun, or in a gentle sand-heat, for three weeks or a month. Then strain off the Vinegar by expression, filter it through paper, and add the Camphire dissolved in a little rectified Spirit of Wine. Keep it for use in a bottle, tightly corked.

The Vinegar of the Four Thieves is antipestilential, and is used successively as a preservative against contagious disorders. The hands and face are washed with it every day; the room fumigated with it, as are also the cloaths, in order to secure the person from infection. *Ibid.*

To make Musk Sugar.

Bruise six grains of Musk and tie them in a piece of Tiffany, lay it in the bottom of a Gallipot, and then fill it with Sugar, and tie it up close, when you have spent that sugar, put in some more, it will be well perfumed.

Ibid.

A Perfume to perfume Starch.

After you have made your starch something thick, put in some rose water, which musk and ambergreese have been steed in all night and it will make your linnen to smell most pleasantly.

The Book of Simples (circa 1650).

244

Fine Sweet Powder for the hair.

Take one pound of the best starch you can get, put into a Bason with half a pint of Rosemary water, as much Rosewater, stir them well together with a spoon, then dry them well in the Sun, then take the searced Powder of Damask Roses, and four grains of Ambergreece, mix it well with your Starch and sift it fine.

The Pearle of Practice (1662).

SCENTED OILS

To make Oyle of Roses three wayes.

The first way is, take a pound of red Rose buds, beat them in a Marble morter with a woodden pestle, then put them into an earthen pot, and poure upon them foure pound of oyle of Olives, letting them infuse the space of a moneth in the Sunne, or in the chimney corner stirring of them sometimes, then heate it, and presse it, and straine it, and put it into the same pot or other vessell to keepe.

The second is take halfe a pound of red Roses, and halfe a pound of Damaske, beate them together in a marble morter, and put them into a pot, and poure upon them foure pounde of oyle, and let them infuse the space of twelve houres, then pour them all into a pan and boyle them two or three boylings, and straine them and presse them in a strong towell in the presse, and in the meane time put in the pot as many more Roses and poure the oyle upon them and so beate them and presse them and

245

put Roses to the oyle three times, and then boyle it
untill all the humidity bee consumed. The third is to
take all Damask Roses and no red and make three in-
fusions as before.

The Charitable Physitian, by PHILIBERT GUIBERT,
Esquire and Physitian Regent in Paris (1639).

Oyle of Jasmine is made thus.

Take of flowers of Jasmine as many as you please, put
them into as much sweet mature Oil as you please, put
them into a glasse close topt, and set them into the
Sun to be infused for the space of twenty dayes, then
take them out, and straine the Oil from the flowers;
and if thou wouldest have the Oil yet stronger, put in
new flowers and do as before.

This is a pleasant perfume, and being mixt with Oils
and ointments, gives them a gratefull smell, it is also used
in the perfuming of Leather.

After this manner may be made Oil of any flowers, but
because I shall keep my self to the Art of distillation only,
I shall not so far digresse as to speak of these kinds of
Oils, only I thought good to set down the Oil of Jasmine
because by reason of its fragrancy it hath some analogie
with Chymicall Oils that are made by distillation.

JOHN FRENCH. *The Art of Distillation* (1652).

Jasmine Oil.

Nothing more is required than to dip the finest cotton
wool in clear olive oil, which must be spread in thin
layers, in a tall glass vessel, with alternate layers of
Jessamine flowers which, in a few days, will impart the
246

whole of their perfume to the cotton. The oil may then be pressed out for use : and the cotton itself may be laid in drawers or band-boxes, where its perfume is wished for. *Practical Economy* (1822).

Pomade Divine.

Clear a pound and a half of beef-marrow from the strings and bone, put it into an earthen pan or vessel of water fresh from the spring, and change the water night and morning for ten days ; then steep it in rose-water twenty-four hours, and drain it in a cloth till quite dry.. Take an ounce of each of the following articles, namely storax, gum-benjamin, odoriferous Cypress powder, or of Florence, half an ounce of cinnamon, two drachms of cloves and two drachms of nutmeg, all finely powdered ; mix them with the marrow above prepared ; then put all the ingredients into a pewter pot, that holds three pints ; make a paste of white of egg and flour, and lay it upon a piece of rag. Over that must be another piece of linen to cover the top of the pot very close, that none of the steam may evaporate. Put the pot into a large copper pot with water, observing to keep it steady, that it may not reach to the covering of the pot that holds the marrow. As the water shrinks, add more, boiling hot ; for it must boil four hours without ceasing a moment. Strain the ointment through a linen cloth into small pots, and, when cold, cover them. Do not touch it with anything but silver. It will keep many years.

A fine pomatum may be made by putting half a pound of fresh marrow, prepared as above, and two ounces of hog's lard, on the ingredients ; and then observing the same process as above. *Domestic Cookery* (1834).

SCENTED GLOVES

*Divers excellent scents for gloves, with their proportions, and
other circumstances, with the manner of performing.*

The Violet, the Orenge, the Lemmon duely propor-
tioned with other sents, perform this wel : so likewise of
Labdanum, Storax, Benjamin. The manner is thus :
First lay your amber upon a few coales, till it begin to
crack like lime : then let it cool of itself, taking away the
coal : then grinde the same with som Yellow ocre, till
you perceive a right colour for a glove : with this mixture
wash over your glove, with a little haire brush upon a
smooth stone in every seame, and all over : then hang
your gloves to dry upon a line : then with gummed
Dragant dissolved in some Rose-water, and ground with
a little oil de Ben, or of sweet Almonds upon a stone :
strike over your glove in every place with the gumme and
oile so ground together : doe this with a little sponge, but
bee sure the gloves bee first thorowly dry and the colour
well rubbed and beaten out of the glove, then let them
hang again till they be dry, which will bee in short time.
Then if you will have your glove to lye smooth and fair in
shew, go over it againe with your spunge and the mixture
of gumme and oile, and dry the glove yet once againe.
Then grind upon your stone two or three graines of good
Musk, with halfe a spoonfull of Rose-water ; and with a
very little peece of a spunge take up the composition
by a little and a little : and so lay it upon your glove, lying
upon the stone. Picke and strain your gum Dragagant
before you use it. Perfume but the one side of your glove

at once, and then hang it up to dry and then finish the other side. Ten grains of Musk will give a sufficient perfume to eight paire of gloves. Note also, that this perfume is done upon a then Lambsleather glove : and if you work upon a Kid's skin or Goat's skin, which is usuall leather for rich perfumes, then you must adde more quantitie of the oyle of Ben to your gum and go over the glove twice therewith.

Sir Hugh Platt. *Delights for Ladies* (1594).

To perfume Gloves.

Take Angelica-water and Rose-water, and put into them the powder of Cloves, Ambergreece, Musk, and Lignum Aloes, Benjamin, and Calamus Amoraticus : boyl these till half be consumed : then strain it and put your Gloves therein ; then hang them in the Sun to dry and turn them often : and thus three times, wet them and dry them again : or otherwise take Rose-water and wet your Gloves therein, then hang them up till they be almost dry ; then take half an ounce of Benjamin, and grind it with the oyl of Almonds, and rub it on the Gloves till it be almost dryed in : then take twenty Grains of Ambergreece, and twenty Grains of Musk, and grind them together with oyl of Almonds, and so rub it on the Gloves, and then hang them up to dry, or let them dry in your bosome, and so after use them at your pleasure.

Gervase Markham. *The English House-Wife* (1625).

To perfume Gloves.

To perfume gloves excellently take the Oyl of sweet Almonds, oyl of Nutmegs, oyl of Benjamin of each a

Dram, of Amber-greece one grain, fat Musk two grains : Mix them all together, and grind them upon a Painter's Stone, and then anoint the gloves there with, yet before you anoint them, let them be dampishly moistened with Damask Rose-water. *Ibid.*

To perfume a Jerkin.

To perfume a Jerkin well take the oyl of Benjamin a pennyworth, oyl of Spike and oyl of olives, half penny-worths of each, and take two Spunges, and warm one of them against the fire and rub your Jerkin therewith, and when the oyl is dryed take the other Spunge and dip it in the oyl, and rub your Jerkin therewith till it be dry, then lay on the Perfume before prescribed for gloves.

Ibid.

To perfume gloves.

Take benjamine, storax, civet, muske and amber-greese with the oyle of sweet balsams : with a little orace flower water grind all these very well upon a painters stone and so wash your gloves with it and put them upon sticks and dry them : the oyle of balsame keeps them supple that they will not dry stiff.

The Book of Simples (circa 1650).

SCENTED TOBACCOS

A pleasant and wholesome Perfume for Tobacco taken in a Pipe.

Take one ounce of the hard Balsom that is in Nuts, *Ambergris* half a dram, Oyl of Anniseeds six drops, Oyl of Cinamon six or seven, or ten drops, Oyl of Cloves three drops ; work all these together by long malaxation in a Mortar warmed a little, into a uniform gummy substance : whereof as much as a Pepper-corn pressed in at the top of a Pipe of Tobacco, will make it taste exceeding well, and perfume the mouth and room very pleasantly, by taking it in smoke.

The Closet of Sir Kenelm Digby Opened (1669).

Another richer Perfume : being pleasant and wholesome, to perfume Tobacco taken in a Pipe.

Take Balm of Peru half an ounce, seven or eight Drops of Oyl of Cinamon, Oyl of Cloves five drops, Oyl of Nutmegs, of Thyme, of Lavender, of Fennel, of Aniseeds (all drawn by distillation) of each a like quantity, or more or less as you like the odour, and would have it strongest ; incorporate with these half a dram of Amber-grease : make all these into a Paste ; which keep in a Box : when you have filled your Pipe of Tobacco, put upon it about the bigness of a Pins Head of this Composition.

It will make the Smoak most pleasantly odoriferous, both to the Takers, and to them that come into the Room, and ones Breath will be sweet all the day after. It also comforts the Head and Brains. Approved by Sir Kenelm Digby.

G. HARTMAN. *The True Preserves of Health* (1682).

SCENTED SNUFFS

The Manner of making the famous Barcelona Snuff, *as it was perform'd at the* Lyon *at* Barcelona. *This is also call'd* Myrtle Snuff.

Take *Seville* snuff, and prepare a dry Barrel, that has not had any Wine in it, or any Scent; then cut the fresh tops of Myrtle, and lay a layer of them at the bottom of the Cask, an Inch or two thick; then lay snuff in that as thick, and lay on more Myrtle, two Inches; then again, put on snuff, and so fill the Barrell in the same Manner, *Stratum super Stratum.* Then press it down with a Board, that will sit, and sit three Weights upon it of a quarter of an Hundred a-piece, and let it stand four and twenty Hours; then turn it out, and sift it, flinging the Myrtle away; then put it into the Cask, as before, with fresh Myrtle, and serve it so three times, and sift it off. When this is done, add to every ten Pounds of snuff, one pound of Orangery Snuff, and mix the whole very well, and after three days, put it into glaz'd Pots, well pressed into them, and stopt close: or else into Leaden Pots; which last is rather the best. *The Country Lady's Director* (1732).

To make Orangery Snuff.

Take Seville Snuff and Orange-Flowers, fresh gather'd early in the Morning. And in a glaz'd earthen Vessel, lay a Layer of the Flowers, then a Layer of Snuff, then a Layer of Flowers; and so on, till the Pot is full. Press it down very gently, and let the Mouth of the Pot be open for twenty-four Hours; then turn all out, and sift your Snuff, and lay in fresh Flowers, with Snuff, in the same manner as before ; and at the end of four and twenty Hours sift it off again, and repeat the same the third time : being sure that the Flowers do not remain longer than twenty-four Hours, else they will sour the Snuff. For making this Snuff you ought to allow at least a pound for Waste, for the Flowers will gather a great deal of it.

Ibid.

Method of scenting Snuff.

The Flowers that most readily communicate their flavour to Snuff are Orange Flowers, Jasmine, Musk Roses, and Tuberoses. You must procure a box lined with dry white paper ; in this strow your Snuff on the bottom about the thickness of an inch, over which place a thin layer of Flowers, then another layer of Snuff, and continue to lay your Flowers and Snuff alternately in this manner, until the box is full. After they have lain together four and twenty hours, sift your Snuff through a sieve to separate it from the Flowers, which are to be thrown away, and fresh ones applied in their room in the former method. Continue to do this till the Snuff is sufficiently scented ; then put it into a canister, which keep close stopped.

Ibid.

Or

Put your Flowers that are placed over each layer of the Snuff, between two pieces of white paper pricked full of holes with a large pin, and sift through a sieve the Snuff that may happen to get between the papers. To scent the snuff perfectly it is necessary to renew the Flowers four or five times. This method is the least troublesome of the two. *Ibid.*

Or

A very agreeable scented Snuff may be made with Roses, by taking Rosebuds, stripping off the green cup, and pistil that rises in the middle, and fixing in its place a Clove; being careful not to separate the Leaves that are closed together. The Rose-buds thus prepared, are to be exposed to the heat of the sun a whole month, inclosed in a glass well stopped, and are then fit for use.

To make Snuff scented with a thousand Flowers, take a number of different Flowers, and mix them together, proportioning the quantity of each Flower, to the degree of its perfume, so that the flavour of no one particular Flower may be predominant. *The Toilet of Flora.*

Perfumed Snuff.

Take some Snuff, and rub it in your hands with a little Civet, opening the body of the Civet still more by rubbing it in your hands with fresh Snuff; and when you have mixed it perfectly with the Snuff, put them into a canister. Snuff is flavoured with other perfumes in the same way.

Ibid.

Snuff after the Maltese Fashion.

Perfume with Ambergrise, in the manner already described, some Snuff previously scented with Orange Flowers. Then grind in a mortar a little Sugar with about ten grains of Civet, and mix by little and little with about a pound of the foregoing Snuff. *Ibid.*

Italian Snuff.

Put into a mortar, or other convenient vessel, a quantity of Snuff already scented with some Flower, pour on it a little White Wine, and add, if agreeable, some Essence of Ambergrise, Musk, or any other Perfume you like best ; stir the Snuff and rub it well between your hands. Scent Snuff in this manner with any particular flavour, and put the different scented Snuffs, in separate boxes, which are to be marked, to prevent mistakes.   *Ibid.*

Snuff scented after the Spanish Manner.

Take a lump of double-refined Sugar, rub it in a mortar with twenty grains of Musk ; add by little and little a pound of Snuff, and grind the whole with ten grains of Civet, rubbing it afterwards well between your hands.

Seville Snuff is scented with twenty grains of Vanilloes only. Keep your Snuff in canisters closely stopped, to prevent the scent from exhaling.

As Spanish Snuff is very fine and of a redish colour, to imitate it nicely, take the best Dutch Snuff, well cleansed, granulated, and coloured red ; beat it fine, and sift it through a very fine lawn sieve. After it has been cleansed, according to the foregoing directions, it is fit to take any scent whatever.

There is no risk in using a sieve that retains the scent of any Flower, to perfume your Snuff with the flavour of Musk, Ambergrise, or any other Perfume. On the contrary, the Snuff receives the Perfume the more readily, and preserves its flavour the longer on that account.

Ibid.

255

Herb Snuff.

Take Sweet Marjoram, Marum Syriacum Leaves, and Lavender Flowers dried, of each half an ounce, Afarabacca Leaves, a drachm. Rub them all into a powder.

Ibid.

Or

Take Betony Leaves and Marjoram, of each half an ounce, Afarabacca Leaves, a drachm. Beat them together into a powder.

Or

Take Marjoram, Rosemary Flowers, Betony, and Flowers of Lilies of the Valley, of each a quarter of an ounce; Nutmegs, a drachm and a half; Volatile Salt, forty drops. Powder, and keep the mixture in a phial, close stopped.

Or

Take Flowers of Lavender, and Clove-july-flowers, of each a quarter of an ounce; Lilies of the Valley, Tiel-tree Flowers, Flowers of Sage, Betony, Rosemary, and Tops of Marjoram, of each half a drachm; Cinnamon, Aloes-wood, Yellow Sanders, and White Helebore-root, of each a drachm; Oil of Nutmegs and Oil of Lemons, of each three drops; mix them into a powder.

A pinch or two of any of these Snuffs may be taken night and morning medicinally, or at any time for pleasure.

Ibid.

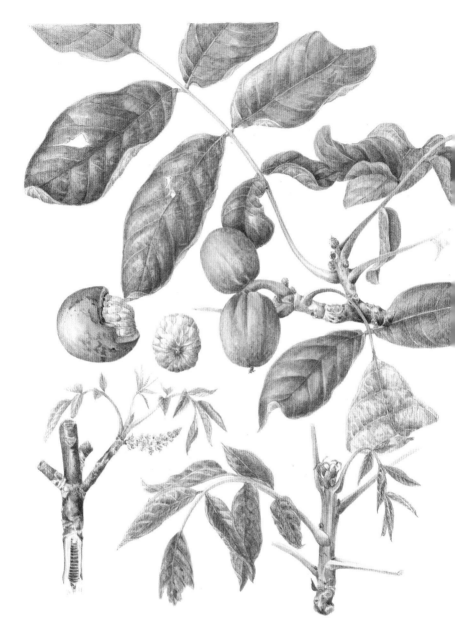

'The leaves of the common ... walnut have, when crushed, a smell which bears no resemblance to that of any other leaf.' *(See page 272)*

SCENTED CANDLES

Candles to perfume the Aire.

Take Benjamin, Storax, of each foure ounces, Frank-incense, Olibanum, of each twelve ounces, Labdanum eighteen ounces, Nigella an ounce, Coriander seeds, Juniper berries, of each halfe an ounce; liquid Storax sixe ounces, Turpentine halfe an ounce, forme them into Candles with gum : dragant and Rose water.

The Charitable Physitian, by Philibert Guibert,
Physitian Regent in Paris (1639).

Odoriferous Candles against Venome and the plague.

Take Labdanum three ounces, Storax ten drams, Benjamin sixe drammes, Frankincense an ounce and a halfe, Staechados two ounces, red Roses, Cloves, of each three ounces, Citron peele, Yellow Sanders, of each three drammes, Juniper berries halfe an ounce, Muske and Ambergreece, of each halfe a scruple : forme them into Candles with gum : dragant dissolved in Rose water.

Ibid.

PLANT LISTS

TREES, SHRUBS AND CLIMBERS

* Signifies hardy only in favoured districts.

NAME.	ORDER.	ORIGIN.	SEASON.	REMARKS.
*Abelia chinensis (syn rupestris)	Caprifoliaceae	China	Summer	Deciduous shrub, 3 feet, suitable for the rock garden. Fragrant white flowers.
*Abelia floribunda	,,	Mexico (int. 1842)	Summer	A fine shrub with pale red sweet-scented flowers. Usually needs the protection of a wall, but in a few favoured localities will grow as a bush.
*Acacia dealbata (Mimosa)	Leguminosae	Australia	February and March	The 'mimosa' of Covent Garden Market. Foliage being evergreen is always attractive. Covered with a sheet of rich yellow deliciously-scented blossoms in early spring. Excellent on walls.
*Akebia quinata	Berberidaceae	China, Corea and Japan (int. 1845)	Summer	Introduced by R. Fortune. Evergreen climber about 10 feet, purplish, very fragrant flowers.
,, var. fl. rosea	,,			A variety with purplish red flowers.
*Aloysia citriodora (Lemon-scented verbena)	Verbenaceae	Chile (int. 1781)	July to Oct.	Requires a sheltered wall.
Artemisia abrotanum and many other species	Compositae	S. Europe	Summer	

Name	Family	Origin	Flowering time	Description
Azara microphylla	Bixaceae	Chile	March and April	The azaras take their name from Joseph Nicolas Azara, a Spanish gentleman, of whom nothing further is known except that he was a patron of science. (See Edward's *Botanical Register*.) Evergreen, 10–15 ft. Shining green box-like leaves. Minute yellow flowers with vanilla-like fragrance. Orange-red berries.
Berberis aquifolium syn Mahonia aquifolium (Oregon grape)	Berberidaceae	West North America	February and March	Evergreen shrub which thrives almost anywhere. Commonest of the berberies. Deliciously-scented flowers followed by an abundance of blue-black fruits which make excellent jam.
Berberis japonica var. Bealii syn B. hyemalis syn Mahonia Bealii	,,	China	February to April	Evergreen, 4–5 feet, with large drooping clusters, yellow flowers with lily-of-the-valley scent. Followed by large fruits.
*Berberis nepalensis	Berberidaceae	Nepaul	Begins flowering in October, at its best in March and April	Rare evergreen with pinnate leaves 2 feet long and clusters of fragrant yellow flowers. Grows 6 feet.

Owing to the large number of new berberises and the hybrids, both natural and intentional, it is impossible to mention more than a few of outstanding merit.

NAME.	ORDER.	ORIGIN.	SEASON.	REMARKS.
Buddleia globosa	Loganiaceae	Chile and Peru (int. 1774)	May and June	Quick growing shrub with orange-coloured ball-like inflorescence, with a peculiar honey scent. Buddleias are not particular as to soil.
Buddleia variabilis	,,	Central and West China	July, August	Beloved by the autumn butterflies—admiral, peacock, etc.
*Bursaria spinosa	Pittosporaceae	Australia (int. 1793)	August	Introduced by the Marchioness of Rockingham. This plant was figured in the *Botanical Magazine* in the year of Waterloo.
Buxus sempervirens and other species	Euphorbiaceae	Britain, S. Europe, N. Africa and W. Asia		Common box. Does well on chalk.
Calycanthus floridus (Carolina Allspice)	Calycanthaceae	S.E. United States (int. 1726)	July to October	Deciduous shrub. Reddish brown flowers and very aromatic leaves and bark.
Calycanthrus occidentalis (syn macrophyllus) (Californian Allspice)	,,	California	July	A larger-leaved variety with strongly-scented crimson flowers. Leaves and wood more powerfully fragrant than C. floridus.
Camellia fragrans	Ternstroemiaceae			A very rare camellia, with deliciously-scented flowers.
*Caryopteris mastacanthus	Verbenaceae	China and Japan	August to October	Flowers are a beautiful clear lavender blue and borne at a time when few shrubs are in bloom. Flowers

Name	Family	Origin	Flowering time	Remarks
				have a slight aromatic scent. Leaves, when bruised, have a strong pungent odour.
Catalpa japonica	Bignoniaceae	Japan	July	Fragrant white flowers. Does not flower in the young state.
Cedrela sinensis (syn Ailanthus flavescens) Chinese Incense tree	Meliaceae	N. and W. China	Summer	Handsome sweet-scented foliage and fragrant white flowers.
Cedrus libani (Cedar of Lebanon)	Coniferae	Mount Lebanon and Cilician Taurus (int. 1676)		Both the leaves and the wood are peculiarly scented. The cones are not produced till the tree is 40 to 100 years old.
Chimonanthus fragrans	Calycanthaceae	China (int. 1766)	January and February	Deciduous shrub, 3–10 feet. Very attractive flowers produced in midwinter. Strong honeysuckle scent. Leaves appear later.
*Choisya ternata (Mexican orange blossom)	Rutaceae	Mexico (int. 1825)	May and June	Evergreen shrub, hardy in south. Rich glistening leaves and fine clusters of fragrant white flowers, both in summer and autumn.
Chionanthus virginica (The Virginian Fringe tree)	Oleaceae	E. United States (int. 1736)	June	Snow-white flowers with very delicate scent.

NAME.	ORDER.	ORIGIN.	SEASON.	REMARKS.
Cistus ladaniferus (Gum cistus)	Cistineae	S. Europe and N. Africa (int. 1629)	July and August	Beautiful shrub, 5 feet. Pure white flowers with maroon blotch at base. White flowers 4 inches across. Leaves and foliage are richly aromatic.
Cistus Cyprius	,,	Cyprus	July and August	Young branches are covered with an aromatic gum. Foliage also aromatic. One of the most beautiful of the rock roses.
Clematis Armandi	Ranunculaceae	Central and W. China	April and May	The variety known as La Mortola is much finer than the type.
Clematis aromatica	,,	Origin uncertain	July, August	About 4 feet. Very fragrant blue flowers.
Clematis cirrhosa	,,	Spain, Algeria and Palestine	December to March	Evergreen climber with greenish bell-shaped fragrant flowers. Does not mind frost but needs protection from cutting winds. Discovered in Spain by Clusius in sixteenth century.
Clematis flammula (Virgin's Bower) var. rubro marginata	,, ,,	S. Europe	July to October ,,	A favourite in gardens since the sixteenth century. Almond-scented white flowers. White flowers with reddish margins.
Clematis paniculata	,,	Japan	August to October	Rapid climber. Loose clusters of hawthorn-scented flowers.
Clematis nutans (syn C. Rehderiana)	,,	W. China	September and October	One of the latest-flowering of the family and invaluable for the autumn garden. Very fragrant bell-shaped yellow flowers.

Name	Family	Locality	Month	Description
Clematis vitalba (Traveller's Joy, Old Man's Beard, Hedge Vine, Maiden's Honesty, etc.)	,,	Europe, Britain	July to October	'Esteemed for pleasure by reason of the goodly shadow and the pleasant scent or savour of its flowers. And because of its decking and adorning waies and hedges where people travel, thereupon have I named it Traveller's Joy.' John Gerard, *The Herball*, 1597.
Clerodendron Fargesii (Glory Tree)	Verbenaceae	Szech'uan	August	Very fragrant white flowers, but chiefly attractive for its pale blue fruit. (Some people find the scent extremely unpleasing.)
Clerodendron foetidum	,,	China (int. 1844)	September, October	One of R. Fortune's introductions. Sickly sweet-scented flowers. Leaves have an intensely disagreeable smell.
Clerodendron trichotomum	,,	China and Japan	August	One of the most beautiful of the Japanese shrubs, 8–10 feet. Deliciously-scented white flowers with purple calyx. Leaves also scented, but not so pleasant.
Clethra alnifolia (Sweet Pepper Bush)	Ericaceae	East N. America (int. 1731)	August and September	Dense-growing shrub. Fragrant white flowers. Foliage when bruised has a peculiar scent. Thrives in damp ground.
Comptonia asplenifolia (Sweet Fern)	Myricaceae	East and North U.S.A.	Summer	Called after Henry Compton, Bishop of London (d. 1713). The foliage has a most pleasant scent.
Corylopsis pauci-flora	Hamamelidaceae	Japan (int. 1864)	March	Deciduous shrub. Leaves are prettily tinted both in spring and autumn. Small pale yellow deliciously-scented flowers borne in catkins before the leaves. Likes sandy loam.

NAME.	ORDER.	ORIGIN.	SEASON.	REMARKS.
Corylopsis spicata	Hamamelidaceae	Japan (int. 1864)	March	Striking shrub, 4–6 feet. Racemes of pale yellow cowslip-scented flowers before the leaves. Foliage, metallic blue in autumn.
Crataegus Oxyacantha (May, Hawthorn, etc.) and many species and varieties	Rosaceae	Europe, Britain, W. Asia and N. America	May	Deciduous tree. Several varieties.
*Cytisus racemosus (syn Genista fragrans)	Leguminosae	Canary Islands	Early summer	Frequently grown in greenhouses. Deliciously-scented yellow flowers. When grown outside in a favoured locality will reach 8–10 feet on a wall and continue blooming till late autumn.

The hardy Cytisus are so slightly scented that they are not included in this list.

NAME.	ORDER.	ORIGIN.	SEASON.	REMARKS.
Daphne blagayana	Thymelaeaceae	Carncola	April	Rare evergreen with sweet-scented very pale yellow flowers.
Daphne caucasica	,,	Caucasus	June and July	A rare deciduous form. Fragrant white flowers.
Daphne Cneorum (Garland flower)	,,	Central and S. Europe	April and May, and again in autumn	Rose-pink sweet-scented flowers. Prostrate habit. Slow growing.
*Daphne genkwa (Japanese lilac)	,,	China and Japan	Spring	Introduced by R. Fortune in 1843. Rare. Lilac-coloured deliciously-scented flowers before the leaves appear.

Name	Family	Region	Time	Description
Daphne laureola (Spurge laurel)	"	Europe, Britain	Early March	Evergreen. Yellowish green flowers with a rather unpleasant smell. Followed by black berries.
Daphne mezereum	"	Europe and Siberia	January to April	Deciduous Bush, 4–5 feet. Does well in any good garden soil, sun or shade. Very fragrant blossoms before the leaves appear. Followed by red berries.
var. alba " atro purpurea				
*Daphne neapolitana (syn fioniana)	"	S. Europe and Asia Minor	March	Evergreen. Bushy habit. Purplish rose, very fragrant flowers.
*Daphne odora syn D. indica ", japonica	"	China and Japan	January to May	The sweetest scented of all the Daphnes.
Daphne pontica	"	Asia Minor	April and May	Evergreen. Quite hardy. Fragrant yellow flowers.
Daphne retusa	"	China	May and June	Compact little shrub about one foot. Very delicately-scented flowers borne on tips of the branches.
Davidia involucrata	Cornaceae	Central and W. China	June	A fugitive scent noticeable in the neighbourhood of the tree at times.
*Decumaria barbara	Saxifragaceae	Texas (int. 1785)	June to August	An almost evergreen climber. Hawthorn-like flowers.
*Drimys aromatica	Magnoliaceae	Tasmania and Victoria	April	Slow growing shrub, about 7 feet. Very attractive leaf-stalks and young shoots have the red colouring of D. Winteri, leaves much smaller. Covered with sweet-scented white flowers in April. Much tenderer than D. Winteri.

NAME.	ORDER.	ORIGIN.	SEASON.	REMARKS.
*Drimys Winteri (Winter's Bark)	Magnoliaceae	Chile	May and June	The bark was brought home by Captain Winter in one of Drake's ships from the Magellan Straits in 1578, introduced as a living plant in 1827. Large leaves, red stems and clusters of ivory-coloured scented flowers. All varieties have leaves strongly scented when crushed.
var. Nandina	,,	Found by Mr. Harold Comber in S. America		
*Edgeworthia chrysantha	Thymelaeaceae	Himalayas	January and February	Common in gardens in S. Europe. Flowers clear yellow and deep yellow in ball-like clusters borne on end of shoots. Only for very favoured districts.
*Ehretia accuminata	Boraginaceae	China and Japan	August	Rare shrub. Large dark leaves, honey-scented white flowers.
Epigaea repens (New England Mayflower)	Ericaceae	N. America, Newfoundland to Saskatchewan, Florida, Wisconsin and Kentucky (int. 1736)	May	Abundant near Plymouth, Massachusetts, where the Pilgrim Fathers landed. Said to have been named by them after their ship the *Mayflower*. Creeping shade-loving evergreen, 3–4 inches high. Sweet-scented white or red flowers. Grows only in arid soils.

Name	Family	Origin	Flowering	Description
Erica arborea	"	Mediterranean and Caucasus (int. 1658)	March to May	Large bush, 4–10 feet. Soft green asparagus-like foliage. Very fragrant flowers covering the bush March to May. Beloved by bees.
*Erica australis (Spanish Heath) var. Mr. Robert	"	Spain and Portugal	Spring	Bush 4–6 feet. Slightly fragrant purplish flowers lasting nearly two months. The white-flowered form.
Erica Veitchii	"	E. Arborea and E. Lusitanica	"	Bush 2–5 feet. Very fragrant white flowers. Best scented of all the hardy heaths.
Escallonia illinita	Saxifragaceae	Chile	Summer	Evergreen. One of the hardiest of the genus. Strong unpleasing scent. Very quick growing.
*Eucalyptus coccifera	Myrtaceae	Tasmania		
*Eucalyptus cordata	"	"	October	Very tender.
*Eucalyptus Gunnii	"	S. Australia and Tasmania		

The Eucalyptus family is included in this list, but with the exception of a Tasmanian form of *E. Gunnii*, known as Whittingamensis after the late Lord Balfour's place, which has proved absolutely hardy there and at Aldenham, the hardiest will only survive until a severe winter comes. All are strongly aromatic.

Name	Family	Origin	Flowering	Description
Eucryphia pinnati-folia	Eucryphiaceae	S. America	August	These lovely flowers have not a particularly pleasant scent.
*Eupatorium Weinmannianum	Compositae	Mexico	Autumn till Christmas	Excellent wall plant in the south. Clusters of fragrant white flowers.

NAME.	ORDER.	ORIGIN.	SEASON.	REMARKS.
Ficus Carica (Fig.)	Urticaceae	W. Asia and E. Mediterranean		Cultivated in this country from very early times. Whole plant has a fugitive attractive smell.
Fothergilla Gardeni (syn F. alnifolia) (American Witch Elder)	Hamamelidaceae	Eastern N. America (int. 1765)	April and May	Deciduous shrub. Spikes of slightly-scented white flowers before the leaves. Good autumn foliage.
Fothergilla major	,,	Alleghany Mts.	May	Fragrant spikes of flowers.
Fraxinus ornus (Manna Ash)	Oleaceae	S. Europe, Asia Minor	May	White flowers with a not particularly pleasant scent.
*Freylinia cestroides			November to March	Rare evergreen, 5–6 feet. Apricot-coloured deliciously-scented flowers. Only for very favoured districts.
Gaultheria procumbens (Partridge Berry, Mountain tea, Creeping Winter Green)	Ericaceae	N. America (int. 1762)	July and August	Evergreen shrub, creeping habit. Flowers and leaves have a pleasant aromatic scent. Attractive red berries in autumn.
Hamamelis mollis	Hamamelidaceae	China	January and February	Peat and shade-loving.
Hamamelis japonica	,,	Japan	January and February	Flowers of both *H. mollis* and *H. japonica* have an interesting dusty Eastern scent.

Name	Family	Origin	Flowering	Description
*Helichrysum antennarium	"	Australia	June	Rare shrub. Hawthorn-like sweetly scented flowers.
*Helichrysum fragrans	Compositae	S. Africa	Summer	Evergreen shrub. Small pink pleasantly scented flowers. If kept dry after picking flowers are almost ever-lasting.
*Heliotropium	Boraginaceae	Peru (int. 1757)	Summer	The well-known 'Cherry Pie.'
*Hoheria populnea	Malvaceae	New Zealand	September	Small handsome tree. Slightly scented flowers.
Holboellia latifolia	Berberidaceae	Himalayas	June, July	Evergreen climber which attains a great height—40 feet and upwards. A most penetrating attractive scent, noticeable at a great distance from the plant.
Hypericum ascyron	Hypericaceae	N. America	July, August	Little garden merit, yellow flowers, leaves have a strong offensive smell.
*Hypericum balearicum	"	Balearic Isles (int. 1714)	June to September	Fragrant flowers.
Hypericum calycynum (Rose of Sharon)	"	Asia	June to September	Leaves slightly scented.
Hyssopus officinalis	Labiabae	S. Europe and W. Asia	July to September	Cultivated at least since the sixteenth century in these islands and probably long before. Aromatic.
Itea virginica (Virginian willow)	Saxifragaceae	N. America (int. 1744)	July to October	Deciduous. One of the prettiest American shrubs. Deep green oblong leaves, sprays of white flowers with a fragrance like the pond lily. Foliage and stems beautifully coloured in autumn.

NAME.	ORDER.	ORIGIN.	SEASON.	REMARKS.
Jasminum officinale	Oleaceae	China, India and Persia	Throughout Summer	Cultivated for centuries in these islands. Date of introduction unknown.
var. grandiflorum				
var. aureum				
Jasminum revolutum	,,	Afghanistan and N.W. Himalayas	Summer	Old-fashioned evergreen, seldom seen. Large rich yellow flowers. Perfectly hardy on a warm wall.
Jasminum Stephanense	,,			Sweetly-scented pinkish flowers.
Juglans nigra	Juglandaceae	Eastern N. America		The leaves of both the common and the American walnut have, when crushed, a smell which bears no resemblance to that of any other leaf.
Juglans regia (Common Walnut)	,,	E. Europe and Asia Minor		
Juniperus sabina	Coniferae	Central and S. Europe		Strong aromatic scent. Perhaps the most strongly scented of the Junipers.
*Laurea Novae-Zealandiae	Monimiaceae	New Zealand		Very sweetly-scented leaves.
*Laurelia semper-virens		Chile	May	Very sweetly-scented leaves.
Laurus nobilis	Lauraceae	S. Europe	Summer	
Lavandula vera	Labiatae	Mediterranean region	July and August	Cultivated in Britain at least since the sixteenth century and possibly since Roman days.
var. alba				
var. nana				

Name	Family	Origin	Flowering time	Notes
Lavandula spica	,,	,,	,,	Yields the oil of spike, which is less pleasantly scented than the oil extracted from L. vera.
Liriodendron tulipifera (Tulip tree)	Magnoliaceae	East N. America (int. 1668)	June to August	One of the most beautiful hardy trees and one of the earliest introduced from N. America. Known to have been grown by Bishop Compton in the garden of Fulham Palace in 1688. Very ornamental foliage, gold in autumn, cup-shaped yellow-green flowers strongly sweet-scented. Thrives in any soil.
Lonicera brachypoda	Caprifoliaceae		July–September	Evergreen. Pale yellow fragrant flowers.
Lonicera caprifolium	,,	Europe and possibly Britain	June, July	Deciduous climber.
Lonicera fragrans	,,	China (int. 1845)	January and February	Introduced by R. Fortune. Cream-coloured, very fragrant flowers.
Lonicera japonica (syn L. Halleana)	,,	Japan and China	July to September	The most sweetly-scented of the honeysuckles.
var. aureo reticulata	,,			A variegated and most attractive variety.
Lonicera perichymenum (Common honeysuckle)	,,	Europe, Britain	June to September	Fragrant reddish yellow flowers in profusion.
var. L. p. belgica (Early Dutch variety) / var. L. p. serotina				The best of the honeysuckles.

NAME.	ORDER.	ORIGIN.	SEASON.	REMARKS.
Lonicera Standishii	Caprifoliaceae	China (int. 1845)	December to March	Introduced by R. Fortune. Cream-coloured fragrant flowers.
Lonicera thibetica	,,	Thibet	May, June	Deciduous shrub. Lilac-coloured fragrant flowers.
Lupinus arboreus	Leguminosae	California	Summer	Date of introduction unknown. Fragrant flowers, especially those of the type—sulphur yellow.
Magnolia acuminata (Cucumber tree)	Magnoliaceae	Eastern U.S.A. (int. 1736)	Early June	Deciduous forest tree. Flowers inconspicuous and faintly scented.
*Magnolia Campbellii	,,	Himalayas	March	Deciduous forest tree. Lovely rose du Barri, fragrant flowers, cup-shaped. Alas! far from hardy.
Magnolia conspicua Yulan, Lily Tree	,,	China (int. 1789)	April	Cultivated in China over a thousand years. One of the best of the large-growing magnolias. Quick growing and free-flowering. Cream white, very slightly-scented flowers.
Magnolia cordata	,,	Eastern U.S.A. (int. 1801)	Spring	
Magnolia compressa (syn M. Michelia compressa)	,,	Japan (int. 1894)		Is still to be proved. Appears to be hardy in the South, having survived several winters in some gardens.
Magnolia Dawsonia	,,	China	Summer	Very slightly scented.
Magnolia Delavayii	,,	Yunnan	Summer	Very faint scent.
Magnolia Fraseri	,,	N. America	May	Rare American species. Large foliage and cream-coloured slightly-scented flowers, 4 to 6 inches across.
Magnolia fuscata	,,	China		
Magnolia glauca (Swamp Bay)	,,	Eastern U.S.A.	Summer	Very faintly-scented flower.

274

Magnolia grandiflora	,,	S. United States (int. early eighteenth century)	July, August, September, October	The well-known laurel magnolia. Lemon-scented, immense blooms 6–10 inches across.
Magnolia Houttei	,,	China and Japan (int. 1884)	Spring	Forest tree. Very powerful sweet scent.
Magnolia hypoleuca	,,		Summer	
Magnolia Lennei	,,	M. conspicua × M. obovata	Spring through June	A magnificent hybrid.
Magnolia Kobus	,,	Japan	Spring	Small flowers sweetly scented.
Magnolia macrophylla	,,	S.E. United States		Largest leaved magnolia known. Fragrant flowers.
Magnolia parviflora	,,	Japan	June, July	A lovely variety. White ball-like flowers which, when expanded, show rose-coloured stamens. Very sweetly scented.
Magnolia Nicholsoniana	,,	China		Has to be proved.
Magnolia nitida	,,	S.E. Thibet, Yunnan, and N.E. Burma		The fruit seeds are reported to be bright orange-red, strongly aromatic and flowers very fragrant. Yet to be proved in this country.
Magnolia obovata	,,	Japan (int. 1790)	May	Slightly scented.

NAME.	ORDER.	ORIGIN.	SEASON.	REMARKS.
Magnolia rostrata	Magnoliaceae	Thibet and China		Probably tender. According to recent correspondence in *The Gardeners' Chronicle* this magnolia is reported to be likely to prove unsatisfactory from a horticultural point of view.
Magnolia rustica	,,	Hybrid		A well-known hybrid.
Magnolia salicifolia	,,	Japan	April, May	Willow-like leaves and fragrant white flowers. Leaves when bruised are fragrant.
Magnolia Sargentiana	,,	China		Related to M. Campbellii. Has attained 25–30 feet in this country but has not flowered yet.
Magnolia Soulangeana Var. nigra and other varieties	M. conspicua ×M. obovata		April	A well-known hybrid. Faint but very sweet scent.
Magnolia stellata	,,	Japan	March	Earliest of the magnolias to flower. Sweetly-scented flowers before the leaves appear.
Magnolia tripetala (Umbrella magnolia)	,,	N. America (int. 1752)	May, June	Immense green leaves 16 inches long and 6 inches wide. Large white flowers with strong unpleasant scent.
Magnolia Thompsoniana	,,	Hybrid	July	Raised in the nursery of a Mr. Thompson about 110 years ago. Apparently a chance hybrid between M. glauca and M. tripetela. Strongly-scented flowers.
Magnolia Watsoni	,,	Japan	July	Probably a hybrid between M. hypoleuca and M. parviflora. Very fragrant, exquisite flowers.
Magnolia Wilsonii	,,	,,	May	Like parviflora. Flowers pendulous instead of erect and come earlier.

Name	Family	Origin	Flowering time	Notes
Michelia compressa *See* Magnolia Michelia compressa				
Myrica asplenifolia *See* Comptonia asplenifolia				
Myrica gale (Sweet Gale Bog Myrtle)	Myricaceae	Europe, Britain		One of the few sweet-scented leaved plants which likes a moist situation.
Myrica cerifera (Wax Myrtle)	"	S.E. United States (int. 1699)		Aromatic leaves. Wax coating of fruits formerly used to make candles.
*Myrtus communis (Myrtle)	Myrtaceae	S. Europe		Grown in these islands since sixteenth century, possibly since Roman days or even before. Evergreen shrub. Fragrant snow-white flowers.
*Myrtus luma (syn Eugenia apiculata)	;	Chile	August to October	
Orixa japonica	Rutaceae	China and Japan		Aromatic leaves.
Osmanthus aqui-folium and varieties	Oleaceae	Japan (int. 1856)	September October	White, very sweetly-scented flowers.
Osmanthus Delavayi	"	Yunnan	April	Beautiful evergreen low-growing shrub. Very sweetly-scented flowers.
Osmarea Burkwoodii			April	See p. 84.

NAME.	ORDER.	ORIGIN.	SEASON.	REMARKS.
Paeonia suffruticosa	Ranunculaceae	China	Spring	Some of the varieties of P. suffruticosa, notably P. vittata and P. s. rosea, are fragrant.
Perowskia atriplic-folia	Labiatae	Himalayas and Afghanistan	August and September	Fragrant leaves.
Phellodendron amurense and other species	Rutaceae	Manchuria		Scented leaves.
Philadelphus Burkwoodii		Hybrid	June	Flowers 2½ inches across. One of the finest of the Philadelphuses.
Philadelphus coronarius (Syringa, Mock Orange, and varieties)	Saxifragraceae	S.E. Europe and Asia Minor	July	Cultivated in this country, at least since sixteenth century. The petals of the scented Philadelphuses are a valuable but uncommon ingredient in pot-pourri.
Philadelphus Delavayi	,,	W. China	Summer	Clusters of fragrant flowers.
Philadelphus Falconeri	,,	Unknown	Summer	Delicately-scented flowers with narrow petals.
Philadelphus incanus	,,	China	Late Summer	Fragrant flowers.
Philadelphus Lemoineci	,,	Hybrid P. coronarius ×P. micro-phyllus	June	A magnificent hybrid. Very fragrant flowers.

Name	Family	Origin	Flowering time	Notes
Philadelphus microphyllus	,,	Colorado, etc.	June	Very fragrant flowers.
Philadelphus pekinensis	,,	North China	June	Slightly-scented yellowish flowers.
Philadelphus purpureo-maculatus	,,	Hybrid	June	Rare. White flowers with purple blotches. Strong scent.
Philadelphus Satsume	,,	Japan (int. 1851)	Summer	Slightly-scented white flowers.
Philadelphus virginale	,,	Hybrid	July	Very vigorous grower with sweetly-scented flowers, produced the whole length of the branches.
Phillyrea angustifolia	Oleaceae	N. Africa and S. Europe	May and June	Cultivated in this country since the sixteenth century. Is mentioned in Gerard's catalogue of his garden. White fragrant flowers.
Phlomis fruticosa (Jerusalem Sage)	Labiateae	S. Europe	July	Leaves have a faint aromatic scent when crushed.
Pieris floribunda	Simarubaceae	S.E. United States	March and April	Flowers have a curious and not very attractive scent.
Plagianthus Lyalli	Malcaceae	New Zealand	June, July	Billows of scented white flowers.
Polygala chamae-buxus var. purpurea	Polygalaceae	Central Europe	April, May	Trailing evergreen, suitable for rock garden in peaty soil and part shade. Fragrant yellow and cream flowers.
Populus balsamifera and its closely allied species	Salicaceae	N. America		Leaves have a strong balsamic perfume, scenting the air around.

NAME.	ORDER.	ORIGIN.	SEASON.	REMARKS.
Populus trichocarpa	Salicaceae	Oregon to B. Columbia	June	Finest of the poplars. In young state leaves scent the air around. Buds coated with a fragrant resin.
Prunus lusitanica	Rosaceae	Spain and Portugal (int. 1648)	April	Flowers have an exquisite and very delicate scent.
Prunus mume (Japanese Apricot) and varieties	"	Korea		
Prunus subhirtella var. autumnalis (syn P. microlepis)	"	Japan	November and December	Fragrant pinkish blossoms during the shortest days of the year.
Ptelea trifoliata aurea (Golden Hop Tree)	Rutaceae	S. Canada and E. United States (int. 1704)	May and June	Seeds have an extraordinarily strong smell.
Pyrus coronaria fl. pl. (American Crab)	Rosaceae	N. America	Spring	Large pale pink flowers with a delicious apple blossom scent.
*Raphiolepis japonica (Japanese Hawthorn)	"	Japan	June	Small shrub about 4 feet. Ovate tough leaves and pure white fragrant flowers.
Rhododendron anthopogon	Ericaceae	Himalayas	April	Leaves strongly aromatic when crushed.

Rhododendron azaleoides syn R. fragrans syn R. odoratum	"	Garden hybrid	June and July	Deliciously-scented flowers.
Rhododendron calendulaceum	"	Eastern N. America (int. 1806)	Early June	Orange-scarlet blossoms. Parent of the orange-coloured garden varieties. Flowers only slightly fragrant.
Rhododendron canadense syn R. Rhodora	"	N. America (int. 1767)	May	Deciduous shrub, rose-purple, sweetly-scented azalea-like flowers. Perfectly hardy and useful in small gardens.
Rhododendron decorum and all forms	"	W. China (int. 1889)	June	Fragrant flowers.
*Rhododendron Edgworthii	"	Himalayas	June	Sweetly-scented flowers.
Rhododendron Fortunei	"	Chekiang (int. 1859)	May	Introduced by R. Fortune. Very fragrant flowers.
Rhododendrum flavum syn luteum	"	Caucasus, Asia Minor, etc. (int. 1793)	May	Richly-scented yellow flowers. Only azalea which is truly a native of Europe. Discovered by Tournefort early in the eighteenth century.
*Rhododendron Griffithianum	"	Himalayas	June	Sweetly-scented flowers.
Rhododendron Lodcri	"	Garden hybrid	May	A magnificent hybrid with scented flowers.

NAME.	ORDER.	ORIGIN.	SEASON.	REMARKS.
Rhododendron occidentale and garden hybrids	Ericaceae	Western N. America	Late June and July	Only azalea found west of the Rockies. Introduced by William Lobb for Messrs. Veitch. Very fragrant white flowers with yellow blotch on upper side. A most valuable summer flowering shrub.
*Rhododendron Schlippenbachii	,,	Manchuria, Korea, etc.	Spring	Lovely soft rose-coloured fragrant flowers. Only for very favoured parts. Perfectly hardy in winter but unfortunately starts into growth too early in this country and gets killed by late spring frosts.
Rhododendron vicsosum (Swamp Honeysuckle)	,,	Eastern N. America (int. 1734)	July	Pink or white flowers, exquisitely fragrant.
Rhus canadensis (Fragrant Sumach)	Anacardiaceae	Eastern U.S.A.	April	Leaves when bruised have a strong aromatic scent.
Rhus cotinus	,,	S. Europe	June	Leaves aromatic when crushed.
Ribes aureum Buffalo Currant var. aurantiacum	Saxifragaceae	U.S.A. (int. 1812)	April	Very aromatic yellow flowers. Deeper coloured flowers.
Ribes nigrum Black Currant and varieties	,,	Europe and possibly Britain	Early Spring	Very aromatic leaves.
Ribes sanguineum and varieties	,,	Western N. America (int. 1826)	Spring	Spicily-scented flowers.

Ribes viburnifolium	"	Lower California	April	Evergreen. Leaves when crushed have a strong aromatic scent rather like turpentine.
Robinia pseudo-Acacia	Leguminosae	E. United States	Spring	Introduced by John Tradescant, Senior.
Roses. See separate list, pages 288 and 289.				
Rosmarinus officinalis	Labiatae	Europe and Asia Minor	February and June	Grown in this country for centuries, possibly since Roman days.
var. prostratus	"	Capri	Summer	Prostrate growth. Much more tender than the type.
Rubus odoratus	Rosaceae	N. America	June to September	Deciduous. Handsome leaves and scented purple-red flowers. Excellent under trees.
Ruta graveolens (Rue)	Rutaceae	S. Europe	June, July	Very strong curious scent.
var. variegata				A most attractive variety.
Salvia officinalis and varieties	Labiatae	S. Europe	June, July	Cultivated for centuries in this country.
Salvia Grahami	"			Very fragrant. Rather tender.
Sambucus canadensis (American or Sweet Elder)	Caprifoliaceae	Eastern N. America	August	Unlike the common elder has a most delicious scent.
Sambucus nigra and varieties	"	Britain	May	Flowers have a very heavy scent. Leaves when crushed emit a pleasant scent.
Santolina chamaecyparissus	Compositae	S. Europe	July	Cultivated for centuries in this country.

NAME.	ORDER.	ORIGIN.	SEASON.	REMARKS.
Santolina viridis (Holy Flax)	Compositae	S. Europe (int. 1727)	July	Less strongly scented than S. chamaecyparissus. Being an ordinary green, it is not so attractive.
Sarcococca ruscifolia	Euphorbiaceae	Central China (int. 1907)	Spring	Dwarf evergreen. Glossy leaves. Fragrant white flowers.
Sassafras officinalis	Lauraceae	Eastern U.S.A. (int. 1633)	May	The whole tree is aromatic.
Satureia montana (Winter Savory)	Labiatae	S. Europe	July	A semi-shrubby plant cultivated for centuries in this country for seasoning.
Schizandra chinensis	Magnoliaceae	E. Asia	April, May	Somewhat aromatic. Dried wood has a particularly agreeable odour.
Skimmia japonica	Rutaceae	Japan	Spring	Evergreen, 2–4 feet, with scented flowers in spring, followed by vivid red berries, which remain throughout the year. S. japonica fragrans is the male form.
*Skimmia laureola	,,	Himalayas		Leaves when crushed have a heavy scent.
Spartium junceum (Spanish broom)	Leguminosae	Mediterranean regions	July, August, September	Deciduous tall shrub with fragrant yellow flowers, very attractive to bees. Grown in this country since sixteenth century.
Symplocos crataegoides	Styraceae	China and Japan	May and June	Deciduous shrub, 6–8 feet. Pannicles of sweetly-scented white flowers.
Syringa vulgaris (Common Lilac)	Oleaceae	Eastern Europe	May	Grown in this country for over 300 years.

It is impossible in this volume to give the long list of Syringa species and varieties. See Mrs. McKelvey's admirable monograph, *The Lilac*.

Teucrium fruticans Shrubby Germander	Labiatae	S. Europe	Summer and autumn	Leaves fragrant when crushed. Introduced by the then Duchess of Beaufort in 1714.
Thymus, all the species, see pages 147 and 148.				
Tilia vulgaris (syn T. europaea Common Lime)	Tiliaceae	Origin uncertain	June, July	Deciduous tree. Fragrant flowers very attractive to bees.
Trachelospermum crocosotomum	Apocynaceae	China (int. 1844)	July and August	Flowers have a very strong, sweet scent.
Ulex europaeus (Furze, Gorse, Whin) var. fl. pl.	Leguminosae	Europe, Britain	Throughout the year	Invaluable for dry banks on sandy soil.
*Umbellularia Californica syn Oreodaphne Californica (Californian Laurel)	Lauraceae	California and Oregon	Summer	Deeper colour and denser growth than the type. Bay-like evergreen with very strongly-scented leaves. In a confined space their pleasant scent can produce very unpleasant effects.
Veronica cupressoides	Scrophulariaceae	New Zealand	June	Cypress-like in appearance, scent of leaves and growth.
Viburnum bitchuense	,,	Japan	May	Very fragrant flowers. Introduced shortly before the war and still rare.

NAME.	ORDER.	ORIGIN.	SEASON.	REMARKS.
Viburnum Carlesii	Scro-phulariaceae	Corea	March and April	Beautiful deciduous shrub with white wax-like strongly-scented flowers. Does best on own roots. The new hybrid, V. Burkwoodii, is better in every way. Tall growing evergreen.
Viburnum fragrans	Caprifoliaceae	China	January	One of the most valuable of the late Mr. R. Farrer's introductions.
Viburnum Lentago (Sheep Berry)	,,	East N. America (int. 1761)	May and June	Cream-coloured flowers, very fragrant.
*Viburnum odoratissimum (syn V. awafuke)	,,	Japan, China, and India	May	A tender handsome evergreen with fragrant white flowers.
Vitex Agnus-Castus (Chaste Tree, Monks' Pepper Tree, etc).	Verbenaceae	S. Europe	August to October	An old favourite seldom seen now. Cultivated in 1570, according to Lobel. Entire plant is aromatic and flowers are fragrant.
Vitis cordifolia Winter or Chicken Grape	Vitacese	N. Eastern America	Early summer	A strong climber, with sweet-scented flowers, succeeded by blue-black berries.
Vitis labrusca (Fox grape)	,,	,,	,,	Parent of many American grapes. Fruit has a curious musk-like scent.
Wistaria chinensis and varieties	Leguminosae	N. China (int. 1816)	May	Finest of the wistarias for colour and fragrance.

Wistaria frutescens	"	S.E. United States	July and August	Fragrant flowers.
Wistaria multijuga and varieties	"	Japan	Summer	Racemes of flowers sometimes 3 feet long.
Zanthoxylum americanum (Toothache tree)	Rutaceae	Eastern U.S.A.		Leaves have a strong aromatic scent.
Zanthoxylum piperitum (Japanese pepper)	"	China and Japan	"	Leaves when crushed have even stronger aroma than the foregoing. The seeds are used by the Japanese as pepper.

THE OLD ROSES

THE following list comprises only those of the old roses which are obtainable now. Collectors of the old roses are continually re-discovering 'lost' varieties. The China Roses, Tea Roses, Hybrid Teas, Hybrid Perpetual, Scotch Briars, etc., are omitted as full lists of these are to be found in most rose catalogues.

R. *centifolia.*

R. centifolia. The Cabbage or Provence Rose. See pp. 16, 107 *et seq.*

R. sulphurea syn R. hemispherica. Yellow Provence Rose. See p. 108 *et seq.*

R. provincialis alba. 'Rose Unique.' The White Provence Rose. See p. 110.

Rose des Peintres. See p. 111.

Rose de Meaux. See p. 111.

Rose de Spong. See p. 111.

Petite de Hollande. See p. 111.

Königen von Denmark. See p. 111.

Rose of the Four Seasons. See pp. 127, 128.

R. *centifolia muscosa.*

R. centifolia muscosa and varieties—the Common Moss, Crested Moss, White Bath, Blanche Moreau, Chapeau de Napoleon, Gloire des Mousseuses, Georges Vibert, Crimson Globe, etc. See p. 112 *et seq.*

Violaceae. See p. 114.

R. *damascena.*

R. damascena. The Damask Rose and varieties. See p. 115 *et seq.*

York and Lancaster Rose. See p. 116.

R. trigenta petala. See p. 117.

Hebe's Lip. See p. 117.

R. *gallica.*

R. gallica and varieties. See p. 117 *et seq.*

Rosa Mundi. See p. 118, 119.

Perle des Panachées. See p. 119.

Oeillet Parfait. See p. 119.

Tuscany. See p. 120.

R. burgundiaca syn. parvifolia. See p. 120.

R. *Alba.*

R. alba. The White Rose of England. See pp. 121, 122.

R. rubra. The Red Rose of England. See pp. 121, 122.

288

R. alba var. rubicunda. Maiden's Blush. The Incarnation Rose.
  See p. 122.
Celestial.

R. moschata.
  For varieties and hybrids. See pp. 123, 127.

  R. cinnamomea. The Whitsuntide Rose. See p. 124.

  R. pomifera. The Apple Rose. See p. 125.

  R. foetida. The Austrian Briar. See p. 125.

  R. virginiana. The Virginian Rose. See p. 126.

  Rose d'Amour. See p. 126.

  R. foliolosa. See p. 126.

R. chinensis.
  R. chinensis var. semper florens. China Monthly. See pp. 126, 127.
  Cramoisie Supérieure. See p. 127.
  Fabvier.
  Fellenberg.
  R. Lawrenciana. See p. 129.

Bourbon Roses.
  Charles Desprez. See p. 128.
  Madame Desprez. See p. 128.
  Souvenir de Malmaison. See p. 128.
  Zephyrine Drouhin. See p. 128.

  R. bracteata. The Macartney Rose. See p. 133.

  R. rugosa. See p. 133.
    and varieties.

  Banksia alba. See p. 133.
  Banksia lutea. See p. 133.
  R. multiflora. See p. 134.
    and varieties—Seven Sisters, Garland Rose, etc. See p. 134.

Native Species grown in our gardens for many centuries :
  R. rubiginosa. Sweet Briar. See p. 94 *et seq.*
    and varieties.
  R. spinosissima. See pp. 98, 99.
    and varieties.

HERBACEOUS PLANTS, ANNUALS, ETC.

NAME.	ORDER.	ORIGIN.	SEASON.	REMARKS.
Abronia fragrans	Nyctaginaceae	Platte River (a tributary of the Missouri) and Eastern flank of Rocky Mts. between 40° × 45° N. Latitude	Summer	Perennial. White flowers with very sweet scent.
Abronia latifolia syn A. arenaria	,,	California	,,	Discovered by Archibald Menzies, surgeon and naturalist in Captain Vancouver's expedition to coast of N.W. America. He also brought from Chile seeds of *Araucaria imbricata* (monkey puzzle tree) in 1798.
Alyssum maritimum (syn A. odoratum, Sweet Alyssum)	Cruciferae	Mediterranean region	April to August	Perennial. In most parts of this country treated as an annual. Scent of new-mown hay.
Angelica officinalis	Umbelliferae	Alps	Summer	So called on account of its healing properties.
Aquilegia fragrans	Ranunculaceae	Kashmir	June	A pale yellow columbine with an exquisite scent. First introduced in 1840.
Arabis albida and other species	Cruciferae	Northern Hemisphere	March and April	So called because Arabia is the home of many of the varieties.

Artemisia dracunculus (Tarragon)	Compositae	S. Europe	July	
Asarum canadens (Wild Ginger)	Aristolo chiaceae	Europe, America	Summer	Very aromatic root. Cultivated in England before 1713 by Bishop Compton at Fulham Palace.
Asperula odorata (Woodruff)	Rubiaceae	Europe, Britain	May	The leaves when dried smell like new-mown hay and keep their scent for years.
Auricula See Primula auricula				
Balm See Melissa officinalis				
Balsamita Alecost, Cost-mary	Compositae	Europe	Summer	Very aromatic leaves.
Basil. See Ocymum				
Calamentha glabella	Labiatae	S. Europe	Summer	Minute herbaceous plant with very fragrant lilac flowers.
Calendula officinalis Pot Mangold	Compositae	Mediterranean and Canary Isles	All the year	Petals were formerly used for flavouring.
Californian poppy. See Romneya Coulteri				
Carnation. See Dianthus caryo-phyllus				

NAME.	ORDER.	ORIGIN.	SEASON.	REMARKS.
Carum Carvi (Caraway)	Umbelliferae	Europe, Britain	May	The roots were formerly eaten as well as the aromatic seeds.
Cedronella (Balm of Gilead)	Labiatae	Western Texas	Summer	So called from the cedar-like scent.
Centaurea moschata (Sweet Sultan)	Compositae	Persia	Summer	Introduced in Charles I's reign, and named by John Parkinson. 'A stranger of much beauty and but lately obtained from Constantinople, where, because (as it is said) the great Turk, as we call him, saw it abroad, liked it, and wore it himself, all his vassals have had it in great regard, and it hath been obtained from them by some that have sent it into these parts. . . . The Turks themselves, as I understand, do call it the Sultan Flower, and I have done so likewise.' John Parkinson, *Paradisus*, 1629. Other old English names for Sweet Sultan were, ' Blackamore's Beauty ' and ' Honey-flower.'
Coriandrum (Coriander)	,,	S. Europe	Summer	The seeds of Coriander become more fragrant with age.
Cheiranthus (Wallflower) and garden hybrids	Cruciferae	N. Hemisphere Mostly S. Europe	Spring	
Dianthus barbatus (Sweet William)	Caryophyll-aceae	Unknown	Summer	

Name	Family	Distribution	Season	Notes
Dianthus caryophyllus and garden hybrids	"	Chiefly S. Europe, N. Africa, and Asia	"	
Dianthus plumarius (Pink) and garden hybrids	"	"	"	
Erysimum (Alpine Wallflower)		Alps, W. Asia and N. America	Spring	
Geranium macrorrhizium	Geraniaceae	Central Europe	Summer	Flowers have a strong aromatic scent.
Hesperis matronalis (Rocket. Dames Violet)	Cruciferae	Europe and Asia	Summer	
Hesperis tristis (Night-scented stock)	"	"	"	So called because it is most fragrant in the evening.
Hop. See Humulus lupulus				
Humulus lupulus (Common Hop)	Articaceae	Europe		'Mee thinkes I myght aptlye compare such men as have grounde fitte for this purpose (growing hops), and will not employ it accordingly, to Alehouse Knightes, partely for the small devotion which both the one and the other have unto Hoppes, but

NAME.	ORDER.	ORIGIN.	SEASON.	REMARKS.
				especially for that many of these Ale-Knightes having good drinke at home of their owne, can be content to drinke worse abroad at an Alehouse so they may pay for it.' 'They which have a Hoppe hyll in derision wyll scant fall out to leave a Moulehyll in reversion.' Epilogue to *A perfite platforme of a Hoppe Garden* by Reynolde Scot, 1578.
Iberis odorata (Sweet scented Candytuft)	Cruciferae	Alps	April onwards	
Lathyrus odoratus including the garden varieties	Leguminosae	N. Hemisphere	Summer	
Linnaea borealis	Caprifoliaceae	Norway and parts of Scotland, Asia, and N. America	,,	Very sweetly scented, especially in the evening.
Lupinus arboreus	Leguminosae	America	,,	Semi-shrubby. Will not tolerate lime.
Lychnis vespertina	Caryophyllaceae	Europe, Britain	,,	
Marjoram *See* Origanum				

Matthiola bicornis (Night-scented Stock)	Cruciferae	Mediterranean region	"	Named after the Italian botanist, Matthioli.
Matthiola incana	"	"	"	
Matthiola sinuata and numerous garden hybrids	"	"	"	
Melissa officinalis	Labiatae	Europe and W. Asia	"	So called because the plant is beloved by bees.
Mentha spicata and many other species	"	Temperate regions	"	
Mignonette See Reseda				
Monarda didyma (Bergamot, Oswego tea)	Labiatae	N. America	"	Called after Nicolas Monardes, the sixteenth century Spanish doctor and author of the first book on American plants—written 19 years before the defeat of the Spanish Armada. '*Dos libros, el veno que trata de odas las casas que traen de nuestras Indias Occidentales* (1569).' Translated into English in 1577 by John Frampton, *Joyfull Newes out of the new founde worlde*.
Myrrhis odorata (Sweet Cicely)	Umbelliferae	Europe	"	An old favourite now rarely seen in gardens.

NAME.	ORDER.	ORIGIN.	SEASON.	REMARKS.
Nasturtium. See Tropaeolum				
Nicotiana alata (affinis)	Solanaceae	America	Summer	Called after J. Nicot, who first introduced this 'weed' into Europe.
*Ocymum (Basil)	Labiatae	Asia, Africa, Chile, etc.	July and August	The aromatic leaves of both the bush basil and the sweet basil were formerly commonly used in salads.
Oenothera biennis (Evening Primrose) var. grandiflora	Onagraceae	America	,,	One of the most exquisite of the evening scents.
Oenothera marginata	,,	,,	,,	Flowers change from white to a delicate pink. Very sweetly scented.
Oenothera trichocalyx	,,	California	,,	Snow-white scented flowers. One of the best of the Oenotheras.
Origanum vulgare and other species	Labiatae	Mediterranean region	,,	
Paeonia	Ranunculaceae	China and Europe	,,	Numerous varieties of the herbaceous peonies are sweetly scented.
Phlox decussata	Polemoniaceae	N. America	,,	
Pink. See Dianthus plumarius				
Polyanthus. See Primula				

Primrose
See Primula vera

Primula auricula, numerous hybrids	Primulaceae	Alps, etc.	Spring	Many of the numerous species and varieties of this large family are sweetly scented.
Primula elatior	,,	Europe, Britain	,,	
Primula polyanthus, numerous hybrids	,,	Hybrid	,,	
Primula veris	,,	Europe, Britain	,,	
Primula vulgaris, numerous hybrids	,,	,,	,,	
Primula anisodora	,,	Yunnan	Summer	Found by Mr. Forrest.
Primula Bulleyana	,,	Garden Hybrid	,,	
Primula chionantha	,,		Late Spring	Drooping, sweetly-scented white blooms, with dark centre.
Primula florindae	,,	S.E. Thibet	Summer	Found by Captain Kingdom Ward at an altitude of 12,000 feet.
Primula involucrata	,,	Himalayas	,,	One of the early introductions from the Himalayas. One of the best scented primulas.
Primula nivalis sino-purpurea	,,	Thibet	,,	
Primula pudibunda	,,	,,	,,	Found by Captain Kingdom Ward at an altitude of 15,000 feet. Pale yellow flowers.
Primula sikkimensis	,,	Himalayas		

Explorers are continually adding to the already long list of Asiatic species of primula. These Asiatic species vary greatly in their degree of fragrance.

NAME.	ORDER.	ORIGIN.	SEASON.	REMARKS.
Pyrola rotundifolia	Ericaceae	Europe	Early Summer	Small herbaceous evergreen with drooping slightly-scented bell-like flowers.
Reseda (Mignonette)	Resedaceae	S. Europe to Persia	Summer	
Rocket. *See* Hesperis metronalis				
Romneya Coulteri (Californian Bush poppy)	Papaveraceae	California	,,	Called after T. Romney Robinson.
Romneya trichocaly	,,	,,		
Salvia Grahami	Labiatae	Mexico	Summer and Autumn	Both the flowers and leaves are scented.
Salvia officinalis and varieties	,,	S. Europe	Summer	So called from its healing properties.
Salvia sclarea (Clary)	,,	,,	,,	Very handsome border plant. Pungent aromatic scent.
Scabiosa atro-purpurea (Scabious)	Dipsaceae	Europe, Asia, and Africa	Late Summer	A peculiarly attractive honey-like ' sunny ' scent.
Stock. *See* Matthiola bicornis, etc.				
Sweet Pea. *See* Lathyrus odoratus				
Sweet Rocket. *See* Hesperis				

298

Sweet William *See* Dianthus barbatus			
Tanacetum vulgare and varieties	Compositae	Europe, N. Asia	Summer
Tropaeolum majus (Nasturtium)	Geraniaceae	S. America	Late Summer and Autumn
Viola odorata (Sweet Violet) and many varieties	Violaceae	Europe, Asia	Spring
Viola tricolor (Hearts-ease, Pansy) and many varieties	"	Alps	"

BULBS, RHIZOMES, ETC.

*Amaryllis belladonna and varieties	Amaryllidaceae	S. Africa	August and September
Anthericum liliastrum (St. Bruno's Lily) var. maximum	Liliaceae	Europe, S. Alps and Pyrenees	Summer

NAME.	ORDER.	ORIGIN.	SEASON.	REMARKS.
Anthericum liliago (St. Bernard's Lily)	Liliaceae	Europe, S. Alps and Pyrenees	Summer	
Convallaria majalis and varieties	,,	N. Hemisphere	Spring	
*Crinum longifolium	Amaryllidaceae	S. Africa	Late Summer	Pale rose, faintly-scented flowers.
Crocus vernus and other species	Iridaceae	Origin unknown	February onwards	
Cyclamen euro-paeum	Primulaceae	Europe	August	
Gladiolus tristis	Iridaceae		July	
Hyacinthus orientalis and garden varieties	Liliaceae	Mediterranean to S. Africa	Spring	
Iris aphylla var. Swertii	Iridaceae	Only known in cultivation	Early May	Much dwarfer than *florentina* and *pallida*
Iris arenaria	,,	Plains of Hungary	April	
Iris florentina and garden hybrids	,,	Form of I. germanica	Spring	
Iris germanica and garden hybrids	,,	Unknown	Spring	
Iris graminea	,,	S. and Central Europe	Spring	Fruit-like scent.
Iris histrioides	,,	Palestine	Early Spring	

Iris reticulata and garden hybrids	,,	See p. 23	February	
Iris stylosa and varieties	,,	Algeria	November to April	
Iris statellae syn chamaeiris	,,	S.E. France and N.W. Italy	Spring	
Iris Xiphium	,,	Spain		
Jonquil. *See* Narcissus		Portugal and N. Africa	Spring	
Lilium auratum and varieties	Liliaceae	Japan (int. 1861)	July	'The golden-rayed lily of Japan.' Mam-yuri (Mountain lily).
Lilium Browni	,,	China and Korea	Early July	One of the earliest Chinese lilies grown in these islands. Reintroduced by Fortune.
Lilium candidum var. speciosum	,,	Salonika	July August	The Madonna lily. Figured in an early eleventh-century copy of the Herbarius of Apuleius. Rare and distinct form. Flowers later and has dark stems.
Lilium carolinianum	,,	Carolina and Georgia		Supposed to be southern form of L. superbum.
Lilium centifolium	,,	China	July and August	Said to have been found in a cabbage-patch in China. According to Mr. E. H. Wilson, a type of leucanthum.
Lilium cernuum	,,	Korea, Manchuria		Flowered for the first time in England in Mr. Amos Perry's nursery at Enfield.

NAME.	ORDER.	ORIGIN.	SEASON.	REMARKS.
Lilium Duchartrei var. Wardii	Liliaceae	Western China	July	Discovered by Père David in 1869.
Lilium giganteum and varieties	,,	Himalayas	July	Discovered by Captain Kingdom Ward. Largest and tallest of the lilies.
Lilium Hansoni and hybrids	,,	Japan	Summer	Very hardy.
Lilium japonicum Alexandrae	,,	,,	,,	Very rare. Said to be a form of L. longiflorum.
Lilium longiflorum	,,	Japan, China, and Formosa	,,	
Lilium Philippinense	,,	Philippine Islands	July	The only lily from the Philippine Islands.
var. formosanum		Formosa	,,	White, suffused wine purple without.
Lilium regale	,,	Min River, Western Szech'uan	July	Discovered by Mr. E. H. Wilson in 1903. 'This Lily has a surprisingly limited distribution, being confined to about fifty miles of the narrow semi-arid valley of the Min River in extreme Western Szech'uan between 2500 and 6000 feet altitude—a region where the summers are hot and the winters severely cold, and where strong winds prevail at all seasons of the year. I never saw it wild outside of this valley, which is walled in by steep mountain slopes culminating in perpetual snows. There it grows in great plenty among grasses and low shrubs and in niches on the bare cliffs.'—E. H. Wilson, *Lilies of Eastern Asia.*

Species	Family	Locality	Season	Notes
Lilium speciosum	"	Japan, Kiangsi Province, China, and N. Formosa		Observed in Japanese gardens by Kaempfer. Flowered for the first time in Europe in the Botanical Gardens, Ghent, in 1832.
Lilium tenuifolium	"	Eastern Siberia and N. China		Introduced into the Botanical Gardens, Petrograd, about 1810. Only slightly scented.
Muscari botryoides (Grape hyacinth)	"	Europe	Spring	
Muscari moschatum	Amaryllidaceae	"	"	Very sweetly scented.
Narcissus jonquilla and hybrids	"		"	
Narcissus Leedsii	"		"	Most of these garden hybrids are sweetly scented.
Narcissus odorus Campanelle	Amaryllidaceae	S. Europe	"	
Narcissus odorus rugulosus	"	"	"	
Narcissus poeticus recurvus (Pheasants' Eye)	"	French and Italian Alps	"	
Narcissus triandrus concolor	"	Probably a natural hybrid	Spring	According to Mr. A. F. Calvert probably a natural hybrid of *triandrus alba* and the sweet-scented single jonquil, which is also found in Spain and Portugal. Unlike other forms of *triandrus*, it is scented.

NAME.	ORDER.	ORIGIN.	SEASON.	REMARKS.
Polygonatum officinale (Solomon's Seal)	Liliaceae	N. Hemisphere	May, June	So called from the 'many-kneed' appearance of the rhizome.
Tulipa, many-scented varieties	,,	Europe, Asia	Spring	

AQUATICS

NAME.	ORDER.	ORIGIN.	SEASON.	REMARKS.
Acorus calamus (Sweet Flag)	Araceae	Europe		Formerly used as a strewing herb.
*Aponogeton distachyon (Water Hawthorn)	Naiadeceae	Cape of Good Hope	From Spring to end of Autumn	Very fragrant hawthorn-like scent.
Nymphaea odorata and varieties	Nymphaeaceae	N. America	Summer	The varieties are all very sweetly scented.

INDEX

☙ *Index* ☙

❧ Index ❧

Printed in Great Britain at the University Printing House, Oxford